COMMUNICATION
BETWEEN
CULTURES

COMMUNICATION
BETWEEN
CULTURES

LARRY A. SAMOVAR

San Diego State University

RICHARD E. PORTER

California State University, Long Beach

Wadsworth Publishing Company
Belmont, California
A Division of Wadsworth, Inc.

Communications Editor: Peggy Randall
Development Editor: Laurie Blass
Editorial Assistant: Sharon Yablon
Production Editor: Karen Garrison
Managing Designer: Donna Davis
Print Buyer: Karen Hunt
Designer: Wendy Calmenson
Photo Researcher: Lindsay Kefauver
Compositor: Omegatype Typography
Cover: Donna Davis
Cover Photograph: TSW/Galen Rowell

Printed in the United States of America   19

          3 4 5 6 7 8 9 10—95 94 93 92

Library of Congress Cataloging in Publication Data

Samovar, Larry A.
     Communication between cultures / Larry A. Samovar, Richard E.
   Porter.
        p.   cm.
     Includes bibliographical references and index.
     ISBN 0-534-15006-3
     1. Intercultural communication.   2. Interpersonal communication.
   I. Porter, Richard E.   II. Title.
HM258.S247   1991
303.48'2—dc20   90-49643

7-7-93

CONTENTS

Preface xi

PART 1 COMMUNICATION AND CULTURE 1

Chapter 1 Intercultural Communication: Interaction in a Changing World   3

The Importance of Intercultural Communication   4
  International Contacts 5
  Domestic Contacts 11
Studying Intercultural Communication   16
Preview of the Book: What Lies Ahead?   18
Summary   19
Activities   20
Discussion Ideas   21
Notes   21

**Chapter 2 Communication: Sharing Who We Are
and What We Know**   **25**

Human Communication 25
    Defining Communication 26
    The Ingredients of Communication 29
    The Characteristics of Communication 31
Summary 41
Activities 42
Discussion Ideas 43
Notes 43

Chapter 3 Culture: Our Invisible Teacher   **47**

Culture 48
    The Basic Function of Culture 49
    Some Definitions of Culture 50
    The Ingredients of Culture 50
    The Characteristics of Culture 54
Summary 63
Activities 64
Discussion Ideas 64
Notes 65

**Chapter 4 Understanding Intercultural Communication:
Principles and Precepts**   **69**

Intercultural Communication 70
    Forms of Intercultural Communication 70
An Intercultural Communication Model 74
The Elements of Intercultural Communication 80
    Perception 80
    Verbal Processes 91
    Nonverbal Processes 94
Summary 96
Activities 97
Discussion Ideas 98
Notes 98

PART 2 THEORY AND PRACTICE 101

Chapter 5 Cultural Diversity in Perception: Alternative Views of Reality   103

Understanding Perception 104
Perception and Culture 105
    Beliefs and Values 107
    World View and Its Effect 116
    World View and Cultural Values 126
    Social Organization 132
Summary 139
Activities 140
Discussion Ideas 140
Notes 141

Chapter 6 Language and Culture: Sounds and Actions   145

The Nature of Language 146
The Importance of Language 149
Language and Meaning 150
Language and Culture 151
Argot 158
    The Nature and Use of Argot 158
    Functions of Argot 160
Foreign Languages and Translation 165
Summary 170
Activities 171
Discussion Ideas 171
Notes 172

Chapter 7 Nonverbal Communication: Sound and Action   175

The Importance of Nonverbal Communication   176
Defining Nonverbal Communication   179
Functions of Nonverbal Communication   180
    Repeating   180
    Complementing   181
    Contradicting   181
    Substituting   181
    Regulating   182
Verbal and Nonverbal Symbol Systems   182
    Similarities   182
    Differences   183
Nonverbal Communication: Guidelines and Limitations   184
Nonverbal Communication and Culture   185
Body Behavior   187
    General Appearance and Dress   187
    Body Movements (Kinesics and Posture)   189
    Facial Expressions   195
    Eye Contact and Gaze   197
    Touch   200
    Smell   203
    Paralanguage   205
Summary   207
Activities   208
Discussion Ideas   209
Notes   209

Chapter 8 Nonverbal Communication: The Messages of Space, Time, and Silence   213

Space and Distance   214
    Personal Space   214
    Seating   216
    Furniture Arrangement   216
Time   219
    Formal Time   219
    Informal Time   219

Silence 223 —
Summary 226
Activities 227
Discussion Ideas 227
Notes 228

Chapter 9 The Influence of Context: Business, Education, and Health Care

231

Context and Communication 232
The Business Context 236
The Education Context 244
    What Cultures Teach 245
    How Cultures Teach 248
    Problems in Educating a Culturally Diverse Population 252
The Health-Care Context 256
Summary 263
Activities 263
Discussion Ideas 264
Notes 264

PART 3 KNOWLEDGE INTO ACTION 269

Chapter 10 Accepting Differences and Appreciating Similarities: A Point of View

271

A Philosophy of Change 272
    The Brain Is an Open System 272
    We Have Free Choice 273
    Communication Has a Consequence 274
Potential Problems in Intercultural Communication 274
    Seeking Similarities 275
    Uncertainty Reduction 276
    Diversity of Communication Purposes 276
    Withdrawal 277

Ethnocentrism 278
Stereotyping and Prejudice 279
Improving Intercultural Communication 283
Know Yourself 285
Consider the Physical and Human Setting 288
Seek a Shared Code 289
Develop Empathy 290
Encourage Feedback 294
Develop Communication Flexibility 296
Seek Commonalities 297
Some Ethical Considerations 298
The Future of Intercultural Communication 301
Summary 306
Activities 308
Notes 309

Glossary 313

Credits 319

Index 321

PREFACE

*Culture, the acquainting ourselves with the best that has been known
and said in the world, and thus with the history of the human spirit.*

MATTHEW ARNOLD

This is a book about communication. More specifically, this
is a book about interpersonal intercultural communication.
Because many who read this book are not communication
majors, we tend to discuss specific communication principles
first in each chapter and then apply the principles to interpersonal aspects of intercultural communication. This book

is intended for anyone whose professional or private life is likely to include encounters with people from cultures or co-cultures different from his or her own. We therefore deal both with communication between international cultures and communication between co-cultures within the United States.

We have worked together in the field of intercultural communication for over twenty years and have seen many changes occur. Culture, we have come to believe, is a personal matter, and we have therefore developed our own philosophy about intercultural communication. We have stated our positions at times and make no apologies for having adopted those positions. We also have tried to keep our own ethnocentrism in check, but for those instances in which it has leaked through, we do apologize.

Rationale

Worldwide interest in intercultural communication grows out of two assumptions. The first is that we live in an age when changes in technology, travel, economic and political systems, immigration patterns, and population density have created a world in which we increasingly interact with people from different cultures. Simply pause and look around to see the truth of this assertion. Second, people now know that these diverse backgrounds influence the communication act in subtle and profound ways. That is to say, one's cultural perceptions and experiences help determine how one sends and receives messages.

Approach

Fundamental to our approach to intercultural communication is the belief that interpersonal communication involves action, that it is something we do with and to one another. Whether we are generating words or movements we are creating and producing action. Any study of communication, therefore, must include information about the interactive behaviors all parties are producing as well as the consequences of those behaviors.

Because we are in control of many of our actions, we can improve communication. Hence, this book takes a very pragmatic view of intercultural communication. We see it as interpersonal interaction in which cultural diversity governs the rules by which people attempt to achieve their communication goals. We have attempted throughout this book to translate ideas and concepts into practice—practice that can improve your communication and foster the attainment of your communicative purposes.

Philosophy

A dual philosophy has guided us in the preparation of this book. First, it is to the advantage of all five and a half billion of us who share the planet to improve our interpersonal intercultural communication abilities. The world has grown so small that we all depend upon each other. What happens in one place in the world touches other places. Second, most of the obstacles to understanding can be overcome with motivation, knowledge, and an appreciation of cultural diversity. We hope to supply you with all three.

Organization

We have attempted to organize the book in manageable increments that build on each other. What you learn in one chapter you must carry into the next series of chapters. Our book is divided into three interrelated parts. Part 1 introduces you to the study of communication and culture. After pointing out the importance of intercultural communication in Chapter 1, we use Chapters 2, 3, and 4 to examine communication, culture, and intercultural communication.

Part 2 puts the theory of intercultural communication into practice. The first chapters in this part explore differences in perception, verbal messages, and nonverbal messages. The final chapter explains the ways in which cultures respond differently to business, education, and health-care contexts.

The final part of the book attempts to extend what we have learned throughout the preceding chapters by converting knowledge into action. In Chapter 10 we offer guidelines for improvement as well as a philosophy for the future, a future we believe will be filled with intercultural experiences.

Assistance

Both of us have been interested in culture since we were sophomores in college. Over time we have come to subscribe to the Buddhist and Hindu notions that we learn from each other and that there are many ways of knowing. Culture reaches below levels of awareness, and we are sure, therefore, that some very special people in our lives have taught us about culture. In this sense, we believe that perhaps we have been both students and teachers to many who have crossed our paths. We know that we have learned a great deal about culture and communication from our contacts with the special people in our lives.

A number of people were instrumental in the preparation of this text. We would like to thank the following reviewers: Gale Auletta, California State University, Hayward; LaRay M. Barna, Portland State University; Nemi C. Jain, Arizona State University; and Armeda C. Reitzel, Humboldt State University. Professor Nemi Jain, in a previous work with us, helped to generate many of the ideas that have found their way into this new project. Susan Hellweg of San Diego State University provided invaluable help. There is not a single chapter in the book that does not reflect her counsel, criticism, encouragement, and friendship. As always, we appreciate the advice and editorial direction of Wadsworth Publishing Company. For this undertaking, we greatly appreciate the conviction, firmness, and charm of Kristine Clerkin and Peggy Randall.

Larry A. Samovar
Richard E. Porter

COMMUNICATION
BETWEEN
CULTURES

I

COMMUNICATION AND CULTURE

Human beings draw close to one another by their common nature, but habits and customs keep them apart.

CONFUCIAN SAYING

Lack of communication has given rise to differences in language, in thinking, in systems of belief and in culture generally. These differences have made hostility among societies endemic and seemingly eternal.

ISAAC ASIMOV

CHAPTER ONE

INTERCULTURAL COMMUNICATION: INTERACTION IN A CHANGING WORLD

When Euripides wrote, "All is change; all yields its place and then goes" in 422 B.C., he probably did not realize that he would be helping to introduce a book on intercultural communication. Yet, the study of intercultural communication is about change. It is about changes in the world and how the people in that world must adapt to them. More specifically, this book deals with the world changes that have brought us into direct and indirect contact with people who, because of their culture, often behave in ways that we do not understand. With or without our consent, the last three decades have thrust upon us groups of people who often appear alien. These people, who appear "different," may live thousands of miles away or right next door. What is special about them is that in many ways they are not like us. This book is about those people and how to understand them and communicate with them.

THE IMPORTANCE OF
INTERCULTURAL COMMUNICATION

Intercultural communication, as we might suspect, is not new. Wandering nomads, religious missionaries, and conquering soldiers have been encountering people different from themselves since the beginning of time. These early meetings, like those of today, were often confusing and hostile. In fact, over two thousand years ago the playwright Aeschylus wrote, "Everyone's quick to blame the alien." In the 1990s intercultural contacts are more common and in many ways more significant than those earlier meetings.

Many of you will find the examples and statistics we offer to document the shifting cultural makeup of the United States and of the world somewhat obvious, for some of you have undoubtedly had firsthand experiences with people from different cultures and already know about the changes taking place in the world. Many of us were bewildered and perhaps even saddened as we watched the Japanese purchase such American institutions as Rockefeller Center, more than five thousand 7-Elevens, and a minor-league baseball team in the Chicago White Sox organization. And think of the irony and the message to the world when we all saw the leader of the "Godless" Soviet Union embracing Pope John II. Although we may have found it humorous, it reflected a new world order.

The above examples, and there are many more, emphasize the need to examine the changes that have taken place throughout the world. Our rationale for such a discussion is twofold. First, many of the events that have brought diverse groups together have been subtle and have transpired over a long period of time. Hence, we believe that many of them might have been overlooked. Second, by demonstrating both the quantity and quality of these changes we might be better able to arouse your interest in intercultural communication. Let us begin, therefore, by looking at some of the specific circumstances, both abroad and at home, that put us into contact with people whose cultural background was often different from our own.

International Contacts

The last thirty years might well be characterized as that period when, in a figurative sense, Marshall McLuhan's **global village** prophecy became a reality. The world has indeed been shrinking. We appear to live in a common "village," and we can no longer avoid each other. We are beginning to realize that a symbiotic relationship links all people together. No nation, group, or culture can remain anonymous. If you touch one part of the world, you touch all parts of the world. It is as if a combination of the following three events has made intercultural contact inevitable: (1) new technology and information systems, (2) changes in the world's population, and (3) a shift in the world's economic arena. All of these issues, because they will help predict the future while telling us about the past, are important enough to consider in some detail.

The new technology.   Trips once measured in days are now counted in hours. Supersonic transports place the tourist, business executive, or diplomat any-where in the world within hours. This ease of mobility has allowed many North Americans to travel overseas. In 1980, for example, 22 million Americans went abroad. That number jumped to 41.2 million in 1988.[1] But this freedom to travel was not the exclusive province of Americans. In 1977, 18.6 million tourists from abroad visited the United States. In 1980 the figure was 22 million, and by 1988 the total topped 30 million. Both groups were discovering that they were coming in contact with people who seemed bizarre, and at times mysterious. Conflicting perceptions went far beyond differences in eating utensils and modes of travel. People were observing cultural idiosyncrasies in the use of time and space, the treatment of women and the elderly, and even the meaning of truth.

New and sophisticated communication systems also encouraged cultural interaction during this period. Communication satellites and digital switched networks allowed people throughout the world to share information and ideas at the same time. Whether it was watching a television program or viewing common stock-market reports, people all over the world could experience the same event at the same time. In addition, a well-organized international film industry was evolving that let one society share its cultural experiences with another.

The new population.   The second catalyst contributing to intercultural con-tacts was the rapid increase in the world's population. In the 1970s and 1980s the world's population grew at a startling rate. We entered the 1970s with a population of around three and a half billion people. By 1974 that figure had grown to four billion. Each year added approximately eighty-three million people to the world. As startling as these figures were, it seemed as if we all took special notice when the United Nations revealed, in July of 1987, that with the birth of a baby boy in Yugoslavia, the world now had five billion residents. Since that milestone the population has increased yet another half-billion, and should reach the 6.3 billion mark before the year 2000. These numbers forced much of the world to reexamine the consequences of a crowded planet, a planet that more than ever before was binding its inhabitants together in crucial ways. The connection of one culture with another was most manifest in the areas of natural resources, pollution, and international conflict.

The earth's apparent inability to yield an endless supply of natural resources was one of the stark realities for this new population. While the United States had but 5 percent of the world's population, it was using nearly 25 percent of the world's natural resources. Our energy consumption alone was staggering: The average American in the 1980s consumed as much energy as 3 Japanese, 6 Mexicans, 18 Chinese, 51 Indians, or 385 Ethiopians. These sorts of statistics presented a vivid example of how we were tied to the rest of the world. Having to buy, borrow, and share resources with other people created serious shortages not only for the United States but for all humankind. As oil, copper, lumber, and uranium became scarce in some parts of the world, we learned the limits of the earth's natural resources. Even a substance as common as water was capable of creating clashes between cultures. For example, two Arab nations threatened to go to war against Turkey as that country's Ataturk Dam diverted 75 percent of the downstream water that had once flowed to Syria and Iraq.

Perhaps the most graphic example of a limited resource was food. Before World War II most countries could produce enough food to feed their own people. But the 1970s and 1980s brought us pictures and stories of how hungry the world was in this new era. The U.N. reported that in the Sudan, for example, over 250,000 people had died of starvation.[2] Even more chilling accounts appeared as the world learned of how "40,000 babies were dying of starvation each day in Third World countries."[3] These harsh facts provided yet another reason for people to come together.

If humanitarian desires failed to rally us, there was always the concern that a hungry world was an unstable world. As the gap between the poor and the rich grew, many feared that if we failed to share our bread we would soon be sharing violence. The World Watch Institute offered a grim prediction: "The overall model suggests that we may be moving into a very difficult situation with food, one where food security may replace military security as the principal preoccupation of many governments of the world."[4] The institute's argument was simple: hungry people are desperate people.

As population increased, it became clear that pollution would not observe geographic and cultural boundaries. A burgeoning population was beginning to emerge as the single greatest threat to the health of the planet. The editors at *Time* magazine believed the problem of global pollution was so great that instead of citing a "Man of the Year" for 1988, they declared that the planet was what deserved our attention. Their thesis was clear: It was not a single nation but the earth that was endangered.[5] With the aid of thirty-three experts from throughout the world, they meticulously documented a long list of environmental concerns that cut across the entire planet. It was indisputable that the people of the world were destroying rain forests, polluting common oceans and rivers, killing off valuable plants and animals (99 percent of the creatures ever to have come into existence had vanished), creating the "greenhouse" effect, dumping toxic wastes, and not enforcing regulations for nuclear plants. The editors' final remarks might well have been written for this textbook: "Rich and poor, north and south, nations must get it together or face common disaster."[6]

As the population of the world increased it became more difficult to remain aloof and isolated from global tensions and conflicts. The 1960s, 1970s, and 1980s were giving credence to the axiom that hostility anywhere had the potential to become hostility everywhere. Places like Lebanon, Iran, Israel, Nicaragua, Panama, Honduras, El Salvador, Afghanistan, and Korea seemed as close as troublesome neighbors, for their internal skirmishes appeared to be right next door, and in many ways they were. *U.S. News and World Report* examined the connectedness of global disorder in an essay called "A World of Continuing Tensions."[7] It listed and discussed thirty-four regions in the world where local conflicts could affect events in the United States and even, perhaps, draw us into armed conflict. We needed to know about these countries so that we could avert a global confrontation.

Cultures throughout the world also began to worry about international hostility as membership in the nuclear weapons club continued to grow. Dangerous and deadly secrets that had once been the private possession of a few powerful nations were now in the hands of countries over which we had no control, and even less contact. It was estimated that fifteen countries had the ability to launch ballistic missiles, and that twenty to thirty nations had developed the capability to produce mustard and nerve gases and other lethal chemicals.[8] Here again were nations that we needed to talk to, and understand, if we were to sustain our culture into the next century. We were beginning to see the validity of John F. Kennedy's observation regarding the urgency of intercultural understanding, for he had reminded us that "irrational barriers and ancient prejudices fall quickly when the question of survival itself is at stake."

The new economic arena.   Shifts in the international business community, coupled with new alignments among import and export cultures, also compelled us to focus on this new era. It is important to remember that when World War II ended, most of the world was in disarray. The war had hurt not only the financial institutions of other countries, but had come right into many people's front yards. Hence, buildings as well as banks had been destroyed. The United States avoided this destruction. We emerged from the war as the only super-power. As a combination father figure and big brother we set the tempo everywhere. Economically we were in control.

In the early 1950s America monopolized high technology and made over 80 percent of the world's automobiles. (We now make 24 percent.) In those days most of the world watched television sets made in the United States. (Now only one American company manufactures TV sets.) We produced as much as 40 percent of the world's wealth with less than 5 percent of its population. Only 5 percent of America's industries faced foreign competition during these glory days. In the 1990s, 75 percent of our companies must compete in this new economic world.[9] Even into the 1960s we were the world's largest exporter of manufactured goods, and we ruled over a vast economic empire. Today that same economic empire is in serious trouble. In 1980, only one Japanese bank ranked among the American-led top ten. Today, the world's ten largest banks are Japanese. In 1985 the United States became a net borrower for the first time in seventy-one years, and in July of 1989 the imbalance between total foreign investments in the United States and American holdings overseas reached $532.5 billion. By 1992 the twelve-nation European Economic Community will replace the United States as the world's largest market, with over 400 million consumers buying from its own "club." With a unified currency and no travel restrictions, the European Economic Community presents the United States with yet another economic battle.

As we enter the 1990s it seems obvious that we must communicate with other cultures if our economy is to remain strong. For whether we like it or not, America must share economic dominance with Japan, West Germany, Great Britain, the Netherlands, Korea, Italy, France, Canada, and a long list of smaller nations that also want the rewards afforded those who do business in the international marketplace.

This new global arena is unique in that most of the participants know that international business, like professional sports, is played both at home and on the courts of the opposition. In order to digest the complexity of this new game let us briefly look at our role overseas and what our rivals have done in the United States.

We begin by restating this economic premise: The United States needs to do business with other cultures in order for its economic system to operate and to survive. We simply cannot consume all that we produce. This is reflected in the fact that over one-third of all corporate profits come from international transactions (and this number is growing). "Four of every five new jobs are created as a result of foreign trade; and the 23 largest banks in the United States derive nearly half of their total earnings abroad."[10] In agriculture, one out of three acres of U.S. farmland is cultivated directly for export. Here is yet another example of how we need other cultures and countries to maintain our lifestyle.

This strong dependence on other countries appears in countless other ways. For example:

- U.S. holdings overseas totaled $308.8 billion in 1987.[11]
- In China alone the United States has committed over $3.5 billion to six hundred joint ventures.
- In the Soviet Union such ventures have swollen from two hundred in 1988 to more than one thousand in 1989.
- Recently IBM has proposed a $1 billion plant in Japan to build advanced versions of computer memory chips.
- More than eight thousand companies now have international operations in foreign countries.
- Mexican border towns have over 1,490 *maquiladoras* (foreign-owned factories that employ Mexican workers).

- To manage and administer all these international holdings over a million Americans apply for business passports each year, and 2.5 million of them now work abroad. (This number does not include military personnel.)
- In addition, more than forty states maintain overseas offices to solicit investments.

As we mentioned earlier, Americans are not the only ones doing business on foreign soil. Foreign companies and international investors now take part in what one magazine called "the globalization of national economics."[12] In the United States this globalization appears on many fronts. For example, more than five thousand foreign firms operate in the United States. Foreigners have invested about $300 billion here and own nearly $1.5 trillion in U.S. assets (about 10 percent of the total worth of this country). This is an increase of almost 200 percent since 1980. In 1988 alone, overseas buyers snapped up $42 billion in American assets, and by the end of the decade overseas concerns controlled 13 percent of American industrial assets. AT&T must prepare thousands of its annual stockholder reports in foreign languages.

This foreign influence, as we have already noted, takes a variety of forms. One is property. For instance, foreign investors own over one million acres of U.S. farmland and 64 percent of all the commercial property in downtown Los Angeles. Foreign firms initiated nine of the twenty corporation mergers and acquisitions in 1988. And foreign companies applied for, and were granted, more U.S. patents than were American firms. In addition, one out of every fourteen Americans now works for a foreign boss.[13]

This new economic arena might well serve as a microcosm showing how much the world has changed. This change, though difficult for some to accept, is quite indisputable. Where Yankee technological know-how and marketing power once dominated world markets, Americans now find themselves jockeying for business amid a throng of muscular new competitors—competitors from different cultures that we need to understand if we hope to be successful in the new world.

Domestic Contacts

As changes throughout the world began to alter and even reconstruct life in the United States, a kind of cultural revolution took place within our own boundaries, a revolution that made us redefine and rethink the meaning of the word

American. The word could no longer be used to describe a single group of people. Americans were now coming in different colors and from different backgrounds. From a variety of directions, and with varying degrees of intensity, new cultures and **co-cultures** were emerging while old ones were demanding to be heard. Some, like the influx of immigrants fleeing from economic and political hardships, arrived and remained silent as their numbers increased. Other groups, who previously had remained in the shadow of the **dominant culture,** were now becoming more visible and vocal. Co-cultures and groups such as Native Americans, homosexuals, the disabled, the poor, the elderly, blacks, and women wanted a new recognition. Many were no longer willing to wait passively for admission into the dominant culture. To understand better the influence of these groups it is beneficial to look at some of the circumstances that gave them new prominence. More specifically, let's briefly examine the impact of these new immigrants and the composition of the groups that were demanding recognition.

Immigration. Legal and illegal immigration into the United States has rapidly and significantly transformed the demographics of this country. From 1980 through 1988, approximately 800,000 refugees were legally admitted to the United States, and millions of others entered illegally. This immigration brought us into contact with more and varied cultures. Although immigrants to the United States arrived from hundreds of different places, the people of Southeast Asia and Latin America most complemented our population. In 1980 the Asian-American population in the United States stood at around 3.5 million. By 1987 it had reached 5.1 million, and estimates suggest that the figure will increase to over 10 million by the year 2000.

The Latin-American population, composed of people from Mexico, Puerto Rico, Cuba, and Central and South America, is now approaching twenty-five million. In the period from 1980 to 1988, this group expanded by 30 percent; and demographic experts predict that it will grow to over thirty-five million in 2000, and account for 13 to 14 percent of the population. Hispanics are also the fastest-growing minority in the United States, expanding at five times the rate of the rest of the population.

It is easy to see, at least by the statistics, that Americans are being thrust into communication situations with people from different backgrounds. By all indications the trend will continue. In fact, many people believe that there will not only be a continuation of what we have been experiencing, but an increase in the number of people coming to America. They argue that the rest of the world is not welcoming foreigners. From Hong Kong to western Europe, foreigners are finding the doors closed. As a recent *Time* magazine article noted, "With millions of people in search of asylum, compassion is drying up."[14] But entry doesn't "dry up" in America. People all over the world know that they can seek refuge in the United States, a country that grants immigration status to twice as many people as all the other countries of the world combined. Hence, many of the world's fifteen to eighteen million refugees will end up in the United States.

It should be clear from this that the population of the United States is changing and shifting, and that these transformations will continue. For example, in 1990 whites will account for approximately 78 percent of the total population of the United States. That figure is expected to drop to 54 percent by 2080.[15] Clearly, ethnic minorities are increasing at a much faster rate than the dominant culture.

American business was quick to adapt to the cultural diversity of their new customers. Sears Roebuck, J.C. Penney, and other large retailers introduced bilingual general catalogs. (Santa Claus could now speak Spanish.) Phone companies started printing their Yellow Pages in different languages, depending on what parts of a city would be receiving the book. During the 1970s and 1980s, nineteen new full-time foreign-language television stations went on the air. Programs were broadcast in languages ranging from Korean to Hebrew as these new Americans sought news and entertainment that focused on their other culture.

Recognition.   Asians and Latin Americans were not the only groups altering the cultural makeup of the country. African Americans were also adding to the amount of contact between co-cultures and the dominant culture. From 1970 to 1988 the black population rose from 22.6 million to over 30 million. Blacks were now 12.3 percent of the population. And not only were they making up a larger portion of the total population, but antidiscrimination legislation and major court decisions gave blacks easier access to events and environments that had earlier been, by either law or tradition, reserved for the dominant culture. A new cultural awareness among blacks also helped them come into contact with the dominant culture. In addition, the entire country had learned from the disturbances of the 1960s that communication needed to replace apathy and prejudice.

Homosexuals, who had for decades remained hidden, were beginning to confront the dominant culture. As they emerged from the "closet," we learned in 1989 that they numbered approximately 23 to 25 million, and that they constituted 9 to 11 percent of the population. We also discovered that they often held values and beliefs that were contrary to those of the dominant culture.

Women were yet another segment of the population that began to tell the dominant culture they wanted to be perceived and responded to in new ways. Their messages were reinforced by numerous affirmative action rulings. Many men found that for the first time in their lives they were having to interact with women in new settings and were even being asked to develop new communication patterns. College classrooms, work stations, and even relationships were adjusted as women told the dominant culture that they no longer wanted to be separated from what many of them sensed was the "governing" culture.

If we add co-cultures such as the deaf (about 17.5 million), people who are incarcerated, gangs, the homeless, prostitutes, and even the elderly to our list, we can begin to appreciate just how many people there are who do not hold all mainstream beliefs, attitudes, and values. These individuals, while residing in the United States, live a life that often differs considerably from the dominant culture. It should be easy to grasp how many of America's institutions, and most of its communication patterns, have been affected by the groups we have been discussing. The new immigrants and their children joined determined co-cultures and began to reshape our educational system, the family, and the work place. In each of these settings intercultural contacts became inevitable.

In many cities such as Chicago, Miami, Los Angeles, Dallas, San Diego, Detroit, Washington, San Francisco, and Albuquerque, minority students now outnumber white students in the public schools. By 1990, 30 percent of the students in public schools were ethnic minorities, and this number is apt to grow. Demographic specialists speculate that if current trends continue, the public schools in more than fifty cities in the United States will draw a majority of their students from the ethnic communities.[16] The intercultural implications of these statistics should be obvious to schoolteachers, parents, and students. These individuals, and others, will be in contact with various cultures every day. That contact, as we shall stress throughout this book, will involve people who, because of their diverse backgrounds, perceive schools differently and act out those cultural perceptions in ways that often conflict with traditional norms.

Marriages between members of different cultures are also on the increase, and hence represent another point of contact for people of diverse backgrounds. Mixed marriages among different racial and ethnic groups now total over one million, and they are doubling every five years. These marriages have produced over 500,000 children, a figure that is also growing.

Even the work place has felt the impact of cultural diversity. In 1970, white males comprised 52 percent of the work force. That number dropped to 49 percent in 1980 and reached an all-time low of 43 percent in 1986. By the year 1995, 75 percent of all those entering the work force will be women and minorities. Even now, in California and other places, ethnic minorities comprise 20 percent of the work force.

The newly fashioned work environment has experienced many of the problems that occur when cultures come into contact. For example, managers who once worked only with a rather homogeneous work force now find themselves confronted with employees who not only speak a different language, but who are motivated by different goals. White employees are also finding that for the first time they have to take orders from minorities. In the last ten years the number of black managers has jumped by over one million.[17] Minorities and women find that old communication habits are creating problems. For instance, a recent study by the U.S. Merit System Protection Board found that 42 percent of women who worked for the federal government said they had been sexually harassed either verbally or physically.[18] Such harassment was so widespread in Los Angeles that the mayor of that city instituted training programs for all government workers. Even American industry has had to offer male employees new guidelines for communicating with women and other minorities.

As we conclude this first section of the chapter we want to repeat and expand on two very important themes of this book—themes that we will return to over and over. One deals with content and the other with philosophy. First, the content. Whether it be negotiating a major contract with the Soviets, discussing a joint venture with a Japanese company, having to take orders from someone of a different gender, counseling a young student from Cambodia, working alongside someone who doesn't speak English, or interviewing a minority member for a new position, we all face people with cultural backgrounds different from our own, backgrounds that can make many of our contacts frustrating and unsuccessful. However, differences in language, food, dress, treatment of time, work habits, socializing, and the like account for only some of the problems associated with intercultural communication. Most misunderstandings go much deeper than the superficial differences that *Parade Magazine* or *Reader's Digest* can explain. We now know that in intercultural communication, the **deep structure** of a culture is often what determines a person's response to events and other people. What members of a particular culture value and their ways of perceiving the universe are usually far more important than whether or not they eat with chopsticks, their hands, or metal utensils. The need to understand these significant differences provides the major stimulus behind this book. Although it may sound trite, we are concerned with those differences that make a difference. More specifically, we are concerned with the information you need to become a successful intercultural communicator. Our goal is to supply you with that information.

Our second theme, because it is less tangible than our first, is harder to explain. For now we are no longer talking about a fund of knowledge we believe you should possess at the conclusion of this book, but rather a philosophical orientation that you should *not* have. Let us explain. We are worried about those people who fail to face the fact that complex changes have taken place in North America. These are people who still say: "I do not want to be part of the global village. I want to communicate only with people who resemble me." The problem is that whether they like it or not, they are in the village, and it troubles us that they are not very good villagers. Our culture has a long history of racism and **ethnocentrism.** Although overt racial and ethnic violence has lessened since the 1960s, we still see countless examples of subtle discrimination aimed at blacks, homosexuals, Asians, Hispanics, women, the poor, and the disabled. This negative behavior is not only contrary to American ideals but is harmful. It cripples both the holder of the prejudice and the target of such narrowness. Hence, throughout this book we shall offer information about diverse cultures as well as a point of view aimed at reducing discrimination and prejudice. We believe that intolerance and bigotry are wrong. To discriminate against someone simply because he or she has a different color skin, prays to a different God, or speaks a different language diminishes the best that is in all of us.

STUDYING INTERCULTURAL COMMUNICATION

Having tried to convince you that the study of intercultural communication is a worthwhile pursuit, we must now alert you to some of the problems you will face as you venture into this exciting area.

The study of human communication is convoluted, multidimensional, and subject to countless variations. When the component of culture is added to this topic, the complexities and the problems facing any systematic study of the two are compounded greatly. The study of culture is as elusive as the study of human communication. Although there are as many problems as there are people, we would nevertheless suggest that most of the obstacles fall into three general categories. Let us briefly look at each of these so that you might be aware of the difficulties and challenges facing anyone who takes on the subject of intercultural communication.

First, because culture lacks a distinct crystalline structure, it is often riddled with contradictions and extremes. As we shall point out in Chapter 3, culture is learned on both the cognitive and affective levels. We are told about our culture, but most of what we learn we simply absorb without being aware of it. Culture is vague and it is specific; it is all of an individual, and it is but part of the individual. Put in slightly different terms, we are much more than our culture. Each human being is unique and is formed by countless factors—culture is but one of them. At any given moment our behavior is a product of millions of years of evolution, our genetic makeup, the groups we have been affiliated with, our gender, age, individual histories, our perception of the other person, the situation we find ourselves in, and a long list of other factors. Although culture is the cardinal context, and also offers us a common frame of reference, none of us is ordinary. Simply put, we are our culture and much more.

Lacking consistencies and any clear-cut distinction between an individual trait and a cultural characteristic, we need to be careful when comparing one culture to another. Johnson made this same point clearly in the introduction to an article comparing Eastern and Western concepts of self:

First, generalizations stressing differences between East and West gloss over the diversity within both Eastern and Western traditions them-selves—over different eras, among different cultures, and as these traditions are differently experienced by individuals. Second, such comparisons between East and West necessarily set aside civilizations and nations whose traditions have not been recorded in a manner permitting equivalent representation.[19]

Johnson's major concern was that monolithic comparisons often led to overstating and even misstating the role of culture in human communication.

We have been trying to stress thus far that cultural generalizations must be viewed as approximations, not absolutes. As our experiences have taught us, sometimes people do not act out the prescribed and accepted modes of cultural behavior. Even though not all human transactions follow a prepared script, the study of culture does help explain much of what takes place between people. It is important at this juncture that we be mindful of oversimplification and remember that all the rules have many exceptions.

A second problem in studying intercultural communication is that culture cannot be manipulated or held in check. Therefore, it is difficult to conduct certain kinds of research when investigating this topic. In most scientific experiments, a researcher controls and manipulates some of the variables, but culture is hard to regulate and impossible to suspend. What we know about intercultural communication, therefore, is not only tentative, but comes from a variety of sources—some highly reliable and some speculative. Once again, intercultural generalizations must allow for exceptions and are best viewed as guidelines rather than absolutes.

Our final obstacle is impossible to overcome, for in this instance we are the problem—or as the famous comic-strip character Pogo once said, "We have met the enemy, and he is us." The problem is simply this: We study other cultures from the perspective of our own culture. Our observations and our conclusions are colored by the specific orientation that we have been exposed to. It is difficult, if not impossible, to see and to give meaning to words and behaviors that we are not familiar with. How, for example, do we make sense of someone's silence if we come from a very verbal culture? There also is a danger that we might allow our judgments to take on evaluative connotations—"How could someone be so insensitive as to be silent at a time like this?" The inclination to believe that our group is superior to all other groups and cultures is called **ethnocentrism.** It not only impedes intercultural communication, but because so much of our ethnocentrism is below the conscious level, it is often difficult to identify. As the authors of this book, we carefully examined our own ethnocentrism as we discussed cultures other than our own. Although we shall return to this concept throughout the book, we urge you to join us in being ever vigilant for ethnocentrism so that it doesn't control your perceptions.

PREVIEW OF THE BOOK: WHAT LIES AHEAD?

To help accomplish our purpose we have divided the book into three interrelated parts. Part 1, which has four chapters, introduces the study of intercultural communication. Chapter 1 had but two objectives: to convince you of the importance of intercultural communication and to alert you to some of the problems you might encounter as you study this topic. Because this is a book about communication, culture, and intercultural communication, Chapters 2, 3, and 4 will examine each of those topics in some detail. Chapter 2 will define communication and discuss its major components. During the course of that discussion we will note that while culture tends to separate people, the ways in which we communicate serve to unite us. Chapter 3 will examine the concept of culture, first by defining culture and then by considering its place in the study of intercultural communication. Chapter 4 looks at intercultural communication. In so doing, it identifies the components that make up this study. This chapter will also offer a model of intercultural communication, a model that will serve as a blueprint for examining the communication behavior of any culture or co-culture.

Part 2 moves us from the theoretical to the practical by dealing with intercultural interaction. The first chapter looks at people involved in intercultural communication and at their attempts to communicate. Specifically, Chapter 5 explores some of the differences in perception found among cultures, and the major forces that shape those perceptions. In the next three chapters the focus shifts to the ways in which people from different cultures attempt to share those perceptions through verbal and nonverbal messages. Looking at the kinds of messages that are exchanged will help us appreciate the responses those messages produce.

Chapter 9, the final chapter in Part 2, acknowledges the importance of two communication principles: first, that communication is rule-governed, and second, that those rules are often tied to a particular cultural setting. Hence, our investigation looks at cultural variations in business, school, and health-care settings. Knowing those rules will help explain differences that people often find when they move from context to context.

Part 3, finally, is concerned with the improvement of intercultural communication skills. In a sense, our entire study focuses on the issue of improvement, but in Chapter 10 you will find specific advice and recommendations. This chapter identifies some problems that often plague the individual who comes into contact with members of different cultures or co-cultures. Hindrances such as ethnocentrism, prejudice, and stereotyping are discussed in detail. In addition, the final chapter suggests some new behaviors and attitudes that will make most intercultural meetings more productive and rewarding.

SUMMARY

The Importance of Intercultural Communication

- New technology, growth in the world's population, and shifts in the global economic arena have contributed to increased international contacts.

- Intercultural contacts have accelerated in the last few decades, and will continue to increase.

- Domestic contacts are increasing because new immigrants and co-cultures are demanding recognition.

- Settings that most feel the influence of these cultural changes are the educational system, the family, and the work place.

Studying Intercultural Communication

- The hazards of studying intercultural communication are overgeneralizing and forgetting the complex nature of human behavior.

Preview of the Book: What Lies Ahead?

- Part 1 serves as an introduction to the study of intercultural communication.

- Part 2 moves from the theoretical to the practical.

- Part 3 is concerned with the improvement of intercultural communication skills.

ACTIVITIES

1. Seek out an informant from another culture, someone who is willing to answer questions about his or her culture throughout the duration of this course. If your class has a good cultural mix, pair up with a classmate; you may also have a friend or relative who fits the bill. If not, try an English-as-a-second-language program on your campus or in your community, or an international students' organization. To make an even exchange, you may want to find someone who wants to practice English conversation or who needs tutoring.

2. In small groups, identify your culture or co-culture. (The typical group will have representatives from at least two co-cultures.) After identifying yourselves, discuss the following: How many in the group identify with the dominant culture of North America? What communication problems have your groups typically had with each other? In what settings do these issues arise (for example, the work place, the family)? Take this opportunity to find out as much as you can about each other in terms of cultural identity.

DISCUSSION IDEAS

1. Describe your current intercultural contacts (international and/or domestic). To what degree do you interact with people from other cultures? In what settings? How successful are your attempts at intercultural communi-

cation? If you have problems, to what do you attribute them? How might you improve these interactions?

2. Explain this statement from Chapter 1 and give examples: "In studying other cultures, we do so from the perspective of our own culture."

3. Give an example of a (co-)cultural behavior that you do not understand. See if anyone in the class can explain it to you. Give an example of a behavior from your culture that someone from another culture might have difficulty understanding.

4. How might new technology, population changes, the new economic arena, immigration, and so on affect you personally? Consider, among other things, your plans for furthering your education and pursuing a career.

5. Give examples of co-cultural differences between men and women in North America.

NOTES FOR CHAPTER 1

1. "Where the Tourists Go," *U.S. News and World Report,* February 26, 1990, 63.

2. *Insight,* April 17, 1989, 27.

3. Thomas A. Sanction, "What on Earth Are We Doing?" *Time,* January 2, 1989, 26.

4. *The San Diego Tribune,* March 21, 1989, A-9.

5. *Sanction,* 27.

6. *Sanction,* 64.

7. "A World of Continuing Tensions," *U.S. News and World Report,* December 26, 1988, 52–53.

8. *Newsweek,* January 16, 1989, 23.

9. Mortimer B. Zuckerman, "What Should Make Bush Run Now," *U.S. News and World Report,* February 6, 1989, 70–71.

10. "International Challenges: Perils and Opportunities," *Center for the Advancement of Foreign Language and International Studies,* December 1989, 4.

11. Monroe W. Karmin, "Economic Outlook: My House Is Your House," *U.S. News and World Report,* November 7, 1988, 65.

12. Karmin, 65.

13. *U.S. News and World Report,* January 2, 1989, 82.

14. *Time,* July 3, 1989, 24.

15. Ben J. Wattenberg, "Tomorrow," *U.S. News and World Report,* February 13, 1989, 31.

16. American Council of Education, "Minority Changes Hold Major Implications for U.S.," *Higher Education and National Affairs,* (1984), 8.

17. *Time,* March 13, 1989, 67.

18. *U.S. News and World Report,* August 1, 1988, 50.

19. Frank Johnson, "The Western Concept of Self," in *Culture and Self: Asian and Western Perspectives,* ed. Anthony J. Marsella, George De Vos, and Francis L. K. Hsu (New York: Travistock Publications, 1985), 91–92.

Use what language you will, you can never say anything but what you are.

EMERSON

What sets us against one another is not our aims—they all come to the same thing—but our methods.

SAINT-EXUPÉRY

CHAPTER TWO

COMMUNICATION: SHARING WHO WE ARE AND WHAT WE KNOW

HUMAN COMMUNICATION

We begin our study of intercultural communication not by taking on the entire topic, but rather by examining the communication component of intercultural transactions. Our rationale is simple: To understand intercultural communication you must first understand human communication. This notion is in no way profound, but it is inescapable. For regardless of the person, culture, or setting, when we share ideas and feelings we are engaging in a communication act. All of us, despite differences in background and culture, perform the same basic activities when we attempt to assign meaning to our experiences and the experiences of another person. Whether we live in a city in Canada, a village in India, or the jungles of Brazil, we all participate in the same activity when we communicate. The results and the methods might be different, but the process is the same. In short, all five and a half billion of us engage in communication events so that we can share our realities with other human beings.

By understanding the communication process, you can improve your own communication behavior and appreciate the behavior of others. That improvement can be facilitated if you know (1) how communication is defined, (2) the major components of communication, and (3) the primary characteristics of communication.

Defining Communication

Having just informed you of the importance of understanding communication, we must now warn you that defining and describing human communication is a difficult task. Although there are many reasons that definitions and descriptions are troublesome, most of the problems fall into two categories: The first is the complex nature of communication, and the second is the problems associated with intentionality and unintentionality. Let us briefly probe these two concerns before we offer a working definition of communication.

Communication is complex.   Think for a moment of all the bodily activity that accompanies even the simple act of saying "Hello" to a friend. From the secretion of the chemicals in your brain, to the moving of your lips to produce sound, thousands of components are in operation (and most of them at the same time). To isolate certain of the variables automatically precludes analyzing countless others. When we ask the single word *communication* to include all these activities we are, as Dance notes, "Trying to make the concept of 'communication' do too much for us."[1] We end up thinking of communication as one activity instead of a multidimensional process. As you might suspect, communication becomes even more complex as we add the cultural dimension to an already complicated process. For as we shall see throughout this book, although all cultures use symbols to share their realities, the realities and the symbols are often quite different. One culture might say "Hello" in a casual manner while another bows formally in silence.

To overcome the problems created by the complexity of communication, most scholars concentrate on those aspects of the process that are most germane to their particular interests. For example, neurologists look at what the brain and the nervous system do during a communication act. Psychologists are apt to examine the issues related to perception, and the linguist inspects the language people use. Each of these disciplines carves out but a piece of the territory called human communication. As writers in the area of intercultural communication, we also have to confront the problem of generalizing from only part of the communication process. Therefore, as you will see later in this chapter, our view and description are primarily concerned with *those elements that most influence interaction when members of two different cultures come together in an interpersonal setting.*

Communication as intentional and unintentional behavior. The dilemma created by intentionality versus unintentionality can be explained by briefly presenting the arguments advanced by both schools of thought. One approach, advanced by Miller and Steinberg, describes communication as the process whereby one person deliberately attempts to convey meaning to another.[2] This perspective holds that we intentionally send messages to change or modify the behavior of other people. The argument is rather basic: When we select our words or actions, we do so with some degree of consciousness. For Miller and Steinberg communication is not a random activity that happens by chance, but rather something that is systematic and planned. The planning might be long-range or instantaneous, but in either case it is conscious.

The second orientation proposes that the intentionality approach is too limiting, and that it fails to allow for all the circumstances in which messages are conveyed unintentionally. Scholars who support this approach believe communication takes place whenever people attach meaning to messages, even if the sender of the message did not expect his or her actions to be considered part of the communication event. They contend that communication influences other people whether we intend it to or not.[3] We would claim that knowing your actions convey many potential messages is important when engaging in intercultural communication. The seemingly innocent acts of showing the soles of your feet to a stranger in Korea, or touching a woman you are introduced to in

Saudi Arabia, could send negative messages that might hamper the rest of the encounter.

You now know some of the problems facing anyone who attempts to study human communication. We, of course, are not immune to the uncertainties we have just discussed. Nevertheless, we shall take our turn at defining communication.

A definition of communication. If communication is complex and multidimensional, then it can be defined in the following way: **Communication** occurs whenever meaning is attributed to behavior or the residue of behavior. When someone observes our actions or their remnants, and decides they mean something, we have made contact and have communicated whether our behavior was conscious or unconscious, intentional or unintentional. As long as what we do has the potential of being a message, we are communicating. In this sense our words, actions, and even silence send messages about the moment and how we are reacting to it.

Behavior residue, which is mentioned in our definition, is what remains as a record of our actions. For instance, this chapter is a behavior residue of many of our past communication events. As authors we had to think, write, type, and operate a computer for you to read these words. This notion of **residue** is extremely important to students of intercultural communication in that it calls attention to some of the consequences of past experiences, experiences that are often culture-bound.

Another example of behavior residue is the odor of cigar smoke lingering in an elevator after the cigar smoker has left. The odor, and our attitudes and perceptions towards it, send us a message. Here again we see the importance of memory and past experiences on communication.

This general definition of communication also highlights the attribution of meaning to behavior. Attribution involves taking meaning we already have and imposing it on behavior we observe in our environment. Try to imagine that somewhere in each of our brains is a meaning reservoir in which we have stored all of the meanings we process at any given moment. These various meanings have developed throughout our lifetime as the outside world has sent each of us trillions of messages, each message to be stored for later use. As Pavese once wrote, "We do not remember days, we remember moments." In this sense meaning is relative to each of us because we all have experienced unique moments in our lives. The notion of individual attributions reminds us of the countless variables that come into play each time we communicate.

The definition we presented should lead you to the conclusion that communication takes place on many levels. That is to say, many of our messages are constructed and sent with *conscious intent* ("I shall smile because I want to look happy"), while others are sent without our even being aware that the behavior is a message (someone sees you walking fast and *assumes* you cannot stop and visit).

The Ingredients of Communication

Embedded in our definition are six common ingredients of communication. Because they help explain how communication works, we have decided to develop them in detail. The six factors usually operate almost instantaneously, but we have had to isolate them in order to talk about them. In their basic form the ingredients are so common and universal that they are found in every culture. That is to say, the constituents of communication are one of the many links that bond all human beings together. Culture and space may separate us, but the need to communicate and the mechanics of communication connect us.

First is the **source**. A source is a person who has a need to communicate. This need may range from a social desire for recognition as an individual to the desire to share information with others so that you can influence their next act. Communication, then, is concerned with the sharing of internal states of being with *varying degrees* of intention to affect the behavior of another person. Although the reasons for communication may vary from person to person and from culture to culture, we all share the same frustrations when we attempt to put feelings and ideas into words and actions.

To be consistent with our definition of communication, we should add that the source could send a message without knowing his or her actions were communicating. For example, in North American cultures a man with a spot of pizza sauce on his tie often conveys an image of a sloppy eater. Even though he dropped the sauce by accident, someone else can read meaning into the stain.

Because internal states cannot be shared directly, we must rely on symbolic representations of our internal states. This brings us to the second ingredient, **encoding**. Encoding is an internal activity in which verbal and nonverbal symbols (a code) are selected and arranged according to the rules of grammar and syntax applicable to the language the creator of the messages is using. Again, even though the process of changing feelings to words and actions is universal, the words and actions selected and how they are strung together are culturally based. A member of one culture observes a close friend and decides to smile, yet in another culture the same *internal state* leads someone to place both hands on the partner's shoulders.

Encoding leads to production of a **message**, which is a set of verbal and/or nonverbal symbols that represents a source's particular state of being at a specific moment. What distinguishes a message from the encoding process is that the message is *external* to sources, while encoding goes on inside the person. The message, a representation of the internal state, must pass from one individual to another. Although all cultures use words and actions as messages, each culture has its own ways of forming messages. One culture might say "Good morning," another "Buenos dias," and yet another "*Oh-hah-yoh goh-zah-ee-mahs.*"

Messages must have a means by which they move from source (Person A) to receiver (Person B). The fourth communication ingredient, the **channel**, provides that necessary connection between these two separate entities. The primary channels are sound and sight. We receive the messages when we listen to or watch each other. The degree to which an individual relies on one channel over another is often a product of culture. In the United States, for example, words are highly valued, while in some Mediterranean cultures touching is a major communication channel. And as we shall see later in the book, some Eastern cultures let silence carry the message.

After a message has been generated and moved along by a channel, it still must have our fifth ingredient—a **receiver**. The receiver is the person or persons who take the message into account and are therefore linked to the message source. Receivers may be those whom the source intended or they may be others who, for whatever reason, come into contact with the message.

In the sixth stage of our description of the communication process, the receiver **decodes** the raw energy he or she takes in from the external world. This operation (the converting of external energies to meaningful experiences) is akin to the source's act of encoding, since it is also an internal activity—an activity often referred to as *information processing*. This stage allows the receiver to attach meaning to behaviors the source has produced. Although all individuals decode, culture largely determines the meaning one gives to the outside world. One culture may find loud laughing in public a sign of happiness, while others might decide such outward displays should be reserved for the privacy of one's home—the same event yet two different meanings. This example, like so many in the book, reflects the wisdom of George Gissing when he wrote, "It is the mind which creates the world about us, and even though we stand side by side in the same meadow, my eyes will never see what is beheld by yours, my heart will never stir to the emotions [by] which yours is touched."

The Characteristics of Communication

We trust that the last few pages have made it clear that human communication is a complex activity. It is indeed even far more intricate and puzzling than our discussion thus far has revealed. To help guide you through some of these complexities we would like to develop the topic in greater detail. However, there are a few points to keep in mind before we start our journey. First, our attempt at cataloging is going to be limited by the fact that communication is composed of much more than we can discuss in the next few pages. Just as a description of the forest that mentions only the trees and flowers does not do justice to the entire setting, our inventory is not exhaustive. We, too, are forced to leave out some of the landscape.

Second, and perhaps more importantly, a great deal about communication is yet to be discovered. New theories, concepts, and opinions are appearing rapidly. We shall offer a summary of what we deem to be the important characteristics of communication that should be implicit in any study of intercultural communication.

Finally, as you explore the characteristics of communication, remember that the order of our listing is arbitrary, not systematic. This means that our slate of characteristics *does not* reflect any attempt to establish a hierarchy. Language is linear; hence we are forced to offer one element at a time, even though this distorts the way communication actually operates. In "real life" things happen all at once, not in a straight line. We are in a very real sense falsifying reality to meet our needs.

Now that we have warned you of the pitfalls that await anyone seeking to understand communication, we are ready to consider those characteristics of communication that are common to all human beings regardless of status, age, rank, gender, country, or culture.

No direct mind-to-mind contact.   We begin with a rather obvious and universal characteristic of communication that has frustrated human beings since before language was invented: It is impossible to share our feelings and experiences by means of direct mind-to-mind contact. Admittedly, in the discussion of encoding and decoding we alluded to this idea, but its profound significance allows for this second reading (and later in this chapter, even a third).

The core of this characteristic is elementary yet fascinating. Simply stated, we are all isolated one from another by the cover of our skin. What we know and feel is inside of us, and thus far in the evolutionary process it is not possible for anyone else to enter this very private domain. It is as if we all lived in sequestered houses with doors and windows that never opened. Perhaps we shall see the day when one of the devices from *Star Trek* becomes a reality and another human being can have direct access to what we are experiencing, but for now we must all live in a kind of solitary confinement. An African proverb makes this point more figuratively: "The earth is a beehive; we all enter by the same door but live in different cells."

Although the inability to have direct mind-to-mind contact is universal, the methods used to adjust to this characteristic are culturally based. For example, later in the book we shall discuss cultures that place great stock in verbal language for sharing reality and others that believe meaning gets shared in a variety of ways, and hence that people need not say very much.

We can only infer.   The next characteristic is a corollary and extension of the first. This characteristic reminds us that because we do not have access to the feelings of other human beings, we can only infer what they are experiencing inside their individual homes. We make these inferences from long speeches, single words, movements, smiles, and simple glances. These words and actions, to continue our earlier analogy, represent an attempt to read a note that has been slipped under a closed door.

Again, we would be remiss if we did not point out that the inferences we draw from the symbols of others are rooted in our culture. We see someone who is foreign-looking and speaking loudly and using a lot of gestures, and we infer that he is angry. Yet we observe people in our culture shouting and gesticulating wildly at a baseball game, and we infer that they are having a good time.

Communication is symbolic. In some ways we might well have combined the first three characteristics under this current heading, for everything we have said thus far leads us to assert that we employ symbols as a way of sharing our internal states. Other animals may participate in the communication process, but none of them has our unique communication capabilities. Through millions of years of physical evolution, and thousands of years of cultural evolution, we are able to receive, store, manipulate, and generate symbols. This sophisticated symbol system allows us to use a symbol (be it a sound, a scratch on paper, a statue, Braille, movement, or a painting) to stand for something else. Reflect for a moment on the wonderful gift we have that allows us to hear the words *The kittens look like little cotton balls,* and like magic have a picture in our head. Or what about the joy we experience when we see the smile of our dearest friend? These two sets of symbols, words and actions, help us let another human being know how we experience the world.

Although all cultures use symbols, they often employ different symbols and usually assign special meanings to them. Not only do Mexicans say *perro* for "dog," but the image they form when they hear the sound is quite different from the one North Americans would form.

Because symbols are at the core of communication, we shall return to this element throughout the book. We have even set aside three chapters that look at symbols in great detail. For now, let us once again remind you that symbols, by virtue of their standing for something else, give us an opportunity to share our personalized realities.

Time-binding links us together. Our fourth characteristic, called **time-binding,** is yet another example of how all the characteristics of communication are woven together. This element is perhaps best reflected in a line from Thoreau: "All the past is here." And it is here because we can make symbols. More specifically, because of the development of our cerebral cortex, and all the neurological structures associated with it, we can use symbols at a level of sophistication not known by any other creature. We can not only transmit knowledge from person to person, but we can pass ideas from generation to generation. In fact, for cultures to survive, each new infant must learn from past generations. None of us needs to start from scratch; instead, we carry around a vast amount of speculations, observations, facts, experiments, and learnings of

millions of people over thousands of years. As Weinberg noted, ". . . the grand insights of geniuses which, transmitted through symbols, enable us to span the learning of centuries."[4] We can be told what from the past we need to know, so that we can live in the present and prepare for the future. As the current generation, we are composing the symbols that will be passed along to those who will succeed us. Although cultures vary in their willingness to accept the idea, we too will be replaced. Yet our symbols will remain.

Intercultural communication makes much more sense if we realize that all of us belong to one species and have the same time-binding potential. Hence, all those you approach, be they friend or foe, walk into your life with a long history that they have acquired through the symbols found in their culture. Your specific encounters with them are, in many ways, a reflection of that history.

We seek to define the world.   All of us, from the moment of birth to the ordeal of death, attempt to define the world that impinges on our senses. We can only imagine what a confusing place this must be to the newborn infant. After spending time in a peaceful environment, the child confronts sights, sounds, tastes, and other sensations that, at this stage of life, have no meaning. It must be, as the psychologist William James noted, a bubbling, babbling mass of confusion that confronts the newborn. But from that first moment on, the search for meaning is a lifelong endeavor. As we move from place to place and person to person, we must decide what each word and action means. Like all of the other characteristics we have examined thus far, the need to define is also universal. The meanings we give to events, however, are culturally based. We see men kissing in public and find it strange and unnatural. Other cultures will perceive the same act as very natural. In some ways this entire book is about how different cultures define the circumstances and people that confront them.

Communication has a consequence.   This next characteristic of communication—that it has a consequence—reminds us that when we receive a message something happens to us. Although we touched on this idea in general terms earlier in the chapter, it is important enough to be treated as a separate element.

The basic assumption behind this attribute is apparent, yet the manifestations of this characteristic have a profound influence over the communication act. We suggest that all of our messages, in one degree or another, do something to someone else. This assertion is not philosophical or metaphysical, but is a

biological fact. It is impossible not to respond to the actions of others. It might be helpful if you visualized your potential responses as if they were on a continuum (see Figure 2-1). On one end of the continuum lie responses to messages that are overt and easy to understand. Someone sends you a message by asking directions to the library. Your outward response is to say "It's on your right." You might even point to the library. In either case the message of the other person produced an *observable response.*

A little farther down the continuum are those messages we receive from other people that produce only a mental response, but a response nevertheless. If someone says to you, "The United States doesn't spend enough money on higher education," and you only think about what was said, you are still responding. You don't have to engage in some observable action before we can call it a response to a message.

As we proceed down the continuum we come to yet another level of responses to communication. Now, however, we are referring to responses that are somewhat harder to judge. These are the messages we often receive through imitation, observation, and interaction. We are generally not even aware that we are receiving these messages. Our parents act out their sex roles and we are receiving messages about our sex roles. People greet us by shaking hands instead of hugging, and without being aware of it we are receiving messages about embracing. In the next chapter we shall spend a great deal of time developing the view that most of our culture is transmitted through these types of messages—messages that are subtle yet have an important influence on us. Ruben summarized this point when he noted, "Most of what makes communication operate as it does occurs below the surface of observable experience."[5]

At the far end of the continuum we find the responses to messages that are below the level of consciousnesses. That is to say, our body is responding even if our cognitive processes are kept to a minimum. Messages can alter our chemical secretions, increase or decrease our heart rate, change the temperature of our skin, modify pupil size, and create a host of other internal responses. Although these biological responses are the most difficult to classify, they do give credence to our intial assertion that communication has a consequence.

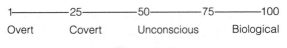

Figure 2-1

Like all of the characteristics we are investigating, this current one is universal. Stated in another manner, all of us receive and respond to messages, yet the nature of that response is rooted in our culture. The grief associated with the death of a loved one is as natural as breathing; each culture, however, determines ways of coping with and sharing the grief. Cultural responses range from wanting the comfort of others to seeking complete and total solitude.

Communication is dynamic.   Like so many of the other concepts in this section, the phrase *communication is dynamic* has more than one meaning. First, and perhaps most importantly, the catchphrase should tell us that communication is an ongoing activity. It, like us, is not fixed. As participants in communication, we constantly are affected by other people's messages (the point of our discussion of the consequences of communication) and, as a consequence, are always changing. The term *transaction,* which we have used throughout this book, is yet another indication that both participants are touched by the dynamic nature of communication. We undergo continual change all through our lives. From the moment of conception through the instant of death, we experience an almost endless variety of physical and psychological changes, some too subtle to notice, others too profound to ignore. But nature and we are not the only things that change: As we shall see in the next chapter, culture is dynamic, and it too changes. It is no wonder that twenty-five hundred years ago Heraclitus wrote, "There is nothing permanent except change."

Second, the phrase *communication is dynamic* also refers to the idea that communication as well as people are changing. Communication is a process. A single word or action does not stay frozen when we communicate; it is immediately replaced with yet another word or action. Communication is like a motion picture, not a single snapshot.

Third, because communication is ongoing and dynamic once an element (word or action) is employed, it cannot be retracted. T. S. Eliot might well have been referring to this transitory aspect of communication when he wrote, "In the life of one person, never, the same time returns." The point is simple: communication is *irreversible.* Once an event takes place we cannot have it over—perhaps a similar event, but not the exact event. The judge who advises the jury "to disregard the testimony just given" knows full well that this is impossible. The words were spoken and they cannot be unspoken.

This same view also helps explain the truism that communication is *unrepeatable*. You know from your own experiences that when you see a movie for a second time it is not the same movie. The reason is obvious—you have already seen the movie. It is the same with communication; it too happens but one time and then becomes part of your history.

Fourth, the changing nature of communication also means that our communication behavior is characterized by a great deal of inattention. Briefly survey your own actions and you come face-to-face with the fact that your mind often doesn't like what it is doing, and hence dashes from idea to idea as it seeks new data. We often shift topics in the middle of a sentence, and research shows that as listeners, our attention span is brief. Like all of the characteristics discussed in this section, the concept of the active brain cuts across all cultures. We can clearly see the universal character of this tendency in the writings of the Buddha. He was so aware of the commonality of this trait that he wrote, "The mind is fickle and flighty, it flies after fancies wherever it likes: it is difficult indeed to restrain."[6]

Communication is contextual.   We interact with others not in isolation but within a **context**, a specific physical surrounding and under a set of specific social dynamics. Put in less bulky terms, the setting and environment help determine how we and others communicate. We all follow a "prescription that indicates what behavior is obligated, preferred, or prohibited."[7] Dress, language, topic selection, and the like are all adapted to the context you find yourself in. You would not attend a university lecture without a shirt, or use profanity or reveal highly personal information there. The context calls for a different mode of behavior. The "regulations" for each context, be it classroom or courtroom, are culturally based, and therefore often shift from culture to culture. That is to say, some cultures may allow a great deal of talking in church, while others perceive the religious setting as one in which to observe strict silence. The role of context in communication is of such importance that later in the book we shall devote an entire chapter to the topic.

Communication is rule-governed.   In our last discussion we noted that the setting and the context influenced the manner in which the participants acted out their various and diverse roles. The current characteristic extends this position beyond the context. We are now suggesting that all phases of the communication act, not only the context, are governed by rules. Put in a slightly different way, we have rules for people as well as places. We learn these rules more by habit than by conscious thought. Think for a moment about some of the rules you follow almost automatically. You know the rules about language that would keep you from cursing in front of your grandparents. You know the rules about good manners that would suggest apologizing if you accidentally bumped someone while racing to the elevator. You know the rules about turn-taking that have you waiting your turn to talk if the person you are interacting with is older than you or is of higher status. You know the rules about the use of time, and can be tardy to some meetings but arrive at the assigned minute for others.

In all of our examples it would be difficult to point to the exact moment in your life when you learned the specific rule. The reason for this is quite clear, and of course speaks to the heart of this textbook. Most rules, like culture itself, are learned below the level of awareness. One culture conducts its business in a whisper, while another speaks in loud and animated voices. We learn such rules early in life and act them out instinctively. In a very real sense this book is about those rules and how they often differ from culture to culture.

Communication is self-reflective.   That communication is self-reflective has its roots in our unique ability to think about ourselves. We can reflect about our past, present, and future. This focus on self can, and usually does, take place while we are communicating with other people. We can simultaneously be participant and observer. More precisely, we can literally watch, evaluate, and alter our performance as a communicator at the very instant we are engaging in the act. We are the only species that can be at both ends of the microscope at the same time.

There is, as you would suspect by now, an intercultural dimension to our capacity to be **self-reflective.** Although it may not always be manifest, some cultures are much more concerned with the self than are others, and therefore devote a great deal of energy to watching and even worrying about the self. The "I" is at the heart of Western psychology, with its strong Freudian influence, while collective cultures put the accent on other people.

The brain is an open system.   This next characteristic of communication directs us to yet another special feature of the human brain. This time it is our ability to learn. It is captivating that our ability to learn new information is endless. We can be told about any subject and have that information be part of our personal fund of knowledge. If you did not know who won the 1990 Kentucky Derby, and we told you it was a horse named Unbridled, you would now know something you did not know before our message arrived. We refer to the brain as an open system because we can continue to take in new data as long as we live—and some world views would suggest even after.

From an intercultural perspective this characteristic is important for two reasons. First, it alerts us to the truism that while each of us can learn new ideas all through life, what we know at any one instant is a product of what the brain has experienced. Obviously, not all brains are exposed to the same experiences. Or as the basic premise of this book would suggest, not all cultures have gathered the same information. In one culture the brain may have received information about how to ride a camel, while in another culture the brain has received information regarding how to drive an automobile. Our rather glaring point is that not everyone has the same fund of knowledge.

Second, the notion of the brain as an open system reminds us that we can learn from each other. One culture's special skill for treating heart disease can be transmitted to a culture lacking that information. A culture that uses acupuncture can teach this art to groups of people who lack the concept in their culture. Yet another culture may transmit the rewards of patience to a culture that is always thrashing from event to event. In short, the best that we have as a people can be shared.

We are alike and we are different. At the beginning of this section we noted that the order in which we presented each element was somewhat random. Perhaps we should have warned you that our disclaimer applied to all but our final characteristic. For we have intentionally saved this final spot for the element that is most difficult to explain. You need only read the heading and you can begin to appreciate our problem. Ask yourself how you would explain a sentence that, at first glance, contains two contradictory ideas. We begin by urging you to view this apparent enigma not as a contradiction, but rather as a sentence that embodies two ideas that are both true.

Let us start by talking about the premise that we are like every other human being. In many ways this entire section has focused on how people are alike. Remember that each of us communicates by employing the same communication components. In addition, we all communicate in ways that manifest the elements we have discussed in the last few pages. However, our commonalties as a species go far beyond the ways we share ideas and information. Even though any inventory of these common qualities will be incomplete, let us nevertheless highlight just a few important threads that join us all together.

We not only share a common communication anatomy, but are identical in other physiological and chemical ways. We all have a heart, lungs, brain, and the like. We are also literally made of the same stuff—part water, part salt, and so on. Our desire to seek pleasure and avoid pain is yet another way we are all similar. This desire characterizes both our physical and our emotional beings. Every human being, and all of the other animals we share this planet with, devotes a great deal of energy to trying to avoid physical discomfort. And should we experience pain, we all suffer in much the same way. A wound to the arm in Peru is much like a wound to the arm in Beverly Hills. Pain is pain; it does not recognize people or cultures.

As we just noted, we also seek pleasure and flee the pain directed at our feelings. Throughout the world, and for thousands of years, people have been protecting their emotional as well as their physical selves. While the word *ego* may be very Western, the concepts behind it (self-respect, vanity, and the like) cut across all cultures. Ego may be called face-saving in China, or being *macho* in Mexico, but it is all the same. In short, human beings seek emotional as well as bodily comforts.

Countless experiences in life seem to elicit a universal response. For example, the whole world perceives the act of childbirth as a magnificent event. In addition, we seem to share a common desire to find a mate. The urge to locate someone to love and care for us is common to all cultures.

There are many other visible ways in which we are similar, but for now let us just conclude by restating the first half of the characteristic: We are similar to other people. Having said that, we now move to the second part of the statement.

Lord Chesterfield once wrote, "There never were, since the creation of the world, two cases exactly parallel." He might have also said that there have never been two people exactly alike. This position is predicated on the simple truism that we experience the world from inside our skin (a point we have made elsewhere in this chapter). Therefore, we respond to the world in our own special way. When you hear a word, or someone touches you, your body reacts from the inside out. The significance behind this important communication characteristic becomes even more apparent if we think about the three actions we engage in when we receive and send messages. First, the external world impinges on our nerve endings and something happens within us. Second, we take what is happening and think about it by employing symbols from our past. Third, we string those symbols together so that we can talk about what was going on inside of us. We admit that this is a rather unadorned and elementary syllogism, but it is nevertheless true.

What we are saying here is that communication is subjective. For example, we have already noted that symbols don't mean the same thing to everyone—they are subjective. This is also true of the messages we produce. It is important to remember that when we talk, we are talking about ourselves. As Ralph Waldo Emerson wrote, "You can never say anything but what you are."

The implications of this final characteristic of communication should be clear. A common anatomy, gender, age, culture, and the like make us comparable, but our isolated and unique bodies keep us apart. Hence, we are alike and we are different. As we have said repeatedly, this book is about those likenesses and those differences.

SUMMARY

Human Communication

- Communication occurs whenever meaning is attributed to behavior or the residue of behavior.

- All communication involves six basic ingredients: (1) a source who (2) encodes an internal state into (3) a message that (4) travels by a channel to (5) a receiver who (6) decodes the message into a usable form.

- Understanding certain characteristics of communication common to all human beings helps clarify how the process works.

- We can never have mind-to-mind communication with another human being. We can only infer what another is experiencing, making most of these inferences from the symbols that we and other people produce. We are bound up in time because of our ability to use symbols.

- Communication is also the way we define our world. We give meaning to events and people, for example, so that we can function in various groups and be members of a common society.

- Our communication behavior has consequences.

- Communication is dynamic; it is ongoing and ever-changing.

- Communication is contextual. Message exchange always takes place in a specific and definable location, not a vacuum.

- Communication is rule-governed; it follows clear and recognizable rules that apply to everything from our selection of topics to the way we dress.

- Communication is reflective; we can watch and evaluate our communication behavior at the same time that we are communicating.

- The brain is an open system; we can learn from each encounter we find ourselves in.

- People are alike and different. We all face the same frustrations forced upon us by the fact that we must live physically isolated from each other.

ACTIVITIES

1. Report a recent attempt at communication with a friend or a stranger. Isolate the ingredients of your particular exchange: the source, the encoding, the message, the channel, the receiver, and the decoding. To describe the decoding, think about the evidence that your message was received. For example:

    Tom Schwartz enters a bakery and says, "I'd like a loaf of French bread, please." The clerk hands the bread to Tom.

SOURCE: Tom

ENCODING: Spoken English

MESSAGE: I'd like a loaf of French bread, please.

CHANNEL: Verbal

RECEIVER: Clerk

DECODING: The evidence for this is that the clerk handed Tom the bread.

2. In small groups, discuss the characteristic of communication referred to as time-binding. What cultural knowledge has been transmitted to your generation? What information from your culture's past helps you live in the present and prepare for the future?

DISCUSSION IDEAS

1. Why is it important to include unintentionality in a definition of communication in an intercultural context?

2. Explain how the statement "People are alike and people are different" relates to intercultural communication.

3. "We can only infer" is another characteristic of communication. Give personal examples of situations in which you inferred what someone else was experiencing. Were your inferences correct? How do you know?

NOTES FOR CHAPTER 2

1. Frank E. X. Dance, "The Concept of Communication," *Journal of Communication* 20 (1970), 210.

2. Gerald R. Miller and Mark Steinberg, *Between People: A New Analysis of Interpersonal Communication* (Chicago: Science Research Associates, 1975).

3. Jurgen Reusch, "Values, Communication, and Culture," in *Communication: The Social Matrix of Psychiatry*, ed. Jurgen Ruesch and Gregory Bateson (New York: W. W. Norton, 1951), 5–6.

4. Harry L. Weinberg, *Levels of Knowing and Existence* (New York: Harper and Row, 1959), 157.

5. Brent D. Ruben, *Communication and Human Behavior* (New York: Macmillan, 1988), 111.

6. Juan Mascaro, *Dhammapada* (New York: Penguin Books, 1973), 40.

7. Susan Shimanoff, *Communication Rules: Theory and Research* (Beverly Hills: Sage Publications, 1980), 57.

Culture is man's medium; there is not one aspect of human life
that is not touched and altered by culture. This means personality,
how people express themselves (including shows of emotion), the
way they think, how they move, how problems are solved, how
their cities are planned and laid out, how transportation systems
function and are organized, as well as how economic and
government systems are put together and function. However, . . .
it is frequently the most obvious and taken-for-granted and
therefore the least studied aspects of culture that influence behavior
in the deepest and most subtle ways.

EDWARD T. HALL

CHAPTER THREE

CULTURE: OUR INVISIBLE TEACHER

People in Paris eat snails, but people in San Diego put poison on them. Why? People in Iran sit on the floor and pray five times each day, but people in Las Vegas sit up all night in front of slot machines. Why? Some people speak Tagalog, others speak English. Why? Some people paint and decorate their entire bodies, but others spend millions of dollars painting and decorating only their faces. Why? Some people talk to God, but others have God talk to them. Why? The general answer to all these questions is the same. People learn to think, feel, believe, and strive for what their culture considers proper. Using the language of the last chapter, people respond to the world in light of the messages they have received, and culture determines the form, pattern, and content of those messages. This omnipresent quality of culture leads Hall to conclude that "there is not one aspect of human life that is not touched and altered by culture."[1] In many ways Hall is correct; culture is everything. And more importantly, at least for the purposes of this book, *culture and communication work in tandem*—they are inseparable. In fact, it is often difficult to decide which is the voice and which is the echo.

Culture dictates who talks to whom, about what, how, when, and for how long. It helps govern the conditions and circumstances under which various messages may or may not be sent, noticed, or interpreted. Our entire repertory of communicative behaviors depends largely on the culture in which we have been raised. Remember, we aren't born knowing how to dress, what toys to play with, what to eat, which gods to worship, or how to spend our money and our time. Culture is both teacher and textbook. From how much eye contact we employ to explanations of why we get sick, culture plays a dominant role in our lives. It is the foundation of communication; and when cultures vary, communication practices may also vary.

Culture and communication are so inextricably bound to one another that some cultural anthropologists (and the authors of this book) believe the terms *culture* and *communication* are essentially synonymous.[2] This relationship between culture and communication is the key factor in understanding communication, and more specifically, intercultural communication. Our ability to recognize the complexities of intercultural communication must begin with a sound grasp of the cultural influences on the way people communicate. To assist you in developing an appropriate perspective for the study of intercultural communication, we plan to do for culture many of the same things we did for communication in the last chapter. We shall explain why cultures develop, define culture, discuss the major ingredients of culture, and isolate the characteristics of culture that most directly relate to communication.

CULTURE

Throughout Chapter 2 we apologized for reducing a topic as complex as communication to simple terms. We fear that here in Chapter 3 we must revert to that same plea. We are now faced with the task of grappling with a concept that is not only complex but, as we just noted, has the potential to include nearly everything. We shall, however, attack the ubiquitous nature of culture in much the same way we did the all-inclusive character of communication. We plan to look only at those aspects of culture that are most germane to the study of intercultural communication.

The Basic Function of Culture

It is believed that our ancestors evolved culture for much the same reason we have cultures today. Both then and now, culture serves the basic need of laying out a predictable world in which an individual is firmly oriented. Culture enables us to make sense of our surroundings. As Thomas Fuller wrote two hundred years ago, "Culture makes all things easy." Although this view might be slightly overstated, culture does ease the transition from the womb to this new life by giving meaning to events, objects, and people in the environment. In this way culture makes the world a less mysterious place.

From the instant of birth, a child is formally and informally taught how to behave. Common behaviors and definable settings allow for automatic responses that can be forecasted. Children, regardless of the culture, quickly learn how to behave in a manner that is acceptable to adults. Conversely, they are also told that if they are good they will be rewarded. Within each culture, therefore, there is no need to expend energy deciding what each event means or how to respond to it. The assumption is that people who share a common culture can usually be counted on to behave "correctly" and predictably. Hence, culture reduces the chances of surprises by shielding people from the unknown. It offers each of its members a common blueprint for all of life's activities. Try to imagine a single day in your life without having access to the guidelines your culture provides. Without the "rules" that govern your actions, you would soon feel helpless. From how to greet strangers to how to spend our time, culture provides us with structure. To lack culture is to lack structure. Without both we would be intellectually defenseless, floundering animals in an unfathomable realm. We might even go so far as to say that "our primary mode of biological adaptation is culture, not anatomy."[3] Culture teaches each of us how to make the most of what we have gained through millions of years of evolution.

Some Definitions of Culture

If culture were a single thing we would need only one definition. We have already indicated, however, that culture, like communication, is ubiquitous, multidimensional, complex, and all-pervasive. Because culture is so broad in its scope, scholars have had a difficult time arriving at one central theory or definition of what it is. As with communication, many definitions have been suggested—perhaps as many as 150 in the literature. These definitions range from those that conceive of culture as an all-encompassing phenomenon ("it is everything"), to those that take a narrower view of the concept ("it is opera, art, and ballet"). Let us examine some of these definitions so that we might better understand the place of culture in intercultural communication.

Hoebel and Frost see culture in nearly all human activity. They define culture as an "integrated system of learned behavior patterns which are characteristic of the members of a society and which are not the result of biological inheritance."[4] For them culture is not genetically predetermined; it is non-instinctive.[5] The reasoning behind this position is twofold. First, people who claim the liberal orientation believe that culture is transmitted and maintained solely through communication and learning.[6] All scholars of culture begin with this same assumption—that is, that culture is learned. It is the second leg of the argument that best identifies scholars who take the sweeping view. These scholars contend that the act of birth confines each individual to a specific geographic location, a location that exposes people to certain messages while at the same time denying them others. All of these messages, whether they be conveyed through a certain language, religion, food, dress, housing, toys, or books, are culturally based; therefore, everything that a person experiences is part of his or her culture.

From a definition that includes all learned behavior we can move to definitions that propose culture has tangible boundaries. But here again scholars have not agreed on the boundaries. Some, such as Triandis, take an expansive view of culture, suggesting that culture "can be distinguished as having both objective (e.g., roads, tools) and subjective (e.g., norms, laws, values) aspects."[7] Those who define culture in this way look at what a culture does to its environment as well as what it does to its people.

Cole and Scribner offer a definition of culture that ties culture to human cognition:

Perception, memory, and thinking all develop as part of the general socialization of a child and are inseparably bound up with the patterns of activity, communication, and social relations into which he enters. . . . His every experience has been shaped by the culture of which he is a member and is infused with socially defined meanings and emotions.[8]

Hofstede has advanced another definition that views culture from a psychological perspective: "Culture is the collective programming of the mind which distinguishes the members of one category of people from another."[9] Both of these definitions stress the mental conditions that cultural experiences impose.

Definitions of culture, like definitions of communication, reflect the specific research emphasis of the person offering the definition. For example, an assessment of culture from a *communication* approach would define culture "as the complex combination of common symbols, knowledge, folklore conventions, language, information-processing patterns, rules, rituals, habits, life styles, and attitudes that link and give a common identity to a particular group of people at a particular point in time."[10]

The lack of agreement on any one definition of culture led anthropologists Kroeber and Kluckhohn to review some five hundred definitions, phrasings, and uses of the concept. From their analysis they proposed the following definition:

Culture consists of patterns, explicit and implicit, of and for behavior acquired and transmitted by symbols, constituting the distinctive achievements of human groups, including their embodiments in artifacts; the essential core of culture consists of traditional (i.e., historically derived and selected) ideas and especially their attached values; culture systems may, on the one hand, be considered as products of action, and on the other as conditioning elements of further action.[11]

Although we believe that the Kroeber and Kluckhohn definition is broad enough to include most of the major territory of culture, we nevertheless have evolved a definition that we believe is most suited to the goals of this book. We define **culture** *as the deposit of knowledge, experience, beliefs, values, attitudes, meanings, hierarchies, religion, notions of time, roles, spatial relations, concepts of the universe, and material objects and possessions acquired by a group of people in the course of generations through individual and group striving.*

The Ingredients of Culture

Our review of definitions of culture should have made it clear that culture is composed of many ingredients. It might be helpful to look at some of these ingredients, and their subcomponents as a way of understanding the composition of culture.

The ingredients of culture, like the definitions, often seem at variance with one another. Most scholars agree, however, that any description should include the three aspects submitted by Almaney and Alwan, who contend that

> cultures may be classified by three large categories of elements: artifacts (which include items ranging from arrowheads to hydrogen bombs, magic charms to antibiotics, torches to electric lights, and chariots to jet planes); concepts (which include such beliefs or value systems as right or wrong, God and man, ethics, and the general meaning of life); and behaviors (which refer to the actual practice of concepts or beliefs.[12]

The authors then provide an excellent example of how these three aspects might be reflected within a culture: "Whereas money is considered an artifact, the value placed upon it is a concept, but the actual spending and saving of money is behavior."[13]

Other inventories usually add to or further partition the three ingredients Almaney and Alwan describe. According to Cateora and Hess, culture is comprised of the following elements:

- Material culture (technology, economics)
- Social institutions (social organizations, political structures)
- Individuals and the universe (belief systems)
- Aesthetics (graphics, plastic arts, folklore, music, drama, dance)
- Language[14]

It should be evident that the word *culture* as well as the reality of culture is complex and multidimensional. It can include everything from rites of passage to concepts of the soul. Think for just a moment of all the beliefs you hold and the objects that have meaning for you because you are a member of one culture or another. Your views of work, dress, etiquette, healing and health, death, play, hygiene, superstition, modesty, sex, status, courtship, and the like are part of your cultural membership.

In Chapter 2 we observed some major problems associated with isolating specific elements for any complex activity. Some of these lessons are worth remembering when we examine the ingredients of culture. First, we asserted that any single listing of ingredients would be incomplete; and second, that the items selected would reflect the point of view of the person preparing the list. These same two qualifications apply to the composition of such a list for culture. For example, the ingredients we have examined so far are general enough to be included in any analysis of culture. However, if we were to move to particular orientations towards the study of culture, we would begin to encounter modifications. Two instances will serve to illustrate this point, one that links culture and international business, and another that links culture to human communication.

Terpstra maintains that any analysis of culture in the *business context* must embrace eight major elements and an array of specific factors. Notice as we list some of these factors how they mirror the business arena:

- Language (spoken, written, official, hierarchical, international, and so on)
- Religion (sacred objects, philosophical systems, beliefs and norms, prayer, taboos, holidays, rituals)
- Values and attitudes (toward time, achievement, work, wealth, change, scientific method, risk-taking)
- Education (formal education, vocational training, higher education, literacy level, human resources planning)
- Social organization (kinship, social institutions, authority structures, interest groups, social mobility and stratification)
- Technology and material culture (transportation, energy systems, tools, science, invention)
- Politics (nationalism, imperialism, power, national interests, ideologies, political risk)
- Law (common law, foreign law, international law, antitrust policy, regulations)[15]

As we offer our second list of cultural ingredients, notice once again how they reflect the perspective of the list maker—in this case someone interested in communication and culture. Dodd identifies the following fourteen elements as common to all cultures: cultural history, cultural personality, material culture, role relationships, art, language, cultural stability, cultural beliefs, ethnocentrism, nonverbal behavior, spatial relations, time, recognition and reward, and thought patterns.[16]

Keep in mind that what Terpstra did for business and culture, and Dodd for communication and culture, others have done with education, health care, and the like. They all end up isolating those aspects of culture that are reflected in the area with which they are most concerned. We, too, shall select parts of culture when we advance our personal inventory.

As we leave this section on the ingredients of culture, we would like you to keep a few things in mind. First, several of the lists we presented contained some of the same items. This is because regardless of the researcher, there is a common core of elements. Second, once scholars list the established elements, they select those portions of culture that most represent their areas of interest. Third, any slate of elements is bound to be insufficient. There are so many elements of culture that one proposal or theory could never contain them all. Finally, although the elements can be found in every culture, the emphasis and manifestation of each element are culturally based. That is to say, all cultures have a language, for example, but each has its own special language.

Having discussed the roots of culture, some of its definitions and ingredients, we are now ready to focus on those aspects of culture that one must understand in order to communicate successfully with someone from a different background.

The Characteristics of Culture

Culture is not innate; it is learned.   We begin with the single most important characteristic of culture, and the one that is hardest to explain. It is the most important because it goes to the heart of what is called culture. It is the most difficult to explain because we must ask the word *learned* to stand for more than one thing. Let's use these two notions as the vehicle to clarify this first characteristic.

Without the advantages of learning from those who lived before us we would not have culture. Babies cut off from all adult care, training, and supervision would instinctively eat, drink, defecate, urinate, gurgle, and cry. But what they would eat, when they would eat, where they would defecate, and the like would be random. Without learning, they would "communicate" even emotional states with gestures and sounds—not language as we know it. Children without information about the past would not have utensils, arts, religion, government, courtship behaviors, and all the other traits that make us human. They would evolve some kind of social order, but one void of a history that could be communicated; they would not be like any other culture. For as we mentioned previously, culture is the collection of life patterns that our elders give us. And while some knowledge conceivably is genetically transmitted, most of our behavior patterns must be learned. As we implied in the title of this chapter, culture is both teacher and subject matter.

Our second introductory assertion regarding the word *learning* is somewhat more enigmatic than our first. The problem is that we all behave as if a word stood for only one thing—and of course there are times when it does. A single word, however, often must stand for many things. Think for a moment of the word *pain*. How different the meaning can be when the word denotes the discomfort from a small splinter in the finger versus the anguish of a burn victim. When we look at the word *learned* as it applies to culture, we find the same problem, for in the context of culture the word has numerous meanings. That is to say, we learn our culture in many different ways. The little boy in North America whose father tells him to shake hands when he is introduced to a friend of the family is learning culture. The Arab baby who is read the Koran when he or she is one day old is learning culture. The Indian child who lives in a home where the women eat after the men is learning culture. The Jewish child who helps conduct the Passover celebration is learning culture.

The term **enculturation** denotes this total activity of learning one's culture. More specifically, enculturation is "conscious or unconscious conditioning occurring within that process whereby the individual, as child and adult, achieves competence in a particular culture."[17] Enculturation usually takes place through *interaction* (your parents kiss you and you learn about kissing—whom to kiss, when to kiss, and so on), *observation* (you watch your father do most of the driving of the family car and you learn about sex roles—what a man does, what a woman does), and *imitation* (you laugh at the same jokes your parents laugh at and you learn about humor—it is funny if someone falls down but doesn't get hurt).

In social psychology and sociology the term **socialization** is often used synonymously with *enculturation*. Regardless of which word is applied, the idea remains the same. From infancy on, members of a culture learn their patterns of behavior and ways of thinking until they become internalized. The power and influence of these behaviors and perceptions can be seen in the ways in which we acquire culture. Our learning through interaction, observation, and imitation can take many forms. The concept is best understood by remembering the words *conscious* and *unconscious* used in the definition we just offered. These two words help explain the broad and sweeping definition of learning we referred to earlier.

Conscious learning is the easier to see and to explain. In its simplest form it involves the ingredients of our culture that we were told about or that we read about. We learned them at the conscious level. A mother tells her young son to take a bath before he goes to bed, and he learns health habits and cleanliness. A father tells his daughter to say "thank you" when someone pays her a compliment, and she is learning. A grandmother tells her grandchild how to play with certain toys, and the child is learning. A young girl reads the rules for bicycle safety, and she is learning. A teacher tells a pupil the correct way to sit in class, and the pupil is learning. In each of these instances (and there are many others), the person is told what to learn. However, it is at the second level of learning, the unconscious level, that we learn the bulk of what we call culture.

Since culture influences us from the very day we are born, we are rarely conscious of many of the messages that we are receiving. This "hidden dimension" of culture leads many researchers to claim that culture is invisible. Ruben, for example, writes that "the presence of culture is so subtle and pervasive that it simply goes unnoticed. It's there now, it's been there as long as anyone can remember, and few of us have reason to think much about it."[18] Most of us would have a difficult time pointing to a specific event or experience that taught us about such things as direct eye contact, our use of silence and space, the importance of attractiveness, our view of aging, our ability to speak one language over another, our preference for activity over meditation, and countless other behaviors that are unique to our particular culture. In all of these cases we were learning the perceptions, rules, and behaviors of membership without being aware of it.

Although learned on the unconscious level, the significant perceptions, rules, and behaviors are given added strength by the fact that members of any culture receive ongoing reinforcement for those aspects of culture that are deemed most crucial. For example, in North America the importance of being thin is repeated with such regularity that we all take this value for granted. In addition, the messages that are strategic for any culture come from a variety of sources. That is to say, parents, schools, plays, folktales, music, art, church, the media, and peers all repeat those assumptions on which any culture operates. Think for a moment of the thousands of ways you have been "told" the importance of being popular and well-liked, or the many messages you have received concerning competition and winning. Our games, sports, toys, movies, and so on all tell us about the need to win. A famous tennis player tells us that he "feels like dying when he comes in second." And the president of a major car company concludes his television pitch by announcing, "We want to be number one—what else is there?"

Although the "carriers" of culture are nearly the same for all of us (parents, peers, church, and so on), the messages they transmit reflect the character of each culture. A case in point is the popular folktale "Cinderella." Although nearly every culture has a version, each culture uses the tale to emphasize a value that is important to that particular culture. For example, the North American version stresses Cinderella's attractiveness as a reflection of her inner qualities. She is also, however, rather passive and weak. In the Algonquin Indian tale the virtues of truthfulness and intellectual honesty are the basis for the Cinderella character. The Japanese story accents the value of intellectual ability and gentleness. In one version there are only two sisters who wish to go to the Kabuki theater. In place of the famous "slipper test" is the challenge of having to compose a song extemporaneously. One sister manages only a simple unimaginative song, which she sings in a loud voice. But Cinderella composes a song that has both meter and metaphor, and she sings it in soft tones. She, of course, is shown to deserve the rewards of such actions. This rather long example shows that the lessons of culture may travel by similar channels—in this case folktales—but they contain different patterns and values.

We conclude our description of this initial characteristic of culture by reminding you of how our discussion directly relates to intercultural communication. First, many of the behaviors we label as cultural are not only automatic and invisible; we often produce them without being aware of our action. For example, in North American culture women smile more than men. Yet they "learned" that behavior below the level of consciousness and perform it almost habitually. Hence, such cultural behavior tends to be unconscious in both its acquisition and expression.

Our second point is a theme we have repeated throughout this chapter: Common experiences produce common behaviors. The sharing of experience and behaviors is what makes a culture unique. Put in slightly different language, culture separates one group of people from another. This separation, and how to understand it, is what this book is all about.

Culture is transmissible from person to person, group to group, and generation to generation.   Much of our discussion to this point has indicated the strong link between culture and communication. This new characteristic—that culture is transmissible—simply adds credence to that position. It also points out that the symbols of a culture are what enable us to pass on the content and patterns of a culture. We can use the spoken word as a symbol and tell others about the importance of freedom. We can use the written word as a symbol and let others read about "the War of Independence." We can use nonverbal actions as symbols and show others that we usually shake hands to greet one another. We can use flags as symbols to claim territory or demonstrate loyalty. We can use automobiles or jewelry as symbols to show others about success and status. We can use a cross to show our love of God. As you would suspect, the use of symbols is at the core of culture. Other animals are limited in their use of symbols and therefore are incapable of developing a culture.

The portability of symbols allows us to package and store them as well as transmit them. The mind, books, pictures, films, videos, and the like enable a culture to preserve what it deems to be important and worthy of transmission. Hence, each individual, regardless of his or her generation, is heir to a massive "library" of information that has been collected in anticipation of his or her entry into the culture. In this sense, culture is historical as well as preservable. Each new generation might write more, but the notes from the past represent what we call culture. As Proust wrote, "The past remains the present."

It is important for any student of intercultural communication to remember that many of the behaviors a culture selects to pass on are universal. However, because culture, like communication, is subjective, there are also countless messages that are unique to each culture. Americans tell each generation to value individualism. In Japan the message is that the group comes before the individual. North Americans tell each generation that competition is valuable. For Mexicans and Native Americans the message is that cooperation is more important than the contest. North Americans tell each generation to value youth. In China the message is to respect and treasure the elderly. Each of these examples makes the same point: *The content of culture is subjective and communicable.*

As we noted earlier, one thing that makes the transferring of culture from generation to generation so interesting is that much of the movement is invisible and unconscious. Jews, to this day, while reading from the Torah, sway backwards and forwards like camel-riders. They have "inherited" this simple act unconsciously from centuries ago, when Jews were prohibited from riding camels. The pretense of riding was developed as a form of compensation. Although the motive for the action is gone, the action gets passed on to each new generation by means of what Hall calls the "silent language" of culture.

Culture is a dynamic system that changes continuously over time.   This current characteristic is yet another example of how communication and culture are alike. For you will recall that in the last chapter we highlighted that communication was not static, but rather was a dynamic, constantly changing process. We now suggest that cultures are also subject to fluctuations, that they seldom remain constant. As ideas and products evolve within a culture, they can produce change. Although cultures change through several mechanisms, the three most common are invention, diffusion, and calamity.

Invention is usually defined as the discovery of new practices, tools, or concepts that most members of the culture eventually accept. In North America the Civil Right's Movement and the invention of television are two good examples of how ideas and products reshape a culture.

Diffusion, or borrowing from another culture, is another way in which change occurs. The assimilation of what is borrowed accelerates as cultures come into direct contact with each other. For example, as Japan and North America have more commerce, we see Americans assimilating Japanese business practices and the Japanese using American marketing tactics.

Although invention and diffusion are the most common causes of change, there are of course other factors that foster shifts in a culture. The concept of **cultural calamity** illustrates how cultures change. Reflect for a moment on how the calamity of the Vietnam War has brought changes to both Vietnam and the United States. Not only did it create a new population of refugees, but it also forced us to reevaluate some cultural assumptions concerning global influence and military power.

From the preceding discussion it should be clear that cultures are very adaptive. History runs over with examples of how cultures have been forced to alter their course because of natural disasters, wars, or other calamities. Events in the last few hundred years have scattered Jews throughout the world, yet their culture has adapted and survived. And think for a moment about the adaptiveness of the Japanese. Their government and economy were nearly destroyed during World War II, yet because they could adapt, their culture endured and they are now a major economic force in the world.

We would be remiss if we failed to indicate that although many aspects of culture are subject to change, the deep structure of a culture resists major alterations. That is to say, changes in dress, food, transportation, housing, and the like, though appearing to be important, are simply attached to the existing value system. However, values associated with such things as ethics and morals, work and leisure, definitions of freedom, the importance of the past, religious practices, the pace of life, and attitudes towards gender and age are so very deep in a culture that they persist generation after generation. Even demands for a more liberal government in countries such as China and the Soviet Union have their roots in the history of those countries. In the United States, studies conducted on American values show that most of the central values of the 1980s are similar to the values of the last two hundred years. In short, when analyzing the degree of change within a culture, you must always consider what it is that is changing. Don't be fooled because downtown Tokyo looks much like Paris or New York. Most of what we call culture is below the surface. It is like the moon—we observe the front, which is flat and one-dimensional, but there is another side and dimensions that we cannot see.

Culture is selective.   Every culture represents a limited choice of behavior patterns from the total of human experience. This selection, whether it be what shoes to wear or how to reach God, is made according to the basic assumptions and values that are meaningful to each culture. Because each individual has only these limited experiences, what we know is but an abstraction of what there is to know. Put in slightly different terms, culture defines the boundaries of different groups.[19]

This characteristic is important to all students of intercultural communication for two reasons. First, it is a reminder that what a culture selects to tell each generation is a reflection of what that culture deems important. In the United States, for example, being healthy is highly valued, and therefore messages related to that idea are isolated. Second, the notion of selectivity also suggests that cultures tend to separate one group from another. If one culture stresses (selects) work as an end (Japan), while another emphasizes work as a means to an end (Mexico), we tend to have a separation.

The various facets of culture are interrelated. This characteristic serves to underscore the complex nature of culture. Hall clearly states the meaning of this sentence when he writes, "You touch a culture in one place and everything else is affected."[20] A good example of this characteristic is the Women's Movement in the United States. Although the phrase is made up of only two words, the phenomenon has been like a large stone cast into a pond. The Women's Movement has brought about changes in sexual practices, educational opportunities, the legal system, career opportunities, and even male-female interaction. Hence, this one aspect of culture has actually altered other patterns and values.

Many mass-communication experts believe that this interconnectedness of culture is at the core of the "cultural imperialism" hypothesis. This hypothesis maintains that by broadcasting American programs to Third World countries, for example, we are actually making them like us. The argument is that if we send programs that glorify material possessions to a culture that stresses spiritual life, we are touching many aspects of their culture. Or put another way, if you interfere with one facet of a culture you alter other facets.

Culture is ethnocentric. The disposition towards ethnocentrism (centeredness on one's own group) might well be the characteristic that most directly relates to intercultural communication. The important tie between ethnocentrism and communication can be seen in the definition of the word itself. Keesing notes that ethnocentrism is "a universal tendency for any people to put its own culture and society in a central position of priority and worth."[21] In other words, ethnocentrism becomes the perceptual prism through which cultures interpret and judge all other groups. These interpretations and judgements include everything from what the "out-groups" value to how they communicate. In this sense ethnocentrism leads to a subjective evaluation of how another culture conducts its daily business. That this evaluation can only be negative is clear if you realize that a logical extension of ethnocentrism is the position that "our way is the right way." Most discussions of ethnocentrism even enlarge the concept to include feelings of superiority. As Keesing writes, "Nearly always the folklore of a people includes myths of origin which give priority to themselves, and place the stamp of supernatural approval upon their particular customs."[22]

As we have pointed out, feelings that "we are right" and "they are wrong" cover every aspect of a culture's existence. Examples range from the insignificant ("earrings should be placed on the ears, not on the nose") to the significant ("we need to fight and die for what is right"). When these kinds of attitudes are carried to their extreme, as they often are, ethnocentrism can be a major hindrance to intercultural understanding. The logical extension of ethnocentrism is detachment and division, which can take a variety of forms, including the severance of co-cultures from the dominant culture, or one major culture avoiding another. How often we see examples of white-collar workers isolated from blue-collar workers, blacks living apart from whites, and those with disabilities removed from our sight. And on an international level, we observe East Indians looking down on the Pakistanis, the Japanese feeling superior to the Chinese, Mexicans unconsciously sequestering their Indian population, and Americans not trusting the Russians.

Our discussion thus far should not lead to the conclusion that ethnocentrism is always intentional, for much of it is not. Like culture itself, ethnocentrism is usually learned at the unconscious level, while we are actually learning something else. If, for example, our schools are teaching American history, geography, literature, and government, they are also, without realizing it, teaching ethnocentrism. For the student, by being exposed only to this single orientation, is developing the view that America is the center of the world, as well as learning to judge that world by North American standards—the standards he or she has been taught. If most of the authors, philosophers, scientists, composers, and political leaders you have learned about are white males, you will use white males to judge other cultures.

What makes the pull of culture so very strong, as we indicated earlier in the chapter, is that the "teaching" begins at birth and continues all through life. Although the language she uses to make this important point is sexist by today's standards, Ruth Benedict nevertheless has offered an excellent explanation of why culture is such a powerful force.

The life history of the individual is first and foremost an accommodation to the patterns and standards traditionally handed down in his community. From the moment of his birth the customs into which he is born shape his experience and behaviour. By the time he can talk, he is the little creature of his culture, and by the time he is grown and able to take part in its activities, its habits are his habits, its beliefs his beliefs, its impossibilities his impossibilities. Every child that is born into his group will share them with him, and no child born into the opposite side of the globe can ever achieve the thousandth part.[23]

Regardless of who or what is the culprit, ethnocentrism can impede intercultural interaction. We shall therefore return to this topic throughout this volume as we offer advice for improving the way you communicate with people from different cultures.

SUMMARY

Culture

- The basic function of culture is to explain the world to each new inhabitant of the culture. The world is a confusing place until we can make some sense of it. Culture, by telling us what to expect, reduces confusion and helps us predict the future.

- We define culture as the deposit of knowledge, experience, beliefs, values, attitudes, meanings, hierarchies, religion, timing, roles, spatial relationships, concepts of the universe, and material objects acquired by a group of people in the course of generations through individual and group striving.

- Culture has many ingredients, such as food preferences, notions of death, housing requirements, and attitudes towards aging.

- Six characteristics of culture that most directly affect communication are that it is (1) learned, (2) transmissible, (3) dynamic, (4) selective, (5) composed of interrelated facets, and (6) ethnocentric.

ACTIVITIES

1. Ask your informant to relate a folktale (or a song, a work of art, or something else appropriate) from his or her culture. What cultural values does it convey? Compare your informant's folktale to one from your culture. Does it stand in opposition to yours, or are there similarities?

2. In small groups, list the North American cultural values mentioned in this chapter (there are several). Add any others you can think of. Then find examples from North American advertising campaigns that reveal these values. An example is an advertising slogan from an athletic shoe manufacturer, "Just do it," which reflects the North American value of activity.

DISCUSSION IDEAS

1. Explain North American views toward these elements of culture: work, dress, hygiene, courtship, sex, and status.

2. Describe a typical day from morning to night in terms of the cultural "rules" that govern your actions. Indicate what you've been trained to do and what you think the cultural "rule" is. For example:

ACTION	RULE
Brush teeth; take shower	Personal odors are offensive in N. American culture
Put on jeans and T-shirt	Comfort and informality are acceptable in educational settings

3. Give additional examples, from recent history, of cultures that have undergone changes through invention, diffusion, and calamity.

4. There are now several fast-food restaurants (such as McDonald's) in France. Does this mean that traditional French values regarding food and eating have changed? Explain your answer.

NOTES FOR CHAPTER 3

1. Edward T. Hall, *Beyond Culture* (Garden City, NY: Anchor, Doubleday, 1977), 14.

2. See Alfred G. Smith, ed., *Communication and Culture: Readings in the Codes of Human Interaction* (New York: Holt, Rinehart, and Winston, 1966), 1–14; Edward T. Hall, *The Silent Language* (Greenwich, CT: Fawcett, 1959); *The Hidden Dimension* (Garden City, NY: Doubleday, 1966); *Beyond Culture* (New York: Anchor Press/Doubleday, 1977).

3. Marvin Harris, *Cows, Pigs, Wars, and Witches: The Riddles of Culture* (New York: Random House, 1974), 84.

4. E. Adamson Hoebel and Everett L. Frost, *Cultural and Social Anthropology* (New York: McGraw-Hill, 1976), 6.

5. Hoebel and Frost.

6. Hoebel and Frost.

7. Harry C. Triandis, "A Theoretical Framework for the More Efficient Construction of Culture Assimilators," *International Journal of Intercultural Relations* 8 (1984), 305.

8. Michael Cole and Sylvia Scribner, *Culture and Thought: A Psychological Introduction* (New York: Wiley, 1974), 8.

9. Geert Hofstede, "National Cultures and Corporate Cultures" (Paper delivered on LIFIM Perspective Day, Helsinki, Finland, December 4, 1984).

10. Brent D. Ruben, *Communication and Human Behavior*, 2d ed. (New York: Macmillan, 1988), 384.

11. A. L. Kroeber and Clyde Kluckhohn, "Culture: A Critical Review of Concepts and Definitions," *Harvard University Peabody Museum of American Archeology and Ethnology Papers* 47 (1952), 181.

12. A. J. Almaney and A. J. Alwan, *Communicating with the Arabs* (Prospect Heights, IL: Waveland Press, 1982), 5.

13. Almaney and Alwan, 5.

14. Philip Cateora and John Hess, *International Marketing* (Homewood, IL: Irwin, 1979), 89.

15. Vern Terpstra, *The Cultural Environment of International Business* (Cincinnati: South-Western, 1978), xiv.

16. Carley H. Dodd, *Dynamics of Intercultural Communication,* 2d ed. (Dubuque, IA: Wm. C. Brown, 1987), 40–49.

17. Hoebel and Frost, 58.

18. Ruben, 396.

19. Hall, 13–14.

20. Hall.

21. Felix M. Keesing, *Cultural Anthropology: The Science of Custom* (New York: Holt, Rinehart, and Winston, 1965), 46.

22. Keesing.

23. Ruth Benedict, *Patterns of Culture* (New York: Mentor Books, 1948), 2.

In modern society different people communicate in different ways,
as do people in different societies around the world; and the way
people communicate is the way they live. It is their culture. Who
talks with whom? How? And about what? These are questions of
communication and culture. A Japanese geisha and a New
England librarian send and receive different messages on different
channels and in different networks. When the elements of
communication differ or change, the elements of culture differ or
change. Communication and culture are inseparable.

ALFRED G. SMITH

CHAPTER FOUR

UNDERSTANDING INTERCULTURAL COMMUNICATION: PRINCIPLES AND PRECEPTS

Having discussed communication in Chapter 2 and culture in the last chapter, we are now ready to link these two concepts together. This connection is crucial, for as Smith emphasizes in the opening quotation to this chapter, culture influences how we send and receive messages. A German, an Egyptian, a youth gang member, or a Brazilian is taught how to communicate through contact with his or her culture. In short, people view the world and respond to the world through categories, concepts, and labels that are the products of experiences—experiences selected by culture.

As cultures differ from one another, the communication practices and behaviors of the individual raised in those cultures also will vary. To understand those variations better we will (1) offer a definition of intercultural communication, (2) canvass some of the forms of intercultural communication, (3) present a model of how it operates, and (4) examine the central elements of intercultural communication.

INTERCULTURAL COMMUNICATION

A number of terms describe various aspects and levels of communication between people of varying backgrounds. As we have already indicated, **intercultural communication** is the overall encompassing term. In its most general sense it refers to those occasions when a member of one culture produces a message for consumption by a member of another culture. More precisely, intercultural communication is communication between people whose cultural perceptions and symbol systems are distinct enough to alter the communication event. Frequently the terms *cross-cultural communication* and *transcultural communication* are used. Although there might be minor shades of differences among all three of these terms, they basically designate the same form of interaction. Other terms, however, are used to focus on varying dimensions and forms of intercultural communication.

Forms of Intercultural Communication

Interracial communication.   **Interracial communication** occurs when source and receiver are from different races. The term *race* pertains to physical characteristics. We know that people vary in the color of their skin, contour of their heads, shape of their eyes, texture of their hair, and the like. Even though some believe that physical traits are becoming blurred, and that the term *racial* might be outdated, racial differences nevertheless often influence communication. And interracial communication may or may not be intercultural. For instance, a third-generation Korean-American whose family has become firmly acculturated into North American culture, talking with a white Anglo-American would be a case of interracial but hardly intercultural communication. On the other hand, a recently arrived Panamanian talking to the same Korean-American would be a case of both interracial and intercultural communication.

The major difficulty encountered in interracial communication is racial prejudice, a problem that can often be traced to the feelings of ethnocentrism we discussed in the last chapter. Strong prejudice leads to stereotyping and suspicion, both of which prevent meaningful interaction.

Another characteristic of interracial communication is that the dominant culture often uses its power to control the degree to which racial groups can be part of the mainstream. In the United States the white race is both the governing and the predominant race, and as such often determines the degree and the extent to which members of other races may act out membership in the reigning culture. Because of its power, the dominant culture (as we shall use the term throughout this book) not only makes most of the important decisions governing the entire culture, but also tends to establish the value system that the media and other institutions transmit. As Folb notes, "When we talk about the concept of dominant culture, we are really talking about power—those who *dominate* culture, those who historically or traditionally have had the most persistent and far-reaching impact on culture, on what we think and say, on what we believe and do in our society."[1]

Our discussion of dominance should indicate that the relative sizes of the subgroups in a culture do not automatically determine who will be dominant. In the Republic of South Africa, a minority white race holds the reins of power and has determined the degree to which the majority black race may mingle or interact in the minority white society.

Interethnic communication. **Interethnic communication** refers generally to situations where the parties are of the same race but different ethnic origins or backgrounds. Ethnicity is usually the result of geographic origin of the minorities of a country or culture. Cubans living in Florida, Mexicans in California, and Haitians in New York might all be citizens of the United States, yet the dominant culture usually doesn't consider them members of the majority culture. Historically they have been isolated and often placed in submissive positions.

The term *interethnic* is also used to denote situations such as in Canada, where there are English-Canadians and French-Canadians. Individuals from both groups are citizens of Canada and even members of the same race, yet they maintain quite different backgrounds, perspectives, goals, and even languages.

International communication.   **International communication** occurs between political structures (nations and governments) rather than between individuals. Often referred to as the communication of diplomacy and propaganda, it frequently involves both interracial and interethnic situations. In the case of international communication, however, interaction is influenced by the policies, aims, needs, and economies of nations. This form of communication is highly ritualized, taking place in formal situations and in places such as the United Nations. International communication is greatly influenced by international law, military strength, treaties, secret agreements, and world opinion. Although we grant its importance as a field of study, we will discuss international communication no further in this book. Our primary emphasis is on people—not on governments. As we have said repeatedly, this is a book about intercultural communication on an interpersonal level.

Intracultural communication.   **Intracultural communication** is communication between members of the same culture. It includes all forms of communication between members of racial, ethnic, or other co-cultures. Although the term *intracultural* can refer to members of the dominant culture sending each other messages, this word is often reserved for communication between co-cultures, which goes by many names and can take a variety of forms. Let's pause for a moment and look at some of the names and forms.

For a number of years the literature employed the word *subculture* when referring to individuals and groups of people who, while living in the dominant culture, had dual membership in yet another culture. In recent years, however, the term has been replaced and the concept itself reformulated. For referring to the *general category* of intracultural communication, the term *co-culture* has come to replace *subculture.* The substitution was based on the rationale that the word subculture implied that members of the nondominant group were inferior in some way or another. Because we believe the switch in language was sound, we shall use the word co-culture when talking about groups or social communities exhibiting characteristic patterns of behavior sufficient to distinguish them from others within an embracing culture.

The term subculture has also been replaced with specific definitions and discussions. For example, instead of treating all co-cultures and groups alike, people talk about them as separate entities. Discussions begin to look at homosexuals, the disabled, youth gangs, the elderly, women, and prostitutes, for example, as groups having unique experiences. The motivation behind examining these groups as separate entities was rather simple. There was now sufficient evidence that the members of these groups often engaged in communication behavior that was markedly different from that of the dominant culture. Their values, and the messages they constructed to represent those values, identified them as individuals who were holding membership in more than one culture.

We need only return to our general analysis of culture to see why these co-cultures have distinct patterns of communication. Remember that at the heart of our earlier analysis of culture was the idea that culture dictated what one experienced. This elementary supposition means that being gay, black, or female exposes a person to a set of messages that helps determine how he or she perceives some aspects of the external world and, just as significant, how he or she communicates those perceptions. Let us explain this point in a little more detail by selecting one co-culture (women) and offering a few examples that justify treating it as a separate culture in the United States. Keep in mind that we could offer the same analysis for any collection of individuals who had shared common experiences over a long period of time.

If we return to the notion that culture is "a relatively organized set of beliefs and expectations about how people should talk, think, and organize their lives"[2], we can appreciate how women and men grow up into two distinct communication cultures. Although they may share common environments and experiences, such as homes, schools, churches, and media, the messages they receive are often quite different. Girls are expected to do indoor chores and boys outdoor jobs. Girls have to stay near the house while boys can go exploring. Girls' games are calm and restrictive; boys engage in aggressive, combative activity. Books, magazines, and television offer stories and pictures that encourage different views of what is important and worthwhile in life. Girls are told to focus on romantic concerns and on being attractive; young boys are told that a man is mechanical, strong, tough, and self-assured. These, and thousands of other messages, produce people who perceive themselves differently (women have lower self-esteem than men), perceive the world differently (women view the world in more anxious and hostile terms), talk differently (women use more tag lines, interrupt less, and so on), and make different use of nonverbal cues (women engage in more eye contact, and use smaller gestures, for example).

As we indicated at the outset of our example, what we have said about women could be applied to any co-culture. What is important for our analysis is not the specific group, but rather the idea that unique experiences generate unique modes of behavior.

AN INTERCULTURAL COMMUNICATION MODEL

Having defined some different forms of intercultural communication, we can now begin to visualize the countless situations we face each day that meet these definitions. A model of a typical encounter can make the intercultural communication process even clearer. This model should assist you in predicting some of the consequences of bringing people together from different cultures or co-cultures.

Figure 4-1 illustrates the influence of culture on individuals, and the problems inherent in the production and interpretation of messages between cultures. Here, three cultures are represented by three distinct geometric shapes. Cultures A and B are purposely similar to one another and are represented by a square and by an irregular octagon that resembles a square. Culture C, which is intended to be quite different from Cultures A and B, is represented both by its circular shape and its physical distance from Cultures A and B.

Within each represented culture is another form similar to the shape of the influencing parent culture. This form represents a person who has been molded by his or her culture. The shape of the person, however, is somewhat different from that of the parent culture. This difference suggests two things. First, other influences besides culture affect and help mold the individual. And second, although culture is the dominant shaping force on an individual, within any culture people vary to some extent from each other.

Message production, transmission, and interpretation across cultures are illustrated by the series of arrows connecting the shapes representing the cultures. When a message leaves the culture in which it was encoded, insofar as it is possible for any message to reflect accurately the meaning of its producer, the message carries the content its sender intended. Actually, the meaning the message conveys is only one-half to one-fourth of what the message producer

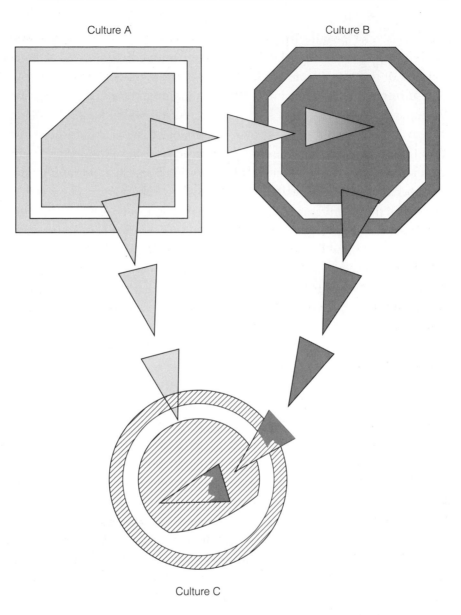

Figure 4-1   Model of Intercultural Communication

intended. This is represented by the arrows leaving a culture having the same pattern inside as that within the message producer. When a message reaches the culture in which it is to be interpreted, the conveyed meaning undergoes further alterations. The meaning the original message conveys is subjected to culturally different repertoires of social reality, communicative behaviors, and meanings that do not necessarily coincide with those of the message producer.

Culture's influence on intercultural communication is a function of the dissimilarity of the cultures. This is indicated in the model by the degree of pattern change in the message arrows. The change that occurs between Cultures A and B is much less than the change between Cultures A and C and between Cultures B and C. This is because Cultures A and B are the most similar. Hence, the repertoires of social reality, communicative behaviors, and meanings are similar and the interpretation effort produces results more nearly like the content of the original message. Since Culture C is represented as being quite different from Cultures A and B, the interpreted message is also vastly different and more yearly represents the pattern of Culture C.

The model suggests that there can be a wide variation in cultural difference during intercultural communication, a variation due in part to circumstances or forms. Intercultural communication occurs in a wide variety of situations that range from interactions between people with extreme cultural differences to interactions between people who are members of the same dominant culture and whose differences are reflected in the values and perceptions of co-cultures, subgroups, or racial groups. If we imagine differences along a minimum-maximum dimension (see Figure 4-2), the degree of difference between two cultural groups depends on their relative social dissimilarity. Although this scale is not refined, it allows us to examine intercultural communication acts and to gain insight into the effects of cultural differences on communication. In order to see how this scale helps us understand intercultural communication, we can look at some examples of cultural differences positioned along the scale.

The first example represents maximum differences—those found between Asian and Western cultures. This may be typified as an interaction between two farmers, one who works on a communal farm on the outskirts of Beijing in China and the other who operates a large mechanized and automated wheat, corn, and dairy farm in Michigan. In this situation, we would expect to find the greatest variation among cultural factors. Physical appearance, religion, philosophy, economic systems, social attitudes, language, heritage, basic conceptualizations of self and of the universe, and degree of technological development would differ sharply. We must recognize, however, that these two farmers also share the commonality of farming, with its rural lifestyle and love of the land. In some

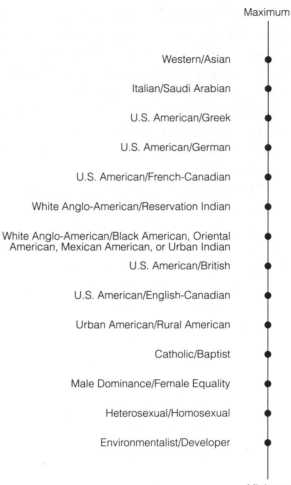

Maximum

Western/Asian

Italian/Saudi Arabian

U.S. American/Greek

U.S. American/German

U.S. American/French-Canadian

White Anglo-American/Reservation Indian

White Anglo-American/Black American, Oriental
American, Mexican American, or Urban Indian

U.S. American/British

U.S. American/English-Canadian

Urban American/Rural American

Catholic/Baptist

Male Dominance/Female Equality

Heterosexual/Homosexual

Environmentalist/Developer

Minimum

**Figure 4-2   Arrangement of Compared Cultures,
Co-cultures, and Subgroups along a Scale of
Minimum to Maximum Sociocultural Differences**

respect, they may be more closely related to each other than they are to members
of their own cultures who live in large cities. In other words, across some cultural
dimensions, the Michigan farmer may share more in common with the Chinese
farmer than with a Wall Street securities broker.

An example nearer the center of the scale is the difference between American culture and German culture. There is less variation; physical characteristics

are similar, and the English language derives in part from German and its ancestor languages. The roots of both German and American philosophy lie in ancient Greece, and most Americans and Germans share some form of the Christian religion. Yet, there are some significant differences. German political and economic systems differ somewhat from those in the United States. German society tends toward formality, but in the United States we tend toward informality. Germans remember local warfare and the destruction of their cities and economy, and they were defeated in two world wars. The United States has never lost a war on its own territory.

Examples near the minimal end of the dimension can be characterized in two ways. First are variations found between members of separate but similar cultures—for instance, between Americans and English-Canadians. The differences are less than those found between American and German cultures, between American and Greek cultures, between American and British cultures, or even between American and French-Canadian cultures, but greater than those generally found within a single culture. Second, there are also minimal differences between co-cultures, subgroups, or racial groups within the same dominant culture. Sociocultural differences may be found between members of the Catholic church and the Baptist church, between ecologists and advocates of further development of Alaskan oil resources, between middle-class Americans and the urban poor, between mainstream Americans and the gay community, between the able and the disabled, or between male dominance advocates and female equality advocates.

Members of cultural groups with minimal differences have more in common than members of groups at the middle or maximum end of the scale. They probably speak the same language, share the same general religion, attend the same schools, and live in the same neighborhoods. Yet, these groups to some extent are culturally unlike; they do not fully share the same experiences, nor do they share the same perceptions. They see their worlds differently. Their lifestyles may be immensely divergent, and their beliefs, values, and attitudes may differ significantly. Because of their cultural similarities, however, they differ primarily in limited aspects of their social perception.

Intercultural communication can best be understood as communication affected by cultural variability in social perception. **Social perception** is the process by which we construct our unique social realities by attributing meaning to the social objects and events we encounter in our environments. It is an extremely important aspect of communication. Culture conditions and structures our perceptual processes so that we develop culturally inspired perceptual sets. These sets not only help determine which external stimuli reach our awareness, but more importantly, they significantly influence the social aspect of perception—the social construction of reality by the attribution of meaning to these stimuli. The difficulties in communication that this perceptual variability causes can best be resolved by knowing about and understanding the cultural factors that are subject to variation, coupled with an honest and sincere desire to communicate successfully across cultural boundaries.

A sincere desire for effective communication is critical. A successful intercultural exchange may be hampered not only by cultural variations but also by unfriendly or hostile attitudes brought about by ethnic or racial prejudices and stereotypes. If these problems are present, no amount of cultural knowledge or communication skill will make an encounter pleasant. This does not mean that unfriendly or hostile persons cannot or should not attempt to communicate. On many occasions unfriendly, even hostile, people must share ideas and feelings, if for no other reason than to understand the other's position. Although this communication situation may not be pleasant, it could reflect an honest and sincere desire to communicate. We must learn not to give up because of prejudices and stereotypes but seek instead to reduce our conflicts through interaction. This may happen if we are willing to recognize our emotional states or feelings and seek clear understanding of and solutions to our problems. People in some cultures, such as the United States, may be able to do this more easily than people in cultures with different cognitive systems, such as those in the Arab world.

We discuss stereotypes and prejudices in Chapter 8, in the hope that recognition of our prejudicial and stereotypic behavior will lead to reflection on our behavior and ultimately a reduction of prejudice and stereotyping. We can, after all, be trained to accept the prejudice in one or both parties in a communication situation and to recognize its undesirable influence. Our major concern, however, is with those situations in which there are cultural differences in the construction of social reality and the production and interpretation of verbal and nonverbal messages during intercultural interaction, and the problems inherent in these varying situations.

THE ELEMENTS OF INTERCULTURAL COMMUNICATION

Culture, as we have presented the concept, is a complete pattern of living. It is elaborate, abstract, and pervasive. Countless aspects of culture help determine and guide communication behavior. These influences on communication, called sociocultural elements, are diverse and cover a wide range of human activity. We have selected those cultural elements that have the potential to affect situations in which people from different backgrounds come together. These elements fall into three general groupings: *perception, verbal processes,* and *nonverbal processes.*

Each of these categories has a number of subsets that we will also examine throughout the book. These sociocultural elements are the constituent parts of intercultural communication. When we combine them, as we do when we communicate, they are like the components of a stereo system—each one related to and needing the other. In our discussion, we will treat the elements as individual categories. In reality, however, they do not exist in isolation, nor do they function alone. Our perceptions (the way we make sense out of the world) are actively involved in all stages of message production and reception. All processes work together in an inextricable matrix of interacting variables that we call intercultural communication. We need to point out again that our analysis will be abbreviated and introductory; in following chapters, each of these categories will be the subject of a separate and detailed analysis.

Perception

In its simplest sense, **perception** is the process by which an individual selects, evaluates, and organizes stimuli from the external world."[3] In other words, perception is an internal process whereby we convert the physical energies of the world outside of us into meaningful internal experiences. Because that world embraces everything, we can never completely know it. As Singer notes, "We experience everything in the world not as it is—but only as the world comes to us through our sensory receptors."[4] Much of what is called perception has its roots in our biology. That is to say, the act of bringing the outside world to our consciousness involves a great deal of our nervous system, with its complex chemistry and anatomy. Although these aspects of perception are important, for our purposes the evaluation and action dimension of perception is most pertinent.

Two important claims arise out of the "people" view of perception. First, people behave as they do because of the ways they perceive the world. Second, one learns these perceptions, and the behaviors they produce, as part of one's cultural experiences. Whether it be the judgment of beauty or the responses to a snake, we react to outside forces primarily because our culture has taught us to do so. We tend to notice, reflect on, and respond to those elements in our environment that are meaningful and significant to us. In the United States we might respond positively to someone who "speaks his mind," yet this same behavior would be frowned upon in many Oriental cultures. In short, the world looks, sounds, tastes, and feels the way it does because our culture has given us the criteria of perception.

In the ideal intercultural encounter, we would hope for many overlapping experiences that could yield a commonality of perceptions. Although it often exposes much of the world to similar events, culture tends also to introduce us to dissimilar experiences, and hence to varied perceptions of the external world. A few cross-cultural examples will help us here.

The manner in which a culture responds to and treats women demonstrates the connections of culture, perception, and communication. In Saudi Arabia, because of strict and specific Islamic laws, women are raised in a style that is bound to influence how people in that culture view them—and in many respects women are outside that culture. One grows up in Saudi Arabia knowing that women have few legal rights and in most instances are not allowed to drive a car or even obtain a passport without the written consent of a male family member. Arranged marriages are still the rule and many men, when asked how many children they have, automatically state the number of sons. As you can see, women's liberation (at least as North Americans perceive it) has not yet arrived in Saudi Arabia. In striking contrast is the way females grow up in the United States. Although the Women's Movement in the United States is still evolving, it is safe to conclude that Saudis perceive females (attribute social meaning to the label *woman*) differently than do people in the United States.

You should be able to observe from the above example how complicated this entire issue of diverse perceptions can be if we include such perceptions as age, space, ethics, work, power, aggressive behavior, self-disclosure, time, and competition—all of which have their roots in culture.

Even co-cultures have specialized ways of teaching their members alternative patterns of perceiving and behaving. Most members of the dominant culture in North America have learned that status often comes from material wealth. In the Mexican-American co-culture, status is reflected through one's family and even service to the group. For prostitutes, one mark of status is speaking well and being manipulative so that they can stay in control of the situation. And in prisons, status is based on strength and on the type of crime one has committed on the outside. Once again we see different experiences creating different ways of viewing the world.

Most communication scholars, while granting that perceptions are part of every communication event, have evolved a fairly consistent taxonomy for isolating those perceptual variables that have the potential to impede seriously the intercultural encounter. The six major sociocultural elements that directly influence the meanings we develop for our perceptions are (1) beliefs, values, and attitudes, (2) world view, (3) social organization, (4) human nature, (5) activity orientation, and (6) perception of self and others.

As we introduce the six ingredients of intercultural perception, keep in mind that these perceptions, and the meanings we develop for them, affect us as individuals—they are the subjective aspects of meaning. All of us can experience the same social event, and can often agree on what it is in objective terms, but what the object or event means can differ considerably. As our earlier example illustrated, both a Saudi and a North American would agree in the objective sense that a particular person is a woman, but they most likely would disagree completely on what a woman is in a social sense, and more importantly, would differ in their response to that woman.

Beliefs, values, and attitude systems.   **Beliefs**, in a general sense, are subjective probabilities that some object or event is related to some other object or event or to some value, concept, or attribute. They are our convictions in the truth of something—with or without proof. In short, an object or event possesses certain characteristics that we believe to be true. We have beliefs about religion (Jesus is the son of God), events (the Vietnam War was necessary), other people (I know John is smart), and even ourselves (I am very witty). Our list of beliefs is endless. We may believe that rain will cause the grass to grow (a causal relationship) or that our next-door neighbor is unfriendly. The degree to which we believe that an event or object possesses certain characteristics reflects the level of our subjective probability and, consequently, the depth or intensity of our belief.

What makes our belief system so very important is that it is learned, and hence subject to cultural interpretation. We might acknowledge that the *New York Times* or the *CBS Evening News* is a good place to discover what is true and what we should believe. We believe these sources because we value them. If you highly value the Islamic tradition you may believe that the Koran is an infallible source of knowledge and thus accept the miracles that it sets forth. Whether we trust the *Times,* the Bible, the Koran, the entrails of a goat, tea leaves, the visions induced by peyote, or the changes specified in the Taoist *I Ching* as sources of knowledge and beliefs depends upon our cultural backgrounds and experiences. If someone believes that the voices in the wind can guide his or her behavior along the proper path, we cannot throw up our hands and declare the belief wrong; we must be able to recognize and to deal with that belief if we wish to gain some insight into how the other person perceives and reacts to his or her world.

Values are the evaluative components of our belief, value, and attitude systems. Evaluative qualities include usefulness, goodness, aesthetics, need-satisfaction ability, and pleasure production. They "represent a learned organization of rules for making choices and for resolving conflicts."[5] Although each of us has a unique set of values, there also are values that tend to permeate a culture. These are called *cultural values.*

Cultural values usually are derived from the larger philosophical issues that are part of a culture's milieu. Hence, they tend to be broad-based, enduring, and relatively stable. Values generally are normative in that they inform a member of a culture about what is good and bad, right and wrong, true and false, positive and negative, and the like. Cultural values define what is worthwhile to die for, what is worth protecting, what frightens people, what are proper subjects for study and for ridicule, and what types of events lead individuals to group solidarity. Most importantly, cultural values guide both perception and behavior.

As we have already indicated, values are learned; they are not universal. In many Native American cultures, where there is no written history, age is highly valued. Older people are sought out and asked to take part in many important decisions. Younger people admire them and include them in social gatherings. This positive value placed on age contrasts sharply to the outlook of the dominant culture of North America. Here the elderly are often shunned and made the brunt of jokes.

The value placed on privacy is another instance of how cultures differ in their view of the external world. The English value privacy highly and do not encourage openness. We can see an opposite disposition towards privacy and openness in the United States. Think of all those occasions when we hear the entire life story of the person seated next to us on an airplane—a person we just met.

Beliefs and values contribute to the development and content of our attitude systems. Formally, we may define an **attitude** as a learned tendency to respond in a consistent manner to a given object or orientation. The intensity of our attitudes is based on the degree of conviction that our beliefs and evaluations are correct. These elements interact to create a psychological state of readiness to react to objects and events in our environment. Thus, if we believe, for instance, that physically abusing another person is wrong or fear being hurt when hit, and further believe boxing has high probability of producing physical abuse, we may have a negative predisposition toward boxing (an attitude) that manifests itself in avoidance of attending or participating in boxing matches.

We have seen how beliefs, values, and attitudes can vary from one culture to another. Intercultural communicators are concerned chiefly with the difficulties that can arise when these beliefs, values, and attitudes come into conflict and clash with one another. Violations of expectations based upon deeply structured value systems can produce hurt, insult, and, as history has shown us, even violence.

World view.   The next perceptual element, though listed second, has the distinction of being both the most important and the hardest to describe. It is most important because **world view** is a culture's orientation toward such things as God, nature, life, death, the universe, and other philosophical issues that are concerned with the meaning of life and with "being." Justice Oliver Wendell Holmes used to say that science made major contributions to minor needs, but religion was at work on the things that mattered most.[6] In short, our world view helps us locate our place and rank in the universe. Perhaps more than any other factor, it influences issues ranging from how we view other people to how we spend our time. Olayiwola argues that world view even influences the social, economic, and political life of a nation.[7] Reflect for just a moment on how your concepts of death, illness, and the environment often direct the choices you make and the goals you seek. The point with regard to intercultural communication should be clear: different concepts produce different choices.

As you can observe, the issues associated with world view are timeless and represent the most fundamental basis of a culture. A Hindu, with a strong belief in reincarnation, will not only perceive time differently than a Christian, but will also have different answers to the major questions of life than will a Catholic, Moslem, Jew, Taoist, or atheist.

World view influences a culture at a very deep and profound level. Its effects often are quite subtle and do not reveal themselves in obvious ways. It might be helpful to think of a culture's world view as analogous to a pebble being tossed into a pond. Just as the pebble causes ripples to spread and reverberate over the entire surface of the pond, world view spreads itself over a culture and permeates every facet of it. Although world view influences all aspects of how a culture perceives its environment, this influence is most profound in three areas: the individual and nature, science and technology, and materialism.

As we just indicated, world view specifies the relationship of humankind to the universe, and more specifically, how human beings fit into the grand scheme of things. As long as there has been the slightest trace of culture, going back to forty thousand years ago, we have been seeking some indication of the connection between nature and ourselves. This relationship, depending on the culture, can take on a host of forms. It can be one of subjugation, in which people are helpless and at the mercy of nature, or one of symbiosis, in which people live in harmony with nature. According to still another view, humans can exercise control over nature for their own benefit.

These differences in conceptualizing the relationship between humanity and nature result in distinct frames of reference for perceiving and understanding human desires, attitudes, and behaviors. In intercultural situations, we can find ourselves clashing with others who do not share our views about how to relate to nature. In areas of conflict throughout the world, technological Western cultures, which hold that they can master nature and modify it for their benefit, come into contact with cultures that have a different orientation. A case in point is the ongoing controversy between the dominant American culture and some American Indian tribes who object to widespread strip-mining of coal because it results in the disfigurement of the earth. The two groups may fail to understand each other's arguments because of differing concepts of God and nature. As

Newsweek has noted, "Environmentalists have long blamed Biblical tradition—specifically God's injunction to man in Genesis to 'subdue the earth'—for providing cultural sanction for the Industrial Revolution and its plundering of nature."[8]

The level of a culture's scientific and technical achievement is not so much a single dominant pattern as it is an effect of many patterns. Cultures that are not activity-oriented, and that tend to believe passive acceptance of the world is in accordance with God's wishes, remain relatively unsophisticated in many aspects of scientific and technical development. This is not to imply that non-Western cultures lack science or technology. On the contrary, some of the world's leading inventions have come from Egypt, India, China, and other non-Western cultures. Our emphasis here is not on discovering new "things," but rather on accepting things as they are.

You can see how a culture's view of science and truth would be influenced by the path the culture had followed. Remember, science is based upon a set of **epistemological assumptions**—assumptions about how we gain knowledge. During the course of human development, cultures have developed varying epistemologies that have become very much a part of their world views. In contemporary Western culture we believe that knowledge is gained primarily by **empirical** means. This is the basis of science and technology, and it begins with the basic assumption that we can observe and measure phenomena in order to understand and explain them. A competing way of knowing, which is characteristic of much of the world, relies heavily on intuition. People from the East believe that true knowledge can come only from within one's self. As we have noted elsewhere, Buddha believed that each of us contained a truth, and that through meditation we could discover that truth.

It is important to appreciate that many non-Western cultures have used other ways of knowing for thousands of years. Hindus believe that knowledge comes through long periods of meditation. Buddhists believe that the goal of knowledge is absolute reality, which cannot be found through the senses. For the Buddhists, **sensory perception** implies a dual relationship between the person and the object of perception; they, like Hindus, believe sensory perception is undependable. The objects of perception are dynamic and constantly changing, and our perceptions of them are illusory and have no permanent reality.

Islam, standing opposite other religious views, holds that the world is totally real, and that it is in fact one of two realities: the divine and the created. Allah, the divine, created the world and everything on it for the pleasure of humankind. World reality is available to all persons, but the divine reality is revealed to only a few as an act of kindness by Allah.

Materialism, our final perceptual component of world view, is a cultural orientation towards material goods. For Americans materialism is an integral part of life. Western civilization is historically based on the desire for concrete possessions. A popular bumper sticker even proclaims, "The person who dies with the most toys wins."Americans believe not only that they should gather these "toys," but that they have a right to them. This view does not prevail in the rest of the world, where most people hold that material well-being is not a right of birth nor even a remote possibility. The cultural perception of well-being may be contentment in being alive and having the minimal necessities of food, water, and shelter to maintain life.

These nonmaterial perceptions tend to produce ingrained cultural attitudes and values that may seem quite strange to people from Western material cultures. What brings happiness and contentment to others may be perceived by people used to a high level of material well-being as backward, underdeveloped, and even primitive. It may lead to questions about how these people can live without cars, cable television, refrigerators, telephones, and computers. Yet the reply from these cultures is often something like, "Who needs them? Material possessions only create greed."

Social organization.   The manner in which a culture organizes itself is directly related to the institutions within that culture. These institutions take a variety of configurations and can be formal or informal. The clubs we belong to and the schools we attend all help determine how we perceive the world and how we behave. It is our family, however, and our government that most influence our perceptions and the way we communicate—our family because it introduces us to the culture, and our government because it tells us what from our past is worth remembering. Let us briefly look at both of these institutions and see their place in any study of intercultural communication.

The Chinese have a proverb that says if you know the family you don't need to know the individual. This saying clearly expresses the importance of family in how each of us sees the world. Remember, it is the family that greets us in this new world once we leave the comfort of the womb. Therefore, the family is charged with transforming a biological organism into a human being who must spend the rest of his or her life around other human beings—human beings who expect the individual to act much like all the other people in that culture.

The family is also important because by the time the other major cultural institutions can influence the child, the family has already exposed the individual to countless experiences. From our introduction to language to our ways of expressing love, the family is the first teacher. Just think for a moment of some of the crucial attitudes, values, and behaviors that the family first initiates. Any list would have to include self-reliance, the pleasing of others, responsibility, obedience, dominance, social skills, aggression, loyalty, sex roles, age roles, and the like. Keep in mind that at the moment of birth, a human being's development can take any of a number of paths. A child born in India perceives many people living together in one house and is learning about extended families. By being in the same house with elderly people the child is also learning a value towards the aged. In the United States the child sees only the immediate family in the house and is learning about the nuclear family. Some people see food being served from a common bowl, while others grow up with each person having his or her own plates. These seemingly insignificant experiences, when combined with thousands of other "messages" from the family, shape and mold the members of each culture.

As with world view, the influence of formal and informal government is hard to pin down. For when we speak of the effect of government, we are talking about much more than a culture's political system. Of course, the Soviet brand of communism produces a different individual than does Norwegian democracy. But the most influential role of any government is as the carrier of history, a role clearly marked by the great British statesman Edmund Burke when he wrote, "History is a pact between the dead, the living, and the yet unborn." This observation could also serve as a definition of culture.

The history of any culture serves as the origin of the cultural values, ideals, and behaviors. History can help answer such questions as why one type of activity evolved over another. The value Mexicans place upon "talk," for example, goes back to the socializing that was part of the marketplace during the Aztec period.

There are countless instances of how the history of a culture determines its view of the world. For example, to understand the modern-day Jew and his or her way of perceiving events and people, you would have to understand the seven thousand years of continuous persecution that members of this culture have suffered. Most Jews live with their eyes fixed on the past when they are called upon to make fundamental choices regarding education, freedom, war, civil rights, and attitudes towards non-Jews. Even the behavior of Russians, and their attraction to communism, makes more sense when we appreciate the connection between history and culture. During the past thousands of years, Russia has been invaded by Germans, Turks, Poles, Swedes, French, English, and many other groups. This history has made the Russians long for security (communism) and fear the rest of the world (their valuing of a strong military).

Within our own culture the links among government, history, and culture also help explain the evolution of specific values and attitudes. Remember, from the War of Independence to a Constitution that tells us we can all own guns, our history has stressed individual freedom and our right to defend that freedom even if it means engaging in acts of violence.

In the next chapter we shall look at a number of examples that show how a culture's history helps direct its actions. But for now it is important once again to remind you that individuals and cultures begin with a fund of knowledge that has been built up over a long period of time.

Human nature. For centuries great thinkers, regardless of the culture, have asked a basic question: What is the character of human nature? Nearly all judgments about human behavior begin with this core question. Understanding a culture's beginnings helps explain why people act as they do. Discussions of human nature usually deal with questions of goodness and rationality.

As we just noted, people have raised questions of good and evil for almost as long as we humans have had a sense of self-awareness. Because answers to this fundamental question differ, it is best to place cultures on a continuum that has three divisions: Evil, Good-and-Evil, and Good. Most people agree that the orientation we have inherited from our Puritan ancestors still influences the way many Americans perceive this issue. For many of them, people are basically evil. Hence, constant control and discipline of the self are required if we are to achieve any real goodness.

Most Oriental cultures hold humanity to be an intricate part of the universe, which they see as an infinite system of elements and forces in balanced dynamic interaction. Good and evil are two of these forces. Since humanity is part of the universe, these forces also are naturally present in humankind.

Cutting across the arguments concerning the good or evil of human nature has been the question of the essential rationality of human nature. Throughout history there has been tension between the mystic and the intellectual. Imagine for a moment the different perceptions of reality if you are French and take the rational approach characteristic of Descartes' philosophy, or are a Maasai tribesman and believe that forces outside of you control much of your thinking and behavior.

Being aware of the different principles, premises, and assumptions of other cultures enables us to understand why other people may not grasp our line of reasoning. They may not necessarily be irrational, but they may use alternative methods to reach conclusions.

Activity orientation.   **Activity orientation** has to do with the way a culture teaches its members to view activity. It is best to conceptualize this orientation as a continuum.

Being————————Being-in-Becoming————————Doing

In North American culture the dominant pattern is doing, or goal-directed activity measurable by external standards. We make lists of things to do and we often greet our friends with questions such as "What have you been doing?" This preoccupation is not so common throughout the rest of the world. In Mexico, for example, people take great delight in the simple act of conversation with family and good friends. Mexicans will talk for hours with their associates, for they believe that the act of "being" is one of the main goals and joys of life.

As you might well imagine, the activity orientation impinges upon several other beliefs and values. Our behavioral definition of activity affects our perceptions of work, efficiency, change, time, and progress.

Perception of self and others.   Our perception of self and others is bound to determine how we communicate. In North American culture the word *self* occupies an important place. We speak of self-concept, self-image, self-esteem, self-reliance, self-help, self-awareness, self-actualization, self-determination, and so on. Listen to our conversations and you will notice the word *I* appearing with great regularity. Many cultures do not share our perception of the self as being at the center of the universe. These differences revolve around perceptions of individualism and self-motivation.

From our legal system to our desire not to be like anyone else, Americans believe in the importance of the individual. In many cultures of the world, however, the individual (the self) plays a much smaller role. In these cultures the group is the primary social unit, not the individual. Russian communes, Israeli kibbutzes, and other social collectives emphasize the group. In Japan the group receives special consideration in all decisions. A person directs his or her loyalty not at the self, but rather at others. In fact, in many Oriental cultures the individual is taught to suspend thoughts of self so that the ego does not impose upon others or interfere with an individual's pursuit of life. The "I" in the Chinese written language looks very similar to the word for selfish. Many axioms of Buddhist philosophy are concerned with teaching devotees the proper mental states in which the ego is lost.

Self-motivation is tied very closely to the concept of self. Cultures that favor the group over the individual minimize self-motivation in the sense of individual development and personal success. This does not imply that people in group-emphasizing cultures lack motivation to work or achieve. On the contrary, people in collective environments can be encouraged by a group spirit and be very industrious and hardworking. The differences are in goal direction and motivation. North Americans tend toward development of the self at the expense of the group or others. People in collective cultures devote themselves to group striving. It is easy to see a series of potential problems when cultures like the Maasai, Japanese, and Mexican—which all stress cooperation—come in contact with North Americans.

Verbal Processes

The phrase *verbal processes,* as we shall use it, refers to two closely related activities, both involving symbols. We are employing the phrase to refer to how we talk to each other and to the internal activities of thinking.

Verbal language.   We begin our preview of language by noting that it is impossible to separate our use of language from our culture. For in its most basic sense, language is an organized, generally agreed upon, learned symbol-system used to represent the experiences within a geographic or cultural community.

Culture teaches us both the symbol (dog) and what the symbol stands for (a furry, domesticated pet). Objects, events, experiences, and feelings have particular labels or names solely because a community of people (a culture) arbitrarily decided to so name them.

If we extend the above notion to the intercultural setting, we can observe how different cultures can have *both different symbols and different responses.* Culture even influences the unadorned word *dog* we used in the last paragraph. In some areas of the world, such as Hong Kong and Korea, dogs are considered to be a culinary delight and often are eaten. In the United States dogs sit on the family couch and are not cooked; hence, the word *dog* conveys a quite different meaning in the United States than it does in Korea. If you take our superficial example and apply it to every word and meaning you know, you can begin to visualize the influence of culture on how we send and receive messages. Think for just a moment about the variety of meanings various cultures have for words such as *freedom, sexuality, trespassing, birth control, social security, leadership, assertiveness,* and *AIDS.*

Even the way people *use* language shifts from culture to culture. In the Arab tradition, "verbal language patterns that emphasize creative artistry by using rhetorical devices such as repetition, metaphor, and simile are highly valued."[9] Yet Japanese culture encourages minimum verbal communication. A Japanese proverb gives credence to this outlook by offering this advice: "By your mouth you shall perish." By multiplying this example across the countless cultures you will come into contact with, you can see how differences in language reflect differences in culture.

People living within the same geographic boundaries can also use language in ways that differ from the dominant culture. In general, women, because they are raised to be polite and to focus on the other person, will ask more questions than men and will let men control the flow of the conversation.

Keep in mind that word usage and meaning are learned, and that all cultures and co-cultures have novel experiences that help frame usage and meaning. A few examples demonstrate this idea. Within prison communities, to *tip* is to leave prison, and *doing a pound* is an eight-year sentence. The co-culture of circus and carnival workers uses the word *dip* to refer to a pickpocket, and a *monkey* is someone who gets fleeced by a con-game. Prostitutes use the word *gorilla* to describe someone who beats them up, and an *outlaw* is a prostitute who works without a pimp. We are all aware of the rich examples that can be drawn from the black community.

Because language is such an integral part of intercultural communication, we have set aside an entire chapter to expand on some of the ideas mentioned in the last few paragraphs.

Patterns of thought.   The mental processes of reasoning and problem solving prevalent in a community are another major component of culture that often influences the intercultural encounter. If you, like most North Americans, use the deductive method of reasoning to solve problems, and you are interacting with someone who is using the inductive method (as is the case in the Korean culture), you are apt to misunderstand each other as you try to agree on what the problem is and what the solution is. You are moving from broad categories to specific examples that rely on "facts," while your associate from Korea is starting with specific observations and extracting generalizations. And many of the Korean's generalizations might be based on "intuitive discovery."

Unless we have had experiences with people from other cultures who follow different patterns of thought, it is quite common to assume everyone thinks in the same way. Even the simple organizational pattern of introduction, body, and conclusion is not universal. We take this scheme for granted, but most of the world does not structure its discourse in this fashion.

In addition, Western thought assumes a direct relationship between mental concepts and the concrete world of reality. This orientation places great stock in logic and rationality. Most Westerners believe that truth is out there and that we can discover it by following scientific methods and engaging in logical calculations. The Eastern view, best illustrated by Taoist thought, holds that problems are solved quite differently. To begin with, people are *not* granted instant rationality. We do not find the truth by active searching and the application of Aristotelian modes of reasoning. On the contrary, one had best wait and be patient, and if truth is to be known it will make itself apparent. Culick describes this disparity between the Occidental rational mode of thinking and the Oriental intuitive approach: "The one develops and disciplines man's emotional nature, his sense of propriety, his aesthetic tastes; the other develops and disciplines the reason and will, the capacity to think and act independently. The one begets a culture of courtesy, the other a culture of realism."[10]

Attitudes toward context and time also affect how cultures reason. The Chinese and Japanese perceive the world largely according to the conditions governing the present, not those that might characterize the future. Because Buddhism strongly emphasizes the here and now, and holds that all things are transitory, these cultures take for granted that what we think and say applies to today's conditions and may have to be reinterpreted tomorrow.

Another major difference between the Eastern and Western views is in the areas of activity and pace. To the Western mind, human activity is paramount and will lead ultimately to the "facts." In the Taoist tradition, however, truth is the active agent, and if it is to be known it will be through the activity of truth making itself apparent. Differences in pace are most extreme between cultures that are impulsive and those that are reflective. In the United States we admire the person who can make quick decisions. The Japanese, however, would not view such a person favorably. They would perceive this person as impulsive, since they believe that correct thinking takes time. Americans trying to do business in Japan are often frustrated when they come face-to-face with this slower method of problem solving.

Nonverbal Processes

The ability to use words to represent feelings and ideas is, as we have indicated, universal. All of us can also use nonverbal symbols to share internal states. Although the process of using our actions to communicate is universal, the meanings for those actions often shift from culture to culture. Hence, nonverbal communication becomes yet another element one must understand if one is going to interact with people from different cultures. This element is significant enough to take up two chapters later in the text. For now, however, let us introduce you to three important nonverbal categories: behavior, time, and space.

Nonverbal behavior. It would be folly for us to try to examine all of the elements of nonverbal behavior. An example or two of the nonverbal elements should enable you to visualize how nonverbal issues fit into the overall scheme of intercultural understanding.

Instances of touch as a form of communication demonstrate how nonverbal communication is a product of culture. In Germany women as well as men shake hands at the outset of every social encounter; in the United States, women seldom shake hands. In the Soviet Union men will often greet each other by kissing and hugging. In Thailand people do not touch in public, and to touch someone on the head is a major social transgression. Even co-cultures differ in their use of touch. In the United States, women give and receive more touch than do men, yet men tend to initiate the touch.

Another illustrative example is a culture's use of eye contact. Arabs tend to engage in more eye contact than do Americans; for the Japanese, however, eye contact is not a hallmark of a successful communicator. In some Native American Indian tribes, young children learn that direct eye contact with an elder is a sign of disrespect. A white schoolteacher working on an Indian reservation was not aware of this and assumed her students were not interested in school because they never looked at her.

Even some of our most elementary gestures are culture-bound. We make a zero with our index finger and thumb as a way of "saying" everything is perfect. Yet this same gesture means money in Japan, is used as an insult in Malta and Greece, and is perceived as an obscene gesture in Brazil. The meaning of the common act of waving can also shift from culture to culture. In many Oriental cultures this action means "Please come here"—not good-bye. And people in the Middle East use this gesture for calling a dog.

As we indicated a few paragraphs ago, cultural differences are so very plentiful that we shall offer many more examples in Chapters 7 and 8. For now, however, it should be clear that there are times when the same action can produce contrary responses.

Concept of time. A culture's concept of time includes its attitude towards the past, present, and future, and the importance, or lack of importance, it places on time. Most Western cultures think of time in lineal-spatial terms. We are timebound. Our schedules and our lists dominate our lives. The Germans and the Swiss are even more aware of time than Americans. Trains, planes, and meals must always be on time. In many parts of the world, however, the activity, not the clock, determines action. Hence, these cultures perceive being tardy in quite different terms.

Even co-cultures use time in ways that often confuse the dominant culture. Hopi Indians pay very little attention to time as we know it. They believe that each thing, whether a person, plant, or animal, has its own time system. And blacks often use what is referred to as BPT (black people's time), or hang-loose time. According to this outlook, what is happening at the instant has priority.

Use of space.   We all know that Arabs and Latins tend to interact more closely than do North Americans, and we also know how uncomfortable we feel when people from these cultures get too close to us. This shows how use of space is yet another behavior that is directly related to past experience. Distance, however, is just one aspect of use of space as a form of communication; physical orientation is also influenced by culture. North Americans prefer to sit face-to-face or at right angles to one another, whereas Chinese generally prefer side-by-side seating. The English and Germans are conditioned to waiting in a straight line when seeking service in public, but Arabs, Mediterraneans, and South Americans see nothing wrong with pushing and shoving to secure the best possible location to be served. This is a clear example of how the use of space can send different messages.

We remind you once again that we have not even begun to discuss nonverbal communication in detail. We have simply tried to demonstrate how culture helps determine nonverbal communication.

SUMMARY

Intercultural Communication

- Intercultural communication is communication between people whose cultural perceptions and symbol systems are distinct enough to alter the communication event.

- Intercultural communication occurs when source and receiver are from different races.

- Interethnic communication refers to situations in which the parties are of the same race but of different ethnic origins.

- International communication occurs between political structures.

- Intracultural communication is communication between members of the same culture, including all members of racial, ethnic, or other co-cultures.

An Intercultural Communication Model

- A model of intercultural communication demonstrates how meaning changes when subjected to culturally different repertoires of social reality and communicative behaviors, and to meanings that are different for the interpreter than for the producer.

The Elements of Intercultural Communication

- One element of intercultural communication is perception, "the process by which an individual selects, evaluates, and organizes stimuli from the external world." Cultural perceptions are based on beliefs, values, and attitude systems.

- Another element is verbal processes, how we talk to each other and the internal activities of thinking.

- Nonverbal processes, the third element, involve the use of actions to communicate. The meanings of these actions shift from culture to culture.

ACTIVITIES

1. Find out as much as you can about the history of your informant's culture/nation. Try to isolate specific examples of how your informant's cultural values have been determined by historical events.

2. In small groups, play a word-association game. Your instructor will compose a list of potentially culture-bound words such as *motherhood, freedom, sex,* and *dog.* He or she will say the words one at a time. Write down the first

thing that comes into your mind for each word. Then compare your reactions. Are there any major differences within the group? Discuss them. Then compare your answers with the entire class and discuss.

DISCUSSION IDEAS

1. Give an example of a situation in which another culture's use of nonverbal communication confused you.

2. Find examples in the news of events that involve interracial, interethnic, international, and intracultural communication, and explain how they are examples of each.

3. Which of the kinds of communication in Question 2 (interracial, interethnic, international, and intracultural) might take place in your classroom? In your neighborhood?

NOTES FOR CHAPTER 4

1. Edith A. Folb, "Who's Got the Room at the Top? Issues of Dominance and Nondominance in Intracultural Communication," in *Intercultural Communication: A Reader*, 5th ed., ed. Larry A. Samovar and Richard E. Porter (Belmont, CA: Wadsworth, 1988), 124.

2. Barbara Bate, *Communication and the Sexes* (New York: Harper and Row, 1988), 35.

3. Marshall R. Singer, *Intercultural Communication: A Perceptual Approach* (Englewood Cliffs, NJ: Prentice-Hall, 1987), 9.

4. Singer, 9.

5. Milton Rokeach, *Beliefs, Values, and Attitudes* (San Francisco: Jossey-Bass, 1968), 161.

6. Hustin Smith, *The Religions of Man* (New York: Harper and Row, 1989), 14–15.

7. Rahman O. Olayiwola, "The Impact of Islam on the Conduct of Nigerian Foreign Relations," *The Islamic Quarterly* 33 (1989), 19–26.

8. *Newsweek*, June 5, 1989, 71.

9. Myron W. Lustig, "Cultural and Communication Patterns of Saudi Arabians," in *Intercultural Communication: A Reader,* 5th ed., ed. Larry A. Samovar and Richard E. Porter (Belmont, CA: Wadsworth, 1988), 102.

10. S. Culick, *The East and West: A Study of Their Psychic and Cultural Characteristics* (Ruthland, UT: Charles Tuttle, 1962), 68.

II

THEORY AND PRACTICE

There never were, in the world, two opinions alike, no more than
two hairs, or two grains; the most universal quality is diversity.

MONTAIGNE

A rock pile ceases to be a rock pile the moment a single man
contemplates it, bearing within him the image of a cathedral.

SAINT-EXUPÉRY

CHAPTER FIVE

CULTURAL DIVERSITY IN PERCEPTION: ALTERNATIVE VIEWS OF REALITY

Perception, as we discovered in the previous chapter, is the means by which we make sense of our physical and social environment. More formally, perception is "the process by which an individual selects, evaluates, and organizes stimuli from the external environment."[1] Because our information about and knowledge of our external physical and social world is mediated by perceptual processes, perception is primary in the study of intercultural communication. We behave and communicate as we do because of the ways in which our external world appears to us. In other words, the meaning that we give to the world, what we eventually say about that world, how we communicate about it, and how we interpret the communication of others is a function of our perceptions.

UNDERSTANDING PERCEPTION

The physical process of perception is pretty much the same in all people. We have sensory organs such as eyes, ears, and noses that permit us to sense our environment. These sensations are routed through our nervous system to our brains, where the sensations are interpreted and endowed with meaning in a two-stage sequence. The first stage is recognition or identification, in which a configuration of light or sound waves is identified as perhaps a car or music. The second stage involves the interpretation and evaluation of that which has been identified. The result of that last step, however, is not the same in all people. This step is a learned process influenced primarily by culture. In other words, although sound waves impinge upon our eardrums and cause nerve impulses to be transmitted through our aural nerves in much the same way, how we interpret and evaluate what we hear is very much a function of our culture. Because culture is so important to our perceptions of the world, we need to look at the link between culture and perception.

Our perceptions of the world are interpretations we learn to make from the nerve impulses that reach our brains. These interpretations are highly individualistic and represent our unique set of experiences in the culture in which we have been raised. Whether one will regurgitate or salivate at the thought of eating the meat of a cow, fish, dog, or snake will depend on how thoroughly one has internalized the attitudes and values of the culture in which he or she has been raised.[2] We learn to interpret the world as we grow up interacting within our culture. By observing the way people around us behave, we learn how to interpret our world. Through this learning process, we not only develop the capacity to identify social objects and events, but to give those objects and events meaning and value. If you grow up in a family that values education and is highly involved in continued learning and self-development, you will most likely learn to perceive activities such as reading books as positive and useful. You not only learn to identify the activity of reading; you learn to give it a value as well. If you grow up in a household in which people constantly belittle a particular ethnic or racial group, the chances are very good that you will grow up believing in the inferiority of that group. Likewise, if you are raised to believe that only one religious perspective is the true perspective, you will quite likely grow up believing people with other religious beliefs to be wrong, cursed, unsaved, doomed, unworthy of conversion, or possibly worse. The point here is that we learn to perceive our environment within the culture in which we are raised.

This may seem to be an obvious point, but we want to emphasize that culture strongly influences the environments in which we are raised. Culture exposes a large group of people to similar experiences and tends to produce similar meanings and similar behaviors in those people. This does not mean, of course, that everyone within a particular culture is exactly the same. There is diversity within cultures just as there is diversity between cultures. Our point here is that culture has an impact on how we learn to perceive and plays a major role in our perceptive behaviors.

PERCEPTION AND CULTURE

Although we are particularly interested in the perception of social objects and events, culture also influences how we perceive physical objects. Or, perhaps, culture attaches some social dimension to physical objects so that we learn to interpret them according to the dictates of our culture. When looking at the moon, for instance, North Americans report seeing a man in the moon, American Indians often report seeing a rabbit, Chinese often report seeing a lady fleeing her husband, and Samoans report a woman weaving. Now, obviously, the moon is a rocklike physical object that orbits the earth; but what we see in that physical object is very much an outcome of the influence our culture had upon us as we learned to perceive the moon.

In the social realm, culture makes a far more dramatic impact on our perceptions. Some examples of cultural diversity in perception will help us better understand just how differently cultures perceive social aspects of the environment. And remember, we are stressing the social aspects of perception, which include not only description but evaluation as well.

Caucasian mothers tend to stress as positive those aspects of their children's speech and behavior that reflect assertiveness, excitement, and interest. On the other hand, Navajo mothers viewing the same behaviors report them as being mischievous and lacking discipline. To the Navajo mothers, assertive speech and behavior are a sign of discourtesy, restlessness, self-centeredness, and lack of discipline. Caucasian mothers tend to report the same behaviors as self-disciplined, exciting to observe, and advantageous for the child.[3]

Another example of culture's influence on perception is in the perception of credibility. Credibility has to do with such qualities as whether people may be trusted, whether they know what they are talking about, and whether they have good intentions. For Americans, a credible person has to be articulate and outspoken. For the Japanese, however, a person who is quiet and spends more time listening than speaking is the more credible. Americans usually hold that it is good to express one's opinion as openly as possible. The Japanese, however, hold that talkativeness is a sign of shallowness. Among Americans, credible people seem direct, rational, decisive, unyielding, and confident. Among Japanese, credible persons are perceived as being indirect, sympathetic, prudent, flexible, and humble. In Japan, social status is another sign of credibility, but Americans downplay social status in favor of competence.

The way in which space is perceived also varies culturally. The English value personal space very highly. Arabs, on the other hand, view space quite differently. In crowded shops, theaters, or train stations, the typical Englishman "queues up" instinctively. An Arab, on the other hand, may crash the line like an NFL inside linebacker attempting to sack a quarterback. The British may perceive this Arabic response to lines and space as uncivil.

Some cultures have emphasized color in their perception of the world. Primitive people of Asia and the ancient Greeks associated color with the sun and with divinity. Life and goodness were represented by bright colors, death and evil by black. Brilliant colors were used everywhere, for they identified things with godliness. In Greece all architecture and sculpture were gaily colored, not for aesthetic reasons or to make sculpture appear more lifelike, but in accordance with the symbolic relevance of each building or piece of art. The Navajo differentiate the mountains that surround them by color: The mountains to the east are represented by white, to the west by yellow, to the north by black, and to the south by blue. The Hopi associate direction with color. For them north is yellow, west green or blue, south red, and east white. The Hindu represent fire with red, water with white, and the earth with black. The Chinese identify yellow with the earth, black with water, red with fire, green with wood, and white with metal.

We come now to a premise about social perception: Humans are essentially social animals, and their perceptions of the universe represent each individual's subjective reality. Culture strongly influences this subjective reality, so that although each individual perceives his or her own individual reality, groups of individuals, through cultural conditioning, tend to perceive the universe in similar ways.

We also must recognize a direct relationship between perception and behavior. Behavior is based on our perceptions of the universe. How we react to our perceptions is almost singly a result of our learning and cultural conditioning. Each of us, as we come into contact with other beings, brings to those situations our unique perceptions of the world. We are therefore affected in our perceptual processes by our culture, which has taught us to perceive the world from our own unique perspective. How we react to social and physical objects in our environment depends upon the beliefs, values, and attitudes that we have internalized as we grew up in and became conditioned by our culture.

Beliefs and Values

In Chapter 4 we introduced you to our system of beliefs and values and provided detailed definitions and descriptions of them. Here we shall reexamine beliefs and values and look in depth at the influence culture exerts in establishing them within each of us. We shall also discover how cultural diversity, through its influence on our beliefs and values, affects, our perceptual processes.

Beliefs.   It is important for us to examine belief systems because they give us a better understanding of the bases of behavior. With this understanding we then are in a position to better understand our own behavior. Furthermore, knowledge of the belief systems of others prepares us to understand their behavior. It is a fundamental axiom that what we believe in large measure determines how we behave and how we relate to our environment. If, for instance, we believe that snakes are slimy, we avoid them. On the other hand, if we believe that only through the handling of snakes can we find God, we handle them and run the risk of venomous bites.

The point here is that the culture in which we are raised predominantly determines our beliefs. The extent to which this is true will be seen in the examples of cultural diversity in beliefs that follow.

People who have grown up in eastern Europe or China may very likely believe that business and the means of production should belong to the state or to the people collectively. On the other hand, someone born in the United States, Canada, or Japan will most likely grow up believing that the means of production should belong to individuals in sole proprietorships, or to several individuals in partnerships, or to numerous people in corporations.

People who grow up in cultures where Christianity is the predominant religion usually believe that salvation is attainable only through Christ. Yet, people who are Jewish, Islamic, Buddhist, Shinto, or Hindu do not hold that belief. They hold other beliefs about life after death, salvation, or what happens to the human spirit when the body dies.

In many Islamic cultures, women must keep their faces covered in public or at least cover most of their heads, leaving only as much of their face visible as is necessary to engage in everyday activities such as seeing, breathing, eating, and talking. In non-Islamic cultures, this is not the case.

The reason beliefs are such an influential factor in intercultural communication is that they are deep-seated in our conscious minds. Our beliefs originate as we grow up in our specific cultures. At early ages we are not prepared to question our social institutions, and we freely accept what they teach us about how to live and interact in our society. Because there seems to be consensus about how to dress, how to speak to our elders, how to eat, what to eat, where to eat, what constitutes furniture, how we attain salvation or damnation, how we should earn our living, and what is the proper social structure, we grow up believing these things with little or no question. In fact, if we do ask questions, we usually receive strong negative reactions from such a large segment of our social world that we immediately drop that line of questioning and either accept the belief or become "mentally ill" social outcasts. In other words, as we grow up in a culture, that culture conditions us to believe what it deems to be worthy and true.

Another important function of belief systems is that they are the basis for our values. In the simplest sense, values are enduring attitudes about the preferability of one belief over another. The great cultural diversity among values is important in the study of intercultural communication.

Values. In the study of human interaction, it is important to look at cultural values, but in the study of intercultural communication it is crucial. An understanding of cultural values helps us appreciate the behavior of other people and recognize how to deal with them. Knowing, for instance, that the Japanese value detail and politeness might cause us to examine carefully a proffered Japanese business card, as the Japanese do, rather than immediately relegating it to a coat pocket. An understanding of cultural values also helps us understand our own behavior. We can, for example, associate impatience with our value of time, aggressiveness with our value for competition, or self-disclosure with our value of friendship and sociability.

A value may be defined formally as an enduring belief that a specific mode of conduct or end-state of existence is personally or socially preferable to an opposite or converse mode of conduct or end-state of existence.[4] An individual's cognitive structure, however, consists of many values that are organized into a value system. "A value system is an enduring organization of beliefs concerning preferable modes of conduct or end-state existence along a continuum of relative importance."[5] A value system also "represents what is expected or hoped for, required or forbidden. It is not a report of actual conduct but is the system of criteria by which conduct is judged and sanctions applied."[6] When we internalize our values, they become consciously or unconsciously a standard or criterion for guiding action, for developing and maintaining attitudes toward relevant objects and situations, for justifying one's own and others' actions and attitudes, for morally judging self and others, and for comparing self with others.

Values, then, are social guideposts that show us the cultural norms of our society and specify in large measure the ways in which we should behave. They provide standards that permit us to make individual decisions about our relationships with self, others, society, nature, and God. In other words, they provide us with a set of rules for making choices and reducing ambiguity. Values also possess a normative dimension. They specify, for instance, what is good, bad, right, or wrong, what ought to be or ought not be, what is useful, useless, appropriate, or inappropriate.

Values are also linked to perception and behavior and are revealed through behavior and expression. Getting up and going to school is a behavior that demonstrates the value of education and responsibility. Saying "Please stay and have some coffee" expresses orally the value of hospitality. Putting part of each paycheck into a savings account demonstrates the value of thriftiness.

Here are examples of typical American values as they are expressed in cultural sayings:

"Cleanliness is next to godliness" expresses the value of cleanliness.

"A penny saved is a penny earned" expresses the value of thriftiness.

"Time is money" expresses the values of time and thriftiness.

"Don't cry over spilt milk" expresses the value of practicality.

"Waste not, want not" expresses the value of frugality.

"Early to bed, early to rise, makes a man healthy, wealthy, and wise" expresses the values of diligence and a strong work ethic.

"Losing sucks" expresses the values of winning and success.

"You've made your bed, now sleep in it" expresses the values of individual responsibility or retaliation.

And finally, "The squeaky wheel gets the grease" expresses the value of aggressiveness.

Besides seeing how values express cultural views, we can also see the relative importance of values within a society. Values can be classified into three levels of cultural importance: primary, secondary, and tertiary. **Primary values** are at the top of the value hierarchy because they are the most important. They specify what is worth the sacrifice of human life, worth war, and worth dying for. In the United States, democracy is a primary value. **Secondary values** are very important, but they are not strong enough for the sacrifice of human life. In the United States, the relief of pain and suffering of other human beings is a secondary value. We care, but we do not apply our full attention and resources to such problems. **Tertiary values** lie at the bottom of our value hierarchies. In the United States, hospitality to guests is an example of a tertiary value.

Whether a value is primary, secondary, or tertiary depends upon the culture in which the value resides. Some examples should demonstrate this. Individuality is a primary value in Western cultures, secondary in black cultures, and tertiary in Eastern cultures. Motherhood is a primary value in black and Eastern cultures, but a secondary value in Muslim and Western cultures. Masculinity, however, is universally a primary value in black, Muslim, Eastern, Western, and African cultures. Punctuality is a primary value in Western cultures, secondary in black cultures, tertiary in Muslim and Eastern cultures, and negligible in African cultures. Respect for elders is a primary value in Eastern, African, and

Muslim cultures, a secondary value in black cultures, and tertiary in Western cultures. Respect for youth, on the other hand, is a primary value in Western cultures and a secondary value in Muslim, African, black, and Eastern cultures. Although human dignity is a primary value in Western and black cultures and a secondary value in Eastern, African, and Muslim cultures, equality of women is a primary value only in Western cultures; it is a secondary value in Eastern and black cultures, tertiary in African cultures, and only negligible in Muslim cultures. As you can see from these examples, our values have much to do with specifying our normative behaviors.

We must be aware that cultural values do change. They are not so strongly cast that they remain the same for all time. A cursory examination of American society will show this change. Look, for instance, at American values regarding women, sex, education, family, careers, and minority rights. During the past fifty years there have been remarkable changes regarding these values. Much of this change can be attributed to the fact that our values tend to be arranged in a hierarchy, with the most important values at the top and the least important at the bottom. In many respects, the values at the top of the hierarchy influence those at the bottom. So, for example, the values of freedom and democracy—which are ranked near the top of American values—predominate and laws are passed to prevent discrimination against minority members of the society. Freedom of choice—another top American value—prevails, and laws prohibiting abortion are overturned. One mistake in the arena of intercultural communication is to assume that cultural values are fixed and thus to develop stereotypes of others. We must also remember that the intensity with which individuals within a culture hold values varies. Some people hold values more intensely than others.

Values are learned.   People learn values in a host of ways. To help complete our picture of the relationship between culture and values, we will look at some of the ways in which we learn them. As we grow up in our homes and our culture, we learn values through our interactions with others and through the normative instructions we receive from our families, friends, and others. We learn some values on the cognitive level, as when we are told how to behave. "Don't lie," "Boys don't cry," "Take your punishment like a man," "Make your bed," "Wash your hands," "Don't talk to your mother that way," "Joyce, you do the dishes while John cleans up the backyard."

We also learn values from the proverbs and sayings of our culture. These are repeated and repeated as we grow up until we accept them as fact. Examine the following sayings from American culture past and present to see how they become a part of our belief system and to recognize the values they impart.

"Nice guys finish last."

"Might makes right."

"A woman's place is in the home."

"All things are possible."

Other cultures also have proverbs and sayings that impart values. The values imparted, however, may differ from those in American culture.

One does not make the wind blow but is blown by it. This Asian view implies that people are guided by fate rather than by their own devices.

The nail that stands out gets hit. This is another Asian view that says nonconformity is not tolerated.

The first man to raise his voice loses the argument. This Chinese saying praises the value of harmony.

Order is half of life. This is a German view that stresses the value of organization, conformity, and structure.

Women have but two residences—the house and the tomb. This expresses an Algerian viewpoint about the place of women within the society.

When a fool is told a proverb, the meaning of it has to be explained to him. This Akan proverb illustrates the extent to which members of that society are expected to be familiar with and to understand the meanings of proverbs.

The mouth maintains silence in order to hear the heart talk. This Belgian saying implies the value of intuition and feelings in interaction.

He who speaks has no knowledge and he who has knowledge does not speak. This saying from Japan demonstrates the value of silence.

A friend to everybody is a friend to nobody. This is a German saying that specifies the value of having only a few close relationships rather than many acquaintances.

Even if it is a stone bridge make sure it is safe. This Korean saying implies the value of going slowly, being cautious, or being reflective.

Nothing done with intelligence is done without speech. This Greek saying emphasizes the importance of talk as a means of communication.

Life is a dance, not a race. This Irish folk saying specifies the value of taking things easy or going slowly.

How blessed is a man who finds wisdom. This Jewish saying expresses the importance of learning and education.

No need to know the person, only the family. This Chinese saying implies the value of the family as a unit and the relative unimportance of the individual.

Beauty passes, wisdom remains. This is a Turkish saying that implies the value of age.

A zebra does not despise its stripes. From the Maasai of Africa, this saying expresses the value of accepting things as they are, of accepting oneself as one is, and of avoiding the envy of others.

This thing is like the dew that showers down. Wealth is dew. Kingship is dew. These three proverbs from the Zulu, Tongan, and Ndebele cultures of Africa all use the image of morning dew to denote the transience of things.

The child has no owner. Another Maasai saying, this one reflecting the value that all children are the collective responsibility of the tribe rather than the individual responsibility of the parents.

Empty cans clatter the loudest. This saying from Indonesia emphasizes the importance of silence. Only the ignorant or stupid "clatter" or speak too much.

The father guides the son, and the husband guides the wife. This is a Chinese Confucian saying that emphasizes the position of women within the society.

From these examples, it is easy to see how we acquire and develop our values. And when we take time to think about it, we realize that we learn most of these values and integrate them into our personalities before we are old enough to think about or question their validity.

We also learn values from folklore. Whether it be ancient myths of our culture or current popular culture, folklore is value-laden and teaches and reinforces values. Whether it be Pinocchio's nose growing larger when he lied, Abraham Lincoln learning to read by drawing letters on a shovel by the fireside, or Rambo or Luke Skywalker defending democracy and fighting for what is "right," folklore constantly reinforces our fundamental values.

We also learn values by watching others. We learn to show affection and whom to give it to by watching others hug and kiss. We learn various roles by watching and imitating our parents. We learn who works inside the home and who works outside. We learn about how to spend our time by watching what others do with their time. Do we spend our time alone, with others, praying, playing, working? We discover this by watching others in our culture. By watching, we also learn the importance of grooming, and more importantly, what constitutes a good and acceptable appearance.

Finally, we learn values from sources as subtle as poetry and art and as ubiquitous as the media. In Asian cultures most art depicts objects, animals, and landscapes. It seldom focuses on people. American and European art, however, emphasizes people. These differences reflect first the Asian view that nature is more powerful and important than people and the American and European views that people are more important than nature and that they have the duty to mold nature to their purposes.

The mass media deliver many values. Sports, war stories, police stories, and many documentaries reflect violence. The language that we use is filled with words that reflect and sanction violence. In sports, war terms such as *fight, kill, blow them away, destroy their defense, never surrender, fight it out in the trenches,* and *victory* are frequently used to describe and depict players' actions and attitudes. Sports fans and viewers often use the same terminology when rooting for their team: *kill'em, stomp'em, break their backs, fight to win, destroy their offense, nice guys finish last,* and *winning is everything, losing sucks.*

War stories and police stories use similar forms of language to imply that violence and fighting are glorious as long as you are on the "right" side. Interestingly, this same language that reinforces the use of violence also sets up the conditions under which violence is acceptable. Obviously, violence is all right when it is used to destroy evil. The difficulty is in the definition of evil. This concept has a tremendous amount of cultural diversity; but in the long run, those defined as evil are perceived as causing harm to righteous people. This form of language often defines the "enemy" as less than human, giving just cause for its destruction. Think for just a moment how frequently this rationale has been used by one group of people to subdue and destroy another. Human history is replete with examples, and people are still using these excuses today. Examine, for instance, white South Africa's view of blacks and other racial groups. Or look at the language North Americans used during the Vietnam War, in which they referred to the North Vietnamese as "gooks," "slopes," "VC," "Charlie," and so on. If you degrade your enemy enough to make them less than human, it is much easier to kill them. The same was just as true in Roman times. It is much easier to kill your enemy if you perceive him or her as a barbarian rather than a civilized human.

Media can also teach other values, for instance the value of gossip. Just check the headlines of the "gossip columns" the next time you check out at the grocery store or when you watch "Entertainment Tonight." In other cultures, media stress other values. In Asian countries media may show that idle gossip is improper and that people should not speak ill of someone who is not in their company.

Media can also teach other values, such as how we ought to perceive the elderly. Most American media proclaim the value of youth. Advertisements, especially, value youth. How many products can you think of that use youthful models as a part of their advertising and suggest that if you buy and use the product you will have the same youthful appearance as the models in the ad? The media have often made old people act and look stupid, but ads featuring "middle-aged" folks are becoming more common as the baby-boomers get older.

Now that we have a general idea about how we learn and obtain our values, we will turn to a number of social areas common to all cultures, areas that serve as the sources of a culture's values. Specifically, we will examine world view, social organization, views of human nature, activity orientations, and concepts of self and others, not only to see how they teach us our values but to discover the rich cultural diversity within these value domains.

World View and Its Effect

Each collection of people has from the very beginning of civilization and regardless of time or location seen the need to evolve what is called a world view. World view is extremely important because it influences the deep structures of society and affects our perceptions of the world and, consequently, strongly affects our belief and value systems as well as how we think. Specifically, world view is a culture's orientation towards God, humanity, nature, the universe and cosmos, life, death, sickness, and other philosophical issues that influence how we see our world. Religion is but one kind of world view, and even the person who says there is no god has answers to the large questions about life and death and what really matters.

World view is not a cosmic constant. Culture determines our view of the world, and each culture perceives a different reality. This is because people need to make observations and gather knowledge that makes sense within their particular cultural perspective. How we view our universe, our position in it, what we value, how we think, and how we behave within that universe are all products of cultural learning. We must decide what is worth noting and what to exclude. Each culture selects data that conform to its particular reality. But because these realities differ, the images of the world and reality will also differ. "Truth" is obscure and inconsistent across cultures. We learn to make verifiable statements about our world, statements called facts. We use "facts" to make sense of our environment, to govern how we construct arguments, to solve problems, to make decisions, and to organize and categorize information.

The gathered facts, however, are not the same in all cultures. When men in New Guinea kill pigs to prepare a feast for their dead ancestors, they are expressing both their view of the world and their value for their ancestors. When a farmer in Peru buries three coca leaves as an offering to the gods before planting his crops, he is expressing his view of the world. Or in Haiti, when a mystical leader dances to the beat of drums to enter a trance so that she might experience god, she again is demonstrating her view of the world.

The study of world view is important because if you can understand a culture's most significant values, you can better understand how and why members of that culture behave as they do. World view produces values that penetrate deep into the culture; so if you know something about world view, you know something about culture. For instance, the Islamic world view gives insight into the Islamic culture. In the writings of the Koran, the world is male-dominated. Men are responsible for women because God has given the one more than the other.

Knowledge of world view can even help us understand a culture's perception of nature. Environmentalists have long blamed biblical tradition—specifically God's injunction to man in Genesis to subdue the earth—for providing cultural and religious sanction for the Industrial Revolution and the misuse of natural resources. Other religious or world views lead to different attitudes. The Shinto religion of Japan suggests that there is an aesthetic appreciation of nature in which the focus is on reality and not heaven, a reality that makes nature supreme. Shintoism prescribes a love of the land as a whole and of each part of it in the form of an aesthetic love of things and places. Every hill and lake, every mountain and river is dear. Cherry trees, shrines, and scenic resorts are indispensable to a full life. People perceive them as lasting things among which their ancestors lived and died. Here their ancestral spirits look on, their families still abide. People preserve nature so that nature can preserve the family.

These examples reflect the view of the world that various people's cultures have given them. Obviously, these views can differ significantly. In fact, their diversity can be so radical that it becomes quite difficult for people to understand and to interact with one another. Part of this difficulty is due to the bizarre appearance of others' behaviors and to cultural diversity in values, and part of it is due to our own rigidity and our failure or inability to recognize the relative cultural appropriateness of someone else's behavior.

We have already said that our world view originates in our culture. But what is the predominant element of culture that gives us our world view? Religion! Whether it be the teachings of the Bible, the Vedas, Koran, Torah, I Ching, or the sign of the stars, people have always felt a need to turn elsewhere for the values by which they live their lives and for instruction about how to view and explain the world. In its host of forms, religion has provided the peoples of the world with advice, values, and guidance from antiquity.

All religions imply in one way or another that human beings do not and cannot stand alone. For well over four thousand years, people have concluded that they depend on powers in nature or elsewhere that are external to themselves. Whether this is through the witnessing of external forces guiding lives or whether it became a convenient construct by which to explain the world, external explanations have prevailed. Dimly, or clearly, people have realized that they are not capable of standing alone and apart from the world.

Religion has helped people explain things that they could not otherwise understand or explain. Whether it be conceptions of a first cause of all things or natural occurrences such as comets, floods, lightning, thunder, drought, disease, or abundance, people have relied on religious explanations for understanding. Religion has also helped people recognize where they come from, why they die, and what happens when they die. The diversity of human behavior in these circumstances depends upon the religious view that has developed and prevailed in a culture. According to the Koran, death is like entering the original Garden of Eden, with abundant fruits and many maidens. The Maasai, on the other hand, may leave bodies out in the pasture to repay the earth.

Religion teaches values, in part, through taboos. The eating of pork, for instance, is a Jewish social taboo; the Jain of India prohibit the eating of all meat. And among the taboos of Islam is a prohibition against the consumption of alcohol. The teaching of taboos serves a useful social function in giving direction for socially acceptable behavior.

In the study of intercultural communication, it is useful to study the religions of the cultures in which we are interested or with whom we wish to interact. Such study gives us insight into the theology of the culture as well as the importance of religion to the culture. In the Arabic world, one of the most commonly used words is *inshalla,* which translates as "God willing." This fact is important for two reasons. First, it gives us a taste of the Islamic theological concept that destiny unfolds according to God's will. Perhaps more importantly, however, it reveals a great deal about the importance of religion in Arabic culture. In India the swamis or heads of temples are major opinion leaders. In the more secular United States, on the other hand, although clergy are opinion leaders, they share this position with politicians, entertainers, and editorializers.

Knowing about religions can also provide insight into values and behavior, or at least offer explanations for perceived behavior. People in Ireland, the United States, and Spain have strong beliefs in the devil, but people in France,

Denmark, and Sweden do not. What impact does this have on the regulation of behavior? People in the United States tend to believe in heaven; Hindus in India believe in reincarnation. How do these belief differences regulate behavior? Or do they regulate behavior? We leave that for you to ponder.

Although there are literally thousands of religions or world views, they can be set into a few major categories, each of which has a view of God, a founder, sacred writings, holy places, holy days, sacred symbols, and the like. If we divide the world's population proportionally into these various categories of religion, we find the following: About 33 percent of the world's population is Christian. The second largest religion and the newest is Islam, with approximately 21 percent. Hinduism is next, with about 15 percent, followed by Buddhism and other Eastern religions with 9 percent. Judaism comprises less than 1 percent, tribal and shamanist traditions 2.5 percent. Nonreligious or atheist views account for approximately 19 percent.

To get a better view of these major religious categories, let us sketch them in order to see how religious world view transfers into values and behavior.

Judaism, the oldest of the religions in practice today, monotheistic, culminating in one supreme being. Jews believe strongly in one God, and they reject the Trinity of Christian belief. The founding of Judaism is attributed to Abraham in approximately 1,300 B.C.; since then, Judaism has spread throughout Israel, Europe, and the Western Hemisphere. The Jewish world view is the basis of its culture. This is expressed in four concepts basic to the Jewish faith: (1) God is one. (2) Human beings are free. (3) The individual's highest aspiration is to serve God. (4) Jews belong to a group, to a nation, whose action is to serve God. Judaism penetrates every area of human existence. It has become a system of communication to combat loneliness by providing humankind with a means of communicating with both the secular and transcendental worlds.[7] It is not simply a religion to serve spiritual needs but a guide in the conduct of worship, ceremonies, and justice between persons, in addition to friendship, kindness, intellectual pursuits, courtesy, and diet. Although Jewish culture is defined to a large extent by its belief system, Judaism is more than a set of legalistic laws. By living these laws, a Jew has communion with God.

Christians believe in a God who is manifested by the Trinity of the Father, the Son, and the Holy Spirit. Jesus, the incarnate Son of God the Father, is the perfect man, the Christ. Christians believe he was fully human, was born to a virgin (Mary), and was crucified, buried, and then resurrected from the dead into a state of eternal life. For the Christian, Christ is the embodiment of God's ability to love and forgive. He is the Messiah; by following Christ's example, human beings, too, can become one with God. By living against God's will and direction, Christians believe, one risks guilt and punishment, or life without God. Christians believe strongly in organized worship as a means of proclaiming God's message.[8]

The Christian tradition begins with the assumption that the world is real and meaningful because God created it. Human beings are significant because God created them in his image. Time is important because it began with God's creation of the Earth and will end when his purpose has been fulfilled. The world, therefore, is God's arena, with each human having only one lifetime to heed God's word. Each person is important to God, which in turn makes individuals important to each other. In fact, because God created humankind in his image, Christians even know what God looks like. Other religions do not worship a God one can see. They may perceive God as the father who looks after his children. Christians believe that the future is important, for heaven is waiting. The secular world, however, is also important. Christianity encourages social action as part of the commitment that people make to their Creator, their fellows, and to society.

Remember that we are just touching the surface of religions and world views to indicate how they influence individual values and behavior. From a Christian perspective, we can see this looking at the Mormons, whose whole way of life stems from their religious convictions. Mormons value the family: For them, family relationships are of prime importance. They believe they are a chosen people, they have a strong work ethic, they have prohibitions against smoking and drinking, and they believe strongly in missionary work. The church is their main interest and the social center of their lives. Noting this relationship between the Mormon church and the Mormon people provides a very good example of how a knowledge of world view can help us understand the people who hold that view.

In the Middle East, we find an orientation that is similar to the one in Western countries. This should not seem surprising, because Islam grew out of the Judaic-Christian tradition.

According to the Islamic faith, Muhammad was the heir to the religious mantle passed down by the prophets of the Bible. Like many of the prophets, Muhammad was concerned with establishing a new social order as well as delivering a religious message. *Muslims* believe that their god, Allah, has spoken to human beings many times in the past: to Adam, Moses, Abraham, and Jesus. But the passage of time and human waywardness have clouded over the message. When Allah spoke to Muhammad, the prophet wrote down the divine words in the Koran, the holy book of Islam. To a Muslim, the Koran is the unique word of Allah, without comparison and beyond question. Muslims believe that in the Koran, Allah has spoken completely, and will not speak again. Thus, Muhammad is the last of the prophets.

The key to our understanding the nature of the Islamic world view comes from the name *Islam. Islam* is the infinitive of the Arabic verb meaning "to submit." The word *Muslim* is the present participle of the same verb. In short, a Muslim is one who accepts and submits to the will of Allah.

Like Christians, Muslims worship a personal God with a profound interest in moral behavior. This God created the universe and calls forth a community of beings and charges them with the responsibility to realize righteousness. But the God of Islam is distinctive because he dominates the world scene and acts in history. He is concerned with whole communities and societies as well as with individuals. Muslims believe that everything, good or evil, proceeds directly from the divine will as it is irrevocably recorded on the Preserved Tablets. This orientation, of course, produces a strong belief in **fatalism:** Whatever happens is according to God's will.

Another important aspect of Islam is that it is as much a way of life as a relationship with God. Muhammad, who was God's messenger, was both a political and religious prophet. Hence, there is no separation of church and state. The wisdom of the Koran, the Islamic holy book, makes it clear that there is not a religious compartment to life, but that religion is life. Islam is a concerted codification of all values and ways to behave in each and every circumstance from child-rearing to eating. In the Arabic world even architecture and art forms stem from Islam.

Islam as a way of life is austere. There is no drinking of alcohol; believers must pray five times each day, and women must be modest and submit to the males. This religious orientation becomes a listing of guidelines that one must follow if one is going to strive for a life that will bring fulfillment. Most religions provide guidelines for moral behavior. (Jews, for instance, follow the Ten Commandments; Buddhists follow the Eightfold Path of Buddha.) Islam has the "Five Pillars" of Islam, which guide proper behavior.

Here are the five pillars of Islam.

1. *Repetition of the creed* "There is no God but Allah, and Muhammad is the Prophet of Allah." These words are heard everywhere in the Muslim world.

2. *Prayer,* which is a central ritual. Muslims pray five times a day—upon rising, at noon, in the midafternoon, after sunset, and before retiring. The prayer ritual is very structured: One must face Mecca, recite a prescribed prayer, and be prostrate with the head to the ground.

3. *Almsgiving,* which began as a voluntary activity and has become codified into Islamic society. All Muslims are legally required to give part of their income to the destitute. This amounts to about two and one-half percent of their incomes.

4. *Fasting,* a tradition observed during a holy month. Muslims are required to fast between sunup and sundown.

5. *Pilgrimage.* Once in a lifetime every Muslim is expected to make a pilgrimage to Mecca.

From the Western perspective, the Islamic tradition is difficult to understand. It touches all aspects of life, it emphasizes fatalistic values, and it is religiocentric. It does not permit the freedom of choice common in the West.

A fourth major religious tradition that influences world view is Hinduism. Hinduism is based upon a fundamental assumption that the material world is not the only reality. Hindus are not satisfied with this world or what it offers; they are not satisfied with what they see. They believe there are other realities that are far more important, realities that reveal the true nature of life, the mind, and the spirit.

This belief in other realities stems from the Hindu notion of deliverance—deliverance from the misleading appearances and experiences of the physical world. Hindus are certain that there are mental and spiritual realms of unshakable reality that guarantee eternal satisfaction once one discovers them. The Hindu spends his or her life in search of these realms.

Like Islam, the Hindu religion is a total way of life. From the Western perspective, Hinduism is difficult to grasp and explain because it is so different from Western tradition. In many respects, Hinduism is a conglomeration of religious thought, values, and beliefs without the benefit of a single founder like Abraham, Jesus, or Muhammad. It does not have a central authority in the form of a single God but recognizes many gods. And it does not have an organizational hierarchy like that of the Catholic church. Among the Hindus one may find magic, nature worship, animal veneration, and limitless deities. In some respects Hindus are among the most religious people in the world because they find the divine in everything. Everything, therefore, takes on religious significance, and rituals are important for showing God in everything. This ritual significance is found in everyday activities such as bathing, eating, and marriage ceremonies.

Several Hindu concepts specifically relate to world view and individual values and behavior. First, intellect is subordinated to intuition. Truth does not come to the individual; it already resides within each of us. Second, dogma is subordinated to experience. One cannot be told about God; one must experience God. Third, outward expression is subordinated to inward realization. Communication with God cannot take place through outward expression; it must occur through internal realization of the nature of God. Fourth, the world is an illusion because nothing is permanent. All of nature, including humankind, is in a constant cycle of birth, death, rebirth or reincarnation. Fifth, it is possible for the human to break the cycle of birth, death, and reincarnation and experience an internal state of bliss called **Nirvana.** One achieves Nirvana by leading a good life so one can achieve a higher spiritual status in the next life. The more advanced one's spiritual life, the closer one is to Nirvana. The path to a spiritual life, and therefore Nirvana, is meditation. The Hindu holds materialism in abeyance and instead practices introspection. **Karma** is the link that ties a person's acts in one life to the next life. Fatalism becomes important as past lives influence each new life.

Another difficult world view for the Western mind to grasp is Buddhism. This is in part because its followers believe that one must abandon views generated by the use of ordinary language and concepts. This notion finds expression in the statement "Beware of the illusions created by words." Buddhists believe that there is a supreme and wonderful truth that words cannot reach or teach. This truth is transmitted outside of ritual and outside of scripture. The basic assumption behind this world view is that life is suffering. Decay of the body, illness, death, hating what we do or despising what we cannot have, separation from what we love, and not being able to obtain what we desire are all examples of suffering.

Buddha was not a god but a man, an extraordinary man who, sometime in the sixth century B.C. in India, achieved **enlightenment**. Once awakened, he devoted his life to helping others achieve enlightenment or Nirvana, the state of spiritual and physical purity necessary to attain freedom from the ongoing cycle of suffering and rebirth. Modern Buddhism directs itself to purification of life and consciousness, not to worship of a God figure. Its followers are taught to realize truth through meditation and "right" living. Buddhism is at once a faith, a philosophy, and a way of life. It attempts to help the individual find purification of life by discovering that everything is appearance, nothing real. Peace, enlightenment, and Nirvana do not come from God; one accepts them as the purity of consciousness that mirrors the emptiness of all existence.[9]

Unhappiness, pain, and suffering are the result of the ego. The craving of the ego is what locks people into seeing and desiring one thing after another for their entire lives. From the Buddhist perspective, one must destroy one's ego in order to achieve happiness and alleviate suffering. To the Western mind, this might seem strange; but even more strange, perhaps, is the Buddhist doctrine that in order for one to achieve Nirvana, the first step is the development of a strong ego. It might seem self-contradictory that the first step toward enlightenment is building the thing that one must destroy. But from the Buddhist perspective, you cannot destroy your ego until it is well developed. Unlike many Western religions, which stress community and direction from the clergy, Buddhism challenges each individual to do his or her own religious seeking: Direct personal experience is the final test of truth.

To help overcome desire and to achieve enlightenment, Buddha taught an Eightfold Path.

1. *Right view* is understanding and accepting the reality and origins of suffering, and the ways leading to the cessation of suffering.

2. *Right thought* is being free from ill will, cruelty, and untruthfulness towards self and others.

3. *Right speech* is abstaining from lying, talebearing, and harsh language.

4. *Right conduct* is abstaining from the taking of life, from stealing, and from sexual misconduct.

5. *Right livelihood* is not harming any living thing, and being free from luxury at the expense of others.

6. *Right effort* is avoiding and overcoming evil, and promoting and maintaining good.

7. *Right mindfulness* is the contemplation of the transitoriness of the body, of one's own and others' feelings, of the mind, and of phenomena.

8. *Right meditation* is complete concentration on a single object and the achievement of purity of thought, free from all hindrances and distractions and eventually beyond sensation.

To find enlightenment within oneself the Buddhist must lead a life that focuses on some of the following behaviors.

Through mindfulness the Buddhist seeks to anchor the mind securely in the present. In the practice of right mindfulness, the mind is trained to remain in the present—open, quiet, and alert while contemplating the present event. All judgments and interpretations have to be suspended, or if they occur, just registered and dropped. During mindfulness, the mind stays with its object and penetrates the object's characteristics deeply.

Buddhism stresses the impermanence of all things. All things, both good and bad, are always changing; everything is impermanent and changeable. Simplicity and wantlessness are states without stress. Envy and desire keep us from being happy and peaceful. The Buddhist must learn to let the things of the universe go in order to be content.

Karma is important in that it sets the tone for ethical standards. Karma has to do with action-reaction and with the law of cause and effect: Good deeds bring good results; evil deeds bring evil results. Nirvana is an ethical state marked by an absence of the desires that bring suffering.

One thing we should recognize from our brief look at different religious world views is that the answers to the significant questions in life have a ripple effect on people's everyday lives. Knowing a person's religious world view helps us know the person. We also should realize that because the religious world view according to which a person is raised has such a strong impact upon him or her, it will lead to the internalization of various values and behaviors that the person will express unconsciously and perceive not only as normal but as right.

World View and Cultural Values

Having examined the impact of culture on world view, we shall now look at examples of diverse cultural values that are derived from world view. We will begin with the United States and see how our values are translated into behavior. First we shall look at twelve dominant American cultural values in order to establish a point of reference for the examination of other cultures.

The first is achievement and success. American culture is marked by competitiveness and a focus on personal and occupational achievement. Americans have long respected the high achiever and the self-made person.

Activity and work are highly important values in the United States. America is a fast-paced society of strenuous competition, of ceaseless activity and agitation. Americans perceive work as purposeful, rational action that dominates social existence.

Third is moral orientation. Americans tend to see the world in moral terms. This does not mean conformity to a detailed prescription of moral behavior, but rather to a moral system by which conduct is judged. The quasi-mythical figure, the "typical American," tends to think in terms of right and wrong, good and bad, ethical and unethical conduct.

Humanitarianism is another important value in American society. It is a somewhat disinterested concern and helpfulness, and includes personal kindness, aid and comfort, spontaneous aid in mass disasters, and impersonal patterns of organized philanthropy.

Next are efficiency and practicality. Americans, in the name of efficiency, emphasize adaptability, technological innovation, economic expansion, being up-to-date, practicality, expediency, and getting things done.

Progress has been a strong American value from the earliest days of our nation. America has developed a diffuse set of beliefs, attitudes, and traits such as optimism, an emphasis upon the future rather than the past or present, receptivity to change, faith in the perfectibility of the common individual. Progress has been a prime article of faith.

Americans also value material comfort. The United States undoubtedly has one of the highest living standards in the world.

Equality has been a persistent theme throughout American history. In interpersonal relations, the value system promotes peer relations rather than superior-subordinate relationships.

Freedom is probably the most highly held American value. It permeates the society and is embedded in the Constitution as an inalienable right.

American valuing of science is reflected in an interest in order, control, objectivity, and calculation that is the hallmark of an engineering civilization. This value follows from the assumption of an ordered universe over which humans may exercise control.

Democracy is a highly held value in American culture. It originates in a complex intersection of such primary beliefs as equality, freedom, humanitarianism, and independence. Democracy stresses majority rule, representative government at all levels, the rejection of an instituted inherited aristocracy, and the reservation of certain inalienable rights.

The value of individuality leads to the American penchants for self-improvement and for protection against invasion of privacy. A person in American culture is considered to be independent, responsible, and worthy of respect. American concepts of identity focus on the individual rather than on the group.

This set of American cultural values we have just reviewed will serve as a backdrop and reference point for looking at how values function in other cultures. We shall now turn our attention to a number of value dimensions and see how they vary from culture to culture.

Geert Hofstede has identified four value dimensions that have a significant impact on behavior in all cultures.[10] These dimensions are masculinity-feminity, individualism-collectivism, uncertainty-avoidance, and power distance.

Masculinity and femininity form a value continuum. Various cultures may be placed along this continuum depending upon the degree to which the masculine or feminine world view prevails. Masculinity is the extent to which the dominant values in a society are male-oriented. It is associated with such behaviors as assertiveness, the acquisition of money and material possessions, and not caring for others or the quality of life. Femininity is the obverse of masculinity and stresses caring and nurturing behaviors. A masculine viewpoint holds that men should be assertive and women should be nurturing. Sex roles in a masculine society are clearly differentiated. In Japan, for instance, despite the high level of economic development, the division of labor still finds most men in the role of provider and most women as "homemaker and breeder."[11] Masculine societies admire the successful achiever, and they appreciate ostentatious manliness, which is sometimes referred to as machismo. Ireland, the Philippines, Greece, South Africa, Austria, and Japan are among countries that tend toward a masculine world view.

A feminine world view holds that men need not be assertive, and that they can also assume nurturing roles. Sex roles in feminine societies are more fluid than in masculine societies. The feminine world view also promotes sexual equality and holds that people and the environment are important. Interdependence and androgyny are the ideal, and people sympathize with the unfortunate. Nations such as Sweden, Norway, Denmark, Yugoslavia, and the Netherlands tend toward a feminine world view.

Another value dimension that affects world view is individualism-collectivism. Individualism implies a loosely-knit social framework in which people are supposed to take care of themselves and their immediate families only. Collectivism is characterized by a tight social framework in which people distinguish between **in-groups** and **out-groups.** They expect their in-group (relatives, clans, organizations) to look after them, and in exchange for that they feel they owe absolute loyalty to the group. In collectivist societies such as Pakistan, Colombia, Venezuela, Taiwan, and Peru, people are born into extended families or clans who protect them in exchange for loyalty. A "we" consciousness prevails, and identity is based in the social system. The individual is emotionally dependent on organizations and institutions. The culture emphasizes belonging to organizations; membership is the ideal. Organizations invade private life and the clans to which one belongs, and individuals trust group decisions.

The Japanese value **collectivism** over individualism and collaboration over competition. They tend toward a homogeneous work force with little differentiation between managers and workers. The strong valuing of the collective leads the Japanese to mutual dependence in a group-oriented environment. The Japanese interact and conduct work activities as group efforts and depend heavily upon one another.[12]

Australia, the United States, Great Britain, New Zealand, and Canada tend toward individualism. In these cultures, everyone is supposed to take care of him- or herself and his or her immediate family. An "I" consciousness prevails, and identity is based in the individual. People tend to be emotionally independent of organizations and institutions. These cultures stress individual initiative and achievement, and they value leadership highly. Unlike the collective perspective, individualism emphasizes the right of every individual to his or her private life and opinions.

Uncertainty and avoidance indicate the extent to which a culture feels threatened by uncertain and ambiguous situations. High uncertainty-avoidance cultures will try to avoid uncertainty and ambiguity by providing greater career stability, establishing more formal rules, not tolerating deviant ideas and behaviors, and believing in absolute truths and the attainment of expertise. High uncertainty-avoidance societies also are characterized by a higher level of anxiety and aggressiveness than in other cultures. Within these cultures, people feel the uncertainty inherent in life as a continuous threat that must be fought. Deviant persons and ideas are considered dangerous and intolerance is high. People in strong uncertainty-avoidance societies have a great concern with security in life; they have a strong need for written rules and regulations. They believe in experts and their knowledge. Nations with a strong uncertainty-avoidance tendency are Portugal, Germany, Peru, Belgium, and Japan.

At the other end of the scale we find countries like Sweden, Denmark, Norway, Finland, and the Netherlands that have a low uncertainty-avoidance need. They more easily accept the uncertainty inherent in life and tend to take each day as it comes. Deviant people and ideas are not so threatening to them, and they tolerate the unusual. People in these countries are more willing to take risks, and they hold that there should be as few rules as possible. They believe not so much in experts as in generalists and in common sense.

Another cultural value dimension is **power distance,** the extent to which a society accepts that power in institutions and organizations is distributed unequally. This dimension is reflected in the values of the less powerful members of society as well as in those of the more powerful members. People in large power-distance countries such as Greece, Venezuela, Mexico, Yugoslavia, and the Philippines hold that people are not equal in this world but that everybody has a rightful place. Social hierarchy is prevalent and it institutionalizes inequality. Subordinates consider superiors a different kind of people. Likewise, superiors consider subordinates a different kind of people. People who are in positions of power should look as powerful as possible. In large power-distance cultures there is latent conflict between the powerful and the powerless.

Small power-distance countries such as Austria, Denmark, New Zealand, and Israel hold that inequality in society should be minimized. To them, a hierarchy is an inequality of roles established for convenience. Subordinates consider superiors to be the same kind of people as they, and superiors perceive their subordinates in the same light. People in positions of power try to look less powerful than they really are, and the powerful and the powerless live in harmony.

In addition to the value dimensions we have just considered, others also play a prominent role in shaping behavior. Formality is such a dimension. Cultures tend to range from very formal to quite informal. The United States is a rather informal culture, while Germany, Japan, Egypt, Turkey, and Iran are examples of quite formal cultures. The degree of formality associated with a culture may be recognized by the way in which people are to interact with one another. In Egypt, Turkey, and Iran, for instance, the student-teacher relationship is very formal. This may be seen from an Egyptian proverb which states that "whoever teaches me a letter, I should become a slave to him forever." In these countries, when the teacher enters the room, students are expected to stand up. When students meet their teachers on the street, they are expected to bow to them. Contrast this with the relaxed, informal student-teacher relationships found in the United States.

The degree of formality found in Germany is, from an American perspective, extreme. The value of formality shows up in so many aspects of German life. Germans eat, dress, address others, visit, and conduct themselves in a very formal manner. At mealtime they hold their fork and knife continental-style; most children do also. Another sign of German formality is the way Germans dress. It is very important for Germans to dress well even if just visiting friends or going to school, but especially when attending church.

German formality is also evident in forms of address. Personal titles are always used whether in face-to-face encounters or in addressing a letter. Germans use titles extensively to identify people and their position in the social structure. If, for instance, a person is both a professor and a physician, he would be referred to as Herr Professor Doktor Kaempfer. As noted earlier, Germany is a male-oriented culture. German women are not addressed by their surname, such as Frau (Mrs.) Kaempfer, but always by their husband's titles. The wife of Herr Professor Doktor Kaempfer, for example, would thus be addressed as Frau Professor Doktor Kaempfer.

We can see one last example of the relationship between cultural values and individual behavior by looking at Filipino culture. Filipinos value above all else freedom, peace, and justice. Although foreign powers have exploited and oppressed them for long periods, this has not deterred their determination to achieve these ideals. Mixed in with the values of freedom, peace, and justice are four major concepts that Philippine society values highly: *amor propio, hiya, utang no loob,* and *pakikisama. Amor propio* translates into English as "harmony" and into oriental languages as "saving face." Unfortunately, neither of these translations clearly reflects the Filipino concept. In the Philippines, *amor propio* refers to a very fragile sense of personal worth and the need to be treated as a person rather than as an object. This personal characteristic leaves the Filipino especially vulnerable to negative remarks from others that may affect his or her standing in society at that moment. Consequently, Filipinos seldom criticize others; and if they do, it is in the most polite manner.

Hiya is shame or embarrassment. It is a painful reaction to feelings of alienation, shyness, and inferiority. *Hiya* is developed in children at a very early age in order to prompt them into proper or acceptable behavior. In adulthood, one experiences the inferiority feelings of *hiya* when one does not succeed. Filipinos will give any excuse to divert blame away from themselves to others in order to avoid this feeling. Also, Filipinos do not criticize other people to the extent that they are pointed out in society.

Utang no loob is a feeling of obligation or indebtedness that develops when someone has done a favor for another. When people seek a favor from someone outside the family, they place themselves in *utang no loob,* or suspended obligation. This means that people can expect to repay a favor with a different sort of favor than they received. Favors are not usually repaid on a single occasion but can be served over a period of time at the request of the creditor. Debtors do not see this as being taken advantage of. They return any favor with sincere gratitude toward the person who initially helped them.

Filipinos see outspokenness and frankness as uncivilized traits and will look down on one who demonstrates them. Instead, they value *pakikisama,* or smooth interpersonal relations. In their communication with others they promote good feelings. They will speak vaguely and ambiguously in a meeting in order to avoid a stressful confrontation. They have high respect for one's feelings and will always agree and keep their reservations to themselves.

Social Organization

Thus far we have explored the effects of beliefs, values, and world view upon perception and behavior. Another factor in how we perceive the people and the social events of our world, and how we behave, is the way in which our world is organized. This is known as social organization.

Our study of social organization begins with three assumptions: (1) Historical events help explain the character of a culture; (2) what a culture seeks to remember and pass on to the next generation tells us about the character of that culture; and (3) if you touch one aspect of a culture, you will influence other aspects of the culture. To help us better understand how social organization leads to diversity in perception, we will look at the roles of history and the family in several cultures.

History.   We shall begin our examination of the role of history with the United States. The United States is unique in that the dominant culture is relatively young and was formed primarily through migration. This has led to what is sometimes referred to as the "melting pot" or "stew" concept of culture: A number of diverse cultures migrated to the United States and intermingled to form our current diverse culture. But this cultural integration did not come about easily. The shared, desperate desire of the American people to be separated from the "Crown," from "Divine Right," and from the Church of England provided the thrust toward unity. The desire for emancipation from cultural dependence upon Britain and Europe inspired the early Americans. This impetus led, in part, to the binding of Germans, Irish, and English together in a social fabric ample enough to contain Catholics, Congregationalists, and Methodists, and to unite North, South, and West within a national framework. Americans wanted to separate alienable rights—those that could be voluntarily surrendered to the government—from inalienable rights, or those that could not be surrendered even to a government of the people. The American fundamental proposition became life, liberty, and the pursuit of happiness for each individual, whose liberties had to be protected against the abusive power of government.

The melting-pot concept is often rightfully challenged by those who claim that there has not been a true melting-pot effect, because the United States has denied rights to some elements of our society and has not permitted assimilation. We must realize that the United States, as it exists today, arose because of a variety of factors. We must consider not only those who immigrated but the enslaved, the conquered, and refugees as well. Not everyone arrived here as an immigrant. The Native Americans became a conquered people; African Americans were enslaved. Many Americans arrived as refugees fleeing a homeland in which they could not remain, only to find themselves in a country in which they would suffer prejudice and discrimination.

The dominant culture of the United States is an amalgamation of the diverse cultures of Europe, to which have been added aspects of Native American, African, Middle Eastern, and Asian cultures. Although the dominant culture has assimilated some aspects of the Native American, African, Middle Eastern, and Asian cultures, it has not accepted the races of Native America, Africa, the Middle East, and Asia as equals in a diverse, multicultural society.

A second historical aspect of American culture is that the people who settled the colonies disliked formality and valued individuality. We can attribute these values to the nature of people who would emigrate to a new world and attempt to stake out a new life. Settling in a new, undeveloped land required a great deal of attention to the daily activities of surviving. This situation did not lend itself to formality or dependency. Life in the colonies was a constant struggle, with no time to waste on the nonsense of rigid European or British rules of formality. Only the independent survived.

These environmental factors also had psychological effects on the settlers. When you develop habits of survival based on individualism and a lack of formality, you soon develop thought patterns, beliefs, values, and attitudes attuned to that environment. And so individualism has come to lie at the very core of American culture. We consider anything morally wrong that might violate our right to think for ourselves, judge for ourselves, make our own decisions, or live our own lives as we see fit.

Another aspect of American history that has shaped the culture is violence. Our history is filled with violence, ranging from taking Indian lands by force, to fighting the War of Independence and the Civil War, to the development of the West. Guns are so much a part of our culture and history that our Constitution guarantees our right to bear arms—a right no other nation grants. It is not our intention here to debate the merit of that heritage but to point out its impact on the development of our culture.

Our notions of freedom and independence and the challenge of developing a sparsely populated land have produced a culture with a strong love of change and progress. "America incorporates the yearnings of both Daedalus and Icarus, constructing miraculous contraptions of every type with the caution of the industrialist, yet audaciously believing there is no place we cannot reach."[13] In a recent commentary on the development of American society, the editors of *U.S. News and World Report* remarked: "Being what we are, it was inevitable that Americans would quickly progress from boats to trains to planes. The Constitutionally restless republic that trampled the American road was bound to clutter the American sky, expansionism being in their blood."[14]

The dominant culture of North America is not the only group that American history has shaped. Other examples also link the past with the present. To begin this contrast to the development of America and American culture from European immigrants, let us turn to African-American culture and its history to trace a different development.

First, and most importantly, Africans were not willing immigrants. They were captured and enslaved in Africa, brought to the United States, and sold to the colonists as laborers and servants. Africans were held together by a common bond of misery that produced companionship and identity. They were forced to adopt a new language and religion, and they became in a sense a group without a culture. One of their defenses against enslavement and the robbery of their culture was to incorporate many aspects of their African heritage into their new language and new religion. During the years of enslavement and afterward, African men were often removed from their families and required to work apart. Thus, African women became a dominant force in the family and contributed to a family structure in which the influence of mothers predominated.

The Jews provide another example of the history and development of a culture. Jewish history is a study of some 3,500 years of persecution, and Jews have come to believe that they must live with their eyes fixed on the past for good reason. When they are called upon to make fundamental choices, they will turn to the past for guidance, where they will see persecution, genocide, and flight.

Throughout their history, Jews have always had to move from place to place to avoid persecution. Consequently, they have developed values related to movement and persecution. They have had good reason for being wary of non-Jews, since non-Jews have persecuted them. Even as recently as fifty years ago in the United States, non-Jews were responsible for an event that many still remember. In 1939, a ship carrying Jewish people away from Germany landed in Miami but was turned back. This action of non-Jewish Americans has become a symbolic event to remember and another lesson in the non-Jews' treatment of Jews.

Russian history is similar to that of the Jews. Like the Jews, the Russians have been historically subjected to invasion, persecution, and suffering. During the past thousand years, Russia has been invaded and occupied time and again by the Mongols, Germans, Turks, Poles, Swedes, French, and English. Russian cities were brutally occupied and tightly governed, and entire towns and villages were slaughtered for failure to pay tribute. In addition, the rulers of Russia historically have been hard on the people. The great suffering of the Russian people at the hands of both their own rulers and invading armies does not let them forget. Consequently, they have developed a perception of the world that includes the inviolability of Mother Russia.

Chinese history adds another dimension to our understanding of perception. To ignore the impact of China's complex and sometimes glorious history would deprive us of a theme that is central to understanding the Chinese. Each Chinese derives his or her strongest sense of identity from history. Whatever people's qualities or quirks, their circumstances or political allegiance, whether they live in China itself or are scattered to distant lands, pride in the Chinese cultural heritage is central and links all Chinese.

Arabian history provides additional insights we might otherwise miss. Arabia is named after Saud, the ruling family. This family of approximately four thousand members dominates every activity in a country of only four to five million. We need to understand this social organization, because Western notions of nepotism and corruption have little meaning in the Arabian world.

Other countries' histories also contribute to our knowledge and understanding. Japan, for example, until post–World War II times, has permitted few outsiders to enter. Historically, the Japanese have always guarded their racial purity; they have not been a melting pot. Their history of feudalism, in which benevolent feudal lords took care of their people, has had a major impact in the development of modern industrial Japan. It was very easy for the Japanese to transfer this tradition of feudal loyalty to large companies because the companies, in a sense, have replaced feudalism. Companies care for their employees, providing them with lifelong employment in a kind of cradle-to-grave social environment. With their history of feudalism and its transfer to the large company in its stead, Japan has been phenomenally successful in becoming one of the premier industrialized nations in the world.

Norway gives us another perspective on how social organization shapes perception. Norwegians, perhaps more than any other people in the world, have been molded by their historical adjustment to the physical conditions and the nature of their country. The sea, mountains, lakes, forests, and fjords of Norway have had a great impact on Norwegian society. Norway is a nation of some four million seafarers and land dwellers spread out over valleys, mountains, and coastlines. City dwelling is a relatively new experience for the average Norwegian, and most city dwellers are only one or two generations removed from country life. Norwegians have developed an aesthetic attachment to their land and a love of nature that borders on the religious. Their perception of the world is based on the beauty of their country, and on their love of the land, and of a good life.

The history of Islamic countries can help us understand their perception of Americans. The Islamic faith teaches that God (Allah) is the master of the universe. The Muslim perception of the United States as a country dominated by science and technology has wounded the pride of Islam. Muslims see the United States as a temporary master of the world. From an Islamic point of view, the United States has upset the course of history, and the people of Islamic faith view the United States as an aberration. Militant Muslims even perceive the United States as the devil's empire.

Although we could cite many more examples of how a culture's history has shaped its perceptions, we will turn our attention to another aspect of social organization, the family.

The family.   The family is, perhaps, the single most influential force in the development of individual values and world view within a culture. "It is the primary or basic institution of any society, . . . without the family human society as we know it could not exist, . . . the family is everywhere, it is universal."[15] Although a culture's values and world view derive primarily from its predominant religious views and cultural history, the family is the primary caretaker of these views and values and transmits them to the new members of the culture.

One reason the family is so important in the perpetuation of a culture and its unique views and values is that it introduces the child to the world. In a sense, each family is charged with the responsibility of transforming a newly born organism into a fully developed human being prepared to spend the rest of his or her life interacting with other human beings within a particular cultural environment. Although the parents themselves have been influenced by other social institutions such as the church and the schools and pass this influence on to their offspring, those institutions have no direct influence on the child during the first few years of its life. It is the family that first exposes children to some of the crucial attitudes, values, and patterns of behavior they will need to exist within the culture. The family instills modes of thought and action that, with reinforcement from society, soon become habitual.

Sex roles are taught at home, and children learn to differentiate between masculine activities and feminine activities at a very early age. In a Japanese family, for instance, the father is the ultimate authority, and all members of the family adopt a strict subservience to his wishes. Children see the father get served first at meals, get the first bath, and receive nods and deep bows from the rest of the family. The Navajo of the American Southwest provide a different example of gender roles. Women and children are charged with taking care of the sheep, which provide food and clothing. Women also process the wool and weave clothing and blankets. The latter are sold for a cash income. Although the men work as silversmiths and fashion jewelry that is also sold for cash income, Navajo women provide most subsistence labor and cash income.

By the time other institutions have an opportunity to shape the individual, the family has already exposed the child to countless experiences that have started to teach it everything from language to sex roles. For instance, a child will begin to develop habits regarding how much emotional support to expect from others—and not only from others, but from specific others. In other words, the child will learn where to turn for needed emotional support as well as where not to turn. This also influences a child's sense of self-reliance. The less supportive an environment, the more self-reliant a child must become to survive.

Through the family, children learn what it is possible and desirable to strive for, as well as how to please others as well as themselves. They also learn very rapidly whom it is advantageous to please and whom they should leave alone.

From early on, the family teaches children responsibility to self as well as to others. Children develop a sense of what is important and worthy of attention and what they may ignore or leave on its own. As a part of their responsibility, children also learn obedience. They learn who and what is authoritative, and they learn to obey that authority—including people and institutions outside the immediate family that demand respect and obedience. In this way they learn about social structure and the relative placement of people within that structure; they learn to recognize people superior to them in the structure and to behave in a manner appropriate to that relationship. Tied into the concept of obedience is the parallel concept of dominance. Children learn who controls them and who or what they may control. One obeys those who are dominant and may disobey or dominate those who are not.

While children are primarily under the influence of their parents and immediate family, they also acquire an understanding of sociability, aggression, and loyalty. They learn about sociability by finding out how to make friends, why it is important to make friends, how many friends one ought to have, and how important communication is in having friends and being successful. While they are learning to make friends, they also learn about aggression. Through aggressive behavior they come to understand concepts of control. They may see that if they are large enough to bully someone, they can have their way with that person, and that if bullying does not work, more subtle means of control may be effective. These subtler approaches can range from talking mother into a snack before dinner to convincing another child to do something that will get him or her into trouble. Families teach loyalty in terms of who deserves one's allegiance. What members of the community deserves loyalty? In the extended families typical of Mexico, Latin America, parts of Europe, the Middle East, and Asia, loyalty extends beyond the immediate family of parents and siblings to include grandparents, cousins, second cousins, third cousins, aunts, uncles, great aunts, great uncles, and even godparents. In a culture such as the United States, loyalty is generally confined to the immediate or nuclear family. Within the nuclear family, there is also the notion that at a certain age, children move out of the house and establish their own household and financial independence. In the extended family, this does not hold: Several generations may live in the same abode and depend upon one another financially. The Greek family thinks and acts as an organic whole, and it is extremely important that no member bring shame or dishonor to the group. Even when family members are physically separated, they maintain close contact.

Age is also a strong value in Japanese culture, and the family is organized on a masculine-superior, age-superior basis. The person of lowest stature in a Japanese family is the wife. She is subservient not only to the husband, but also to her own parents and to her husband's parents. Thus the young wife is at the bottom of a hierarchy in terms of both gender and age. Her goal in life is to become old enough to have her son's wife subservient to her.

Finally, the family also teaches the relative importance of self. Some cultures are very adult-oriented, and children are relatively unimportant. Families in England and India send the message to children that they are not very important. The saying "Children should be seen and not heard" reflects this orientation. As a contrast, in Jewish culture children are very important—to the extent that parents will make many personal sacrifices to ensure that their children are not wanting. As a cultural expression of their importance, Jewish children also take an active role in religious ceremonies at an early age.

We hope these examples show you the importance of the family in children's development. From whether one draws his or her food from a common bowl to who talks at the dinner table, the family instructs us about what is important.

SUMMARY

Understanding Perception

- Although the physical process of perception is almost the same in everyone, culture influences the final step of interpretation and evaluation.

Perception and Culture

- Culturally determined beliefs largely determine how we behave and how we relate to our environment.

- Values are enduring attitudes about the preferability of one belief over another.

- World view is a culture's orientation towards God, humanity, nature, the universe, life, death, sickness, and other philosophical issues concerning our being. Religion is the predominant element of culture that gives us our world view.

- Social organization also contributes to diversity in perception. Social organization springs from a culture's history and from the role of the family as caretaker of the culture's values and world view.

ACTIVITIES

1. Ask your informant for English translations of sayings from his or her culture similar to the North American ones listed in this chapter. With your informant, try to determine the cultural values they express. Alternatively, you may want to show the list in this chapter to your informant and see if he or she can come up with similar or opposing sayings.

2. In small groups, make up an ideal culture. Indicate which of the values discussed in this chapter would be **primary** in the value hierarchy of your culture. Try to accommodate the interests of all group members. Give your culture a name. Time permitting, describe the outward manifestations of your cultural values (for example, dress, work, play, food preferences, roles).

DISCUSSION IDEAS

1. Discuss North American cultural perceptions surrounding colors. What do North Americans associate with the following?

   black

   white

   red

   pink

   blue

Do any other colors have particular associations in North American culture? Does the cultural mix of your class lead to any differences in these associations?

2. Find examples of sports and military terms that are used in North American business settings. Interview a corporate employee and/or read a weekly business magazine or the business section of your local newspaper. Explain what the terms mean and why you think they are used in this context.

3. Explain how understanding the religious aspect of a particular culture's lifestyle might help you better communicate with a member of that culture.

NOTES FOR CHAPTER 5

1. Marshall Singer, "Culture: A Perceptual Approach," in *Readings in Intercultural Communication,* vol.1, ed. David S. Hoopes, 6.

2. Singer, 1.

3. George Guilmet, "Maternal Perceptions of Urban Navajo and Caucasian Children's Classroom Behavior," *Human Organization* 38 (1979), 87–91.

4. Milton Rokeach, *The Nature of Human Values* (New York: Free Press, 1973), 5.

5. Rokeach, 5.

6. Ethel Albert, "Value System," in *The International Encyclopedia of the Social Sciences,* vol. 16 (New York: Macmillan, 1968), 32.

7. Prime Time School Television, *The Long Search,* Chicago, 1978.

8. *The Long Search.*

9. *The Long Search.*

10. Geert Hofstede, *Culture's Consequences: International Differences in Work-Related Values* (Beverly Hills, CA: Sage, 1980).

11. Hyoriko Meguro, Address to the World Affairs Council, San Diego, CA, June 16, 1988.

12. D. P. Cushman and D. D. Cahn, *Communication in Interpersonal Relationships* (New York: State University of New York Press, 1985), 136.

13. *U.S. News and World Report,* March 20, 1989, 9.

14. *U.S. News and World Report,* March 20, 1989, 9.

15. F. I. Nye and F. M. Berardo, *The Family: Its Structures and Interaction* (New York: Macmillan, 1973), 30.

The notion that thought can be perfectly or even adequately
expressed in verbal symbols is idiotic.

ALFRED NORTH WHITEHEAD

The sum of human wisdom is not contained in any one language,
and no single language is capable of expressing all forms and
degrees of human comprehension.

EZRA POUND

CHAPTER SIX

LANGUAGE AND CULTURE: SOUNDS AND ACTIONS

To state that language is important is to declare the obvious, yet because we can all talk we often overlook the profound influence language has on human behavior. Our use of sounds and symbols enables us to give life to our ideas. Or as Henry Ward Beecher once wrote, "Thought is the blossom; language the opening bud; action the fruit behind it."

Language diversity is perhaps one of the most difficult and persistent problems we find in intercultural communication. Language may be either verbal or nonverbal. We shall discuss nonverbal language, or what is frequently referred to as nonverbal behavior, in Chapters 7 and 8. Our task at this point is to develop an understanding and appreciation of **verbal language** as it applies to intercultural communication. This chapter will deal with the relationship between verbal language and culture, and how that relationship influences communication and understanding. We shall look at the nature of language, the importance of language, language and meaning, language and culture, the use of argot, and foreign language and translation.

THE NATURE OF LANGUAGE

As we have progressed through the various issues that affect intercultural communication, we have directed our attention to culturally influenced internal states that affect our behavior and perception. In fact, if we think about it for a moment, other than our physical self, everything that we are is internal. Most of this internal state is an electrochemical mélange residing within our brains. Here is the residence and locus of our beliefs, values, attitudes, world views, emotions, and myriad other aspects of our selves and personalities. In essence who and what we are is locked up inside of us.

If what we are is within us, how then do we share ourselves with others? As we pointed out earlier, we do not have a mechanism by which we can connect ourselves with others and have a direct electrochemical transfer that forms a physical communication link. This type of sharing is not yet possible. We can convey some aspects of ourselves nonverbally by touching, but to get to the deeper issues within us, we must resort to a method of symbolic substitution.

We already know that the purpose of communication is to be able to share ourselves with one another, and that intercultural communication is the special circumstance in which the sharing occurs between people of different cultures. This sharing happens through our use of language, which is our medium of exchange for sharing our internal states of being with one another.

In the simplest sense, a language is a set of symbols, with rules for combining the symbols, that a large community uses and understands. Verbal languages are the principal means by which we express our thoughts and feelings.

Verbal languages use word symbols that stand for or represent various concrete and abstract parts of our individual realities. Words, consequently, are abstractions of our realities; they are incapable of eliciting reactions that embody the totality of the objects or concepts they represent. Take, for instance, the word *dog*. What does that word represent? Dogs come in a variety of breeds and sizes. Are we talking about a small lap dog or perhaps a large guard dog? Are we representing a collie, a German shepherd, a poodle? Are we referring to a female or a male animal? Now notice the word that ended the last sentence, the word *animal*. This word is even more of an abstraction than the word *dog*. It could be referring to a dog, to a cow, to a horse, to a rat, or to a human being. Words are abstractions of the things they represent and are, therefore, always incomplete representations.

We may envision a verbal language as consisting of sounds, words, combinations of words, and communicative purposes. These dimensions of language are referred to as the phonemic, semantic, syntactic, and pragmatic.

The smallest unit of speech sound is called a phoneme. Hence the **phonemic** level of language is comprised of the sounds that are meaningful to a community of language users. Languages do not contain all of the same phonemes, nor do they make the same distinctions about the manner in which the sounds are produced. In the English language there are approximately forty-five phonemes, and we do not pay particular attention to minor differences in the way most of these sounds are produced. But in tonal languages such as Chinese, a minor difference in the way a phoneme is produced can be what distinguishes meaning.

The **semantic** level of language refers to the meanings that are attached to words. This level of language is critical to the process of translation, in which it is crucial to understand the meanings associated with words.

The **syntactic** level of language is the rules that govern the use of words. These rules specify what constitutes phrases, sentences, and larger sequences of words. They also specify such things as how a language expresses possession.

Finally, the **pragmatic** level of language contains the rules that govern language for the accomplishment of desired communicative goals. Here are specified the rules that determine whether a message will be persuasive, express anger or scorn, reveal feelings, or enforce social relationships.

If we include culture as a variable in the process of abstraction, the problems become all the more acute. When you are communicating with someone from your own culture, the abstraction process of using words to represent your experiences is much easier, because within a culture people share a number of similar experiences. But when the communication event involves people from different cultures, many experiences are different, and consequently the abstraction process is more troublesome. To illustrate, let us again use the word *dog*.

Most of us think of an animal that is a companion and that possibly serves some useful purpose such as guarding our home. But to many Pacific Islanders and Southeast Asians, the word *dog* may represent a delicacy. Culture exerts a tremendous influence on this process of abstracting our realities into words.

Word symbols are governed by rules that tell us how to use them best to represent our experiences. These rules dictate both language structure in the form of grammar and syntax and how language is regulated through rules that govern turn-taking, feedback, and the like. Language, however, is much more than a mere set of word symbols governed by rules. It is far more complex than that because the language symbols are only abstractions of the real states of our being and, as such, are inadequate substitutes. But language symbols are all that we have, and we have learned to do relatively well using them. We are able to share symbolically our experiences with others and to achieve various levels of mutual understanding, at least among members of a particular language-using community.

The most common form of language that we use is the one with which we are most familiar: spoken language. Written language is merely a convenient way of recording spoken language by making marks on paper or some other suitable surface. If we recall our history, we remember that before paper was invented, language was recorded on clay tablets, papyrus, copper sheets, and many other surfaces that permitted humankind to record, share, and store knowledge for future use and for transmission to future generations.

For many of us, English is our primary language. It consists of symbols (words) and rules (grammar and syntax)—but so do Spanish, Swahili, Chinese, German, and French. If we study another language, we soon discover that not only are the words different, but so are the rules. In English we live in a *house.* In Spanish, we live in a *casa.* In English, we show the possessive form by use of an apostrophe and say "Mary's house." In Spanish, the rules do not permit the use of an apostrophe to form a possessive, so in Spanish we learn to say *"la casa de Maria,"* or *"the house of Mary,"* to form the possessive.

One of our most unusual characteristics as humans is our faculty and capacity to make sounds and marks serve as substitutes for things and feelings. That seemingly effortless process in which we all engage is at the very core of being human. Over millions of years we have evolved the anatomy necessary to produce and to receive sounds, and within a much shorter span of time have created a system whereby those sounds took on meaning by standing for things, feelings, or ideas. This evolution has led to the development of a four process that enables us to use sounds to our advantage: We have learned to receive, store, manipulate, and generate symbols. These four steps, working in combination, set humankind apart from other animals. The extent to which we use language is one of our most singular features.

THE IMPORTANCE OF LANGUAGE

It is through language that we reach out and make contact with our surrounding realities. And it is through language that we share with others our experiences of that reality. If we survey a normal day we will soon see that we use words for a variety of reasons. Even the first few minutes we are awake might find us using language for some of the following purposes.

"Good morning!" Here we use words as a way of becoming reunited with the world outside our skin, as a means of keeping in touch with other people.

"Let me tell you about the horrible dream I had last night. . . . I was almost seduced by a strange creature in a flying saucer." In this case, we use words to share an experience. We even use words to get support from others so that we might feel better. This example also demonstrates how we employ words so that we can deal with the *past,* so that we can talk about something that has already happened.

"Please pass the salt and pepper." In this instance we use words so that we can exercise some control over the *present.* We each seek to affect our environment, to influence many of the daily situations in which we find ourselves. Words, and how we manipulate them, permit us to make those alterations through symbolic transactions with others. We use words to persuade, to exchange ideas, to express views, to seek information, or to express feelings as we maintain contact with other people.

We also use words to form an image of the *future.* "Well, I guess I've got to go to work now. I've an important meeting with Jane today, but I dread seeing her, as I know she's going to be angry about the changes I'm going to make in her work schedule." Here we see how our word-using ability allows us to predict and to describe the future. Although our pictures of the future are not always accurate, at least language enables us to think about, talk about, and anticipate the future.

The ability to communicate with others depends not only upon our language faculty, but upon there being enough commonality of experience among people that the words they use basically mean the same things. The wider and more divergent the language communities from which people come, the more difficult mutual understanding becomes. Although both British and Americans speak English, they come from different language-using communities, and they may not always understand each other.

LANGUAGE AND MEANING

As children, most of us asked our parents, "What does that word mean?" Chances are we asked that question many times, and perhaps still ask it on occasion. This question reflects the way we view language. It suggests that we tend to look for meaning in the word itself. But we err if we think that words possess meaning. It is more accurate to say that people possess meaning and that words elicit the meanings in people. We can all have different meanings for the same word. Take the word *grass*, for instance. To one person it might mean something in front of the house that is green, has to be watered, and must be mowed once a week. To another person grass may mean something that is rolled in paper and smoked. There is no "real" meaning in this example, because all people, from their own personal backgrounds, decide what a word symbol means to them. People have similar meanings only to the extent that they have had or can anticipate similar experiences. Witness how various backgrounds and experiences can alter meanings. If our past experience is in baseball, a *rope* is a line drive. If our background lies in the rock music world, *monster* is not something ugly or evil, but rather a very successful record. And finally, it is likely that we and a physician respond differently to the word *cancer*.

A word, then, can elicit many meanings. Linguists have estimated that the five hundred most often-used words in the English language can produce over fourteen thousand meanings. This diversity of meanings suggests that words not only mean different things to different people, but also that words mean different things at different times and in different contexts. We simply have many more ideas, feelings, and things to represent than we have words to represent them. Tennyson said the same thing poetically when he wrote, "Words, like Nature, half reveal / And half conceal the Soul within."

LANGUAGE AND CULTURE

One of the most important theoretical formulations concerning language is the Sapir-Whorf hypothesis, which in essence states that language is a guide to social reality. This implies that language is not simply a means of reporting experience but more importantly a way of defining experience. Sapir wrote in 1929:

> Human beings do not live in the objective world alone, nor alone in the world of social activity as ordinarily understood, but are very much at the mercy of the particular language which has become the medium of expression for their society. . . . The real world is to a large extent unconsciously built up on the language habits of the group. No two languages are ever sufficiently similar to be considered as representing the same social reality. The worlds in which different societies live are distinct worlds, not merely the same world with different labels attached.[1]

From this position, we can see that language is distinctly a form of human cultural behavior. It is important that we realize the cultural dimension of language for several reasons. Language helps us understand not only one another but culture as well, for it is a reflection of its parent culture. If one is to use a language well, one must know the culture that uses the language. Each language presents us with a unique way of perceiving the world and interpreting experience. As Whorf has so frequently pointed out, the structure of our language influences the manner in which we understand our environment.

Our perceptions of the universe shift from tongue to tongue, and the forms of that shifting are worth considering. We shall look at but a few of literally thousands of examples that demonstrate the influence of culture on language.

In learning to use language, we have evolved elaborate, culturally diverse linguistic forms that assist in our efforts to represent our world symbolically. One such form is high and low context.[2] High-context communication is that form in which most of the information to be conveyed is contained in the physical context or is internalized within the people who are communicating. Very little information is in the coded symbols that form the transmitted message. Many Asian and Middle Eastern nations prefer **high-context** communication. **Low-context** communication, on the other hand, contains almost all of the information to be shared in the explicit coded message. Low-context communication is the form found primarily in Western nations.

Cultural diversity in message context leads to differences in people's attitudes toward the function of verbal messages, and these differences in attitude can affect how communication is perceived. In low-context cultures, the primary function of language is to express thoughts, feelings, and ideas as clearly and logically as possible. Low-context cultures want to identify messages with specific speakers, so the speakers may be recognized for their ability to influence others. In high-context cultures, messages function to enhance social equality and to downplay the importance of individual speakers.

Language usage follows culturally determined patterns. These patterns not only influence the order in which people use words to form phrases; they also influence thinking patterns. The use of language to describe time, for instance, differs from culture to culture. Western societies perceive time as something that can be kept, saved, lost, or wasted. Being on time is extremely important. In other societies, time takes on different values that are reflected in language. In the Vietnamese language, the verb system is such that only context can indicate time. The Sioux Indian language contains no words to represent the concepts of late or waiting. Some adherents of Zen Buddhism perceive time as an infinite pool in which acts cause waves or ripples that eventually subside. Time is a place with no past, no present, no future.

Language reflects the patterns of reasoning prevalent in a culture. The inductive and deductive reasoning patterns of the Western world, for instance, are very different from those of the Arabic world. The Arabic language tends to combine ideas through the use of conjunctions. The result is a lack of efficiency when speakers of Arabic use the English language because it is very difficult for English speakers to locate the main idea in an Arab's message. Western forms of linear thinking thus cause difficulty for Arabic speakers using the English language. And conversely, those same patterns cause difficulty for someone who uses the thought patterns associated with the English language if that person is conversing in Arabic.

Nations tend to have their own national languages. Arensberg and Niehoff spell out the role of spoken language in distinguishing a culture.

Nothing more clearly distinguishes one culture from another than its language. We sometimes confuse writing systems with the spoken language of the people, otherwise we could say that the infallible sign of a separate culture is a separate language and the inevitable result of a separate language is a separate culture. For example, England, the United States, and Ireland all use English today as a literary written language, but they speak British, American, and the 'brogue" (when not Gaelic). They are, in fact, three separate, though related, cultures. It is the spoken, not the written language that is basic.[3]

That countries tend to have unique national languages is only partly true, however. For instance, both French and English are national languages in Quebec, Canada. English, French, and Spanish are national languages in over twenty countries. And more than a dozen countries share Arabic as a national language.

Because more than one nation uses a particular language, there will be some obvious cultural carryover between those countries; but in most cases the extension of a language has resulted from imperial conquest and the forcing of the language on the territory as its official language. Sharing the same official language, however, is no guarantee that nations share the same culture. In most instances where conquest has established English as the official language, most of the people in the country do not speak it. Such is the case in India and other former British colonies.

Besides in national languages, countries also differ in the languages used within their boundaries. Although there are something like one hundred recognized official languages, at least three thousand languages are currently spoken in the world. In Zaire, for instance, there are over one hundred spoken tribal languages. Each tribal group's language not only identifies it but also separates it from other groups. India has several hundred spoken languages, with many of the same inherent problems.

Languages differ not only in the word symbols they use, the rules that govern them, and their phonemic structure, but also in how language serves adaptive functions. The Thai language contains many adaptations necessary for addressing members of the different levels in the hierarchical social system of Thailand. The Thai written language consists of forty-four consonants and thirty-two vowels. The sounds are combined with five different tones to produce a melodious language. Different classes use different pronouns, nouns, and verbs to represent rank and intimacy. There are at least forty-seven pronouns, including seventeen "I's" and nineteen "you's." Because it contains different forms for different classes, it is possible to distinguish four Thai languages: the royal one, the ecclesiastic one, the polite everyday type, and a slang.

The tonal dimension of the Thai language is typical of Asian languages. It produces a great deal of difficulty for someone who is not used to the tonal differences because the same sound pronounced with different intonations has distinctly different meanings. An American official visiting Vietnam discovered this while speaking to a Vietnamese audience. To show his respect to the Vietnamese, he wanted to say something in their language. He intended to make a patriotic declaration—"Vietnam for a thousand years!" But his tonal pronunciation was wrong, and the audience began to laugh when what the official actually said meant "The duck wants to lie down."[4] A similar problem occurred when the Coca Cola Company introduced Coca Cola in China. The Mandarin Chinese words selected to refer to Coca Cola translated into something akin to "Eat the wax tadpole."

Spanish is becoming by far the most widely spoken of the modern Romance languages. As a commercial and diplomatic language, it is quickly taking over the position long enjoyed by French. One important cultural group that speaks mostly Spanish is the eighty-five million Mexicans. Mexicans want to maintain the purity of their language, because they believe that Spanish without a mixture of English is a means of expressing their feelings of solidarity as well as their culture.[5] The following examples show how the Spanish language expresses these feelings.

First of all, Mexicans cherish the art of conversation. They delight in verbal play, making wide use of double entendres, turns of phrases, and old quotations expressed at the right moment in an otherwise ordinary conversation.[6] If there are opportunities to engage in talk, the Mexican is ready. Even among casual acquaintances, the Mexican seems anxious to lower his or her defenses and share in conversation. Once an emotional bond is established, he or she is open and generous, willing to confide and be very hospitable.[7]

The Spanish language tells us a great deal about the Mexican notion of the future through the structure of the future tense. To say "I will go to the store," a Mexican might say, *"Ire al la tienda."* To the speaker of English, however, this means "I *may* go to the store." Spanish statements made about the future reveal its uncertainty by inferring probability.

The Spanish language reveals the strong male dominance of Mexican culture. The Spanish language is replete with gendered nouns and pronouns. A group of men, for instance, would be referred to as *ellos,* and a group of women as *ellas,* the *o* ending being masculine and the *a* ending being feminine. But if a group contains several men and one woman, the group is *ellos*—masculine gender. On the other hand, if a group contains several women and one man, the group is still *ellos.* A group of girls is called *niñas,* but a group of girls with a single boy is called *niños.*

The Spanish language also expresses formality. There are separate verb conjugations for formal and informal speech. Because Mexicans value formality, they use almost another language to carry on formal conversations. The pronouns meaning "you" differ between the formal and the informal or familiar forms of speech. In formal speech the pronoun *usted* is used, while in familiar speech the pronoun *tu* is appropriate.

Oriental languages provide another perspective on the relationship between language and culture. Asians use language cautiously, as they show in their high-context fondness for moderate or suppressed expression of negative and confrontational messages. They tend to be concerned more with the overall emotional quality of the interaction than with the meaning of particular words or sentences. Courtesy takes precedence over truth, and this is consistent with the cultural emphasis on the maintenance of social harmony as the primary function of speech. For certain Asian languages such as Chinese, Japanese, and Korean, the language structures themselves promote ambiguity. In the Japanese language, verbs come at the end of sentences, preventing one from understanding what is being said until the whole sentence has been uttered.

The Japanese language has borrowed from several other cultures. However, even though its writing system is derived from Chinese, grammatically Japanese is very unlike Chinese. It does share much with Korean, including an ancient use of vowel harmony. The Japanese language makes no sharp distinction between singular and plural. It does not distinguish masculine, neuter, and feminine nouns, and it has no articles.

The Japanese use language to communicate who belongs where and to support a carefully established hierarchy. This is perhaps the most significant difference between Japanese and Western communication. In Japan, the very structure of the language requires the speaker to focus primarily on human relationships, whereas Western languages focus on objects or referents and their logical relationships.

Not only do words that men and women use differ in Japanese, but a number of words take different forms for different situations and relationships between the speaker and the listener—or the person being talked about. There are many words for "you": *omae, kimi, ariata, kisama,* and *anata-sama.* Certain words are used only between a husband and wife to express their delicate conjugal relationship. For example, a man uses the word *omae* (you) in two cases: when calling rudely to another man and when addressing his wife. Thus, *omae,* when the "you" is female, can be used only by a husband addressing his own wife. Only one man in the world, therefore, can call a woman *omae*—her husband.

Arabic gives us yet another perspective on the relationship between culture and language. First, the Arabic language helps to bond the Arab countries together linguistically. Anyone who speaks Arabic as a native is considered an Arab regardless of national origin.

Arabs attribute an exceptionally high value to rhetorical artistry, and this strongly influences communication patterns. Arabic is a language that can exercise an irresistible influence over the minds of its users. The language itself can be persuasive to the point that actual words used to describe events are often more significant than the events themselves. Common rhetorical patterns include exaggeration, overassertion, and repetition. Sometimes words are used more for their own sake than for what they are understood to mean, and it is often difficult to obtain direct answers to questions. Someone may offer an answer such as *inshalla,* which means "God willing," because of the belief that God plays an integral role in all actions. No matter how badly someone wants something to happen, it will occur only if God wills it.

Although virtually every Saudi Arabian speaks Arabic, those who engage in international activities are usually fluent in English as well. As most intercultural communication between Saudis and Westerners is likely to utilize English, it is necessary to know about the transference of Arabic communication patterns into the English language. Arabs using English frequently transfer three facets of Arabic to their use of English: intonation patterns, a tendency toward overassertion and exaggeration, and the use of Arabic organizational logic. Native Arabic speakers tend to transfer certain preferred patterns of intonation when speaking English that may make it difficult for the English speaker to comprehend what the speaker is saying. This may be manifest by **intonation** and **stress** patterns transferring unwanted affective meanings because they sound aggressive or threatening to an English listener. The transfer of the flat Arabic intonation pattern to English declarative sentences can result in a monotonous voice pattern that native English speakers often feel demonstrates a lack of interest.

In social discourse, Arabs typically use an exaggerated speaking style. Where a North American can adequately express an idea in ten words, the Arabic speaker will typically use one hundred words. Boasting about the superiority of one's abilities, experiences, or friends is expected. Arabs ordinarily do not publicly admit to deficiencies in themselves. They will, however, spend hours elaborating upon the faults and failures of others who are not members of their clique.

The Greek language tends to express much of Greek culture in a variety of key sayings. In a sense these sayings are proverbs because they have the Greek morality attached to them and serve as a sort of generic form of expression that summarizes much meaning in a short phrase. For example, Greeks look harshly upon a lack of gratitude. A Greek who feels slighted might respond, "I taught him how to swim and he tried to drown me." When a Greek is at fault and has no excuse, he or she is liable to say, "I want to become a saint, but the demons won't let me." Greek men have a tendency toward arrogance and tend to boast often. If one succeeds in putting a halt to the bragging of another, he will say, "I cut out his cough." Greeks have a somewhat cavalier attitude toward the truth. This is expressed in proverbial sayings such as "Lies are the salt of life" and "Only from fools and children will you learn the truth."

Even the English language, with which we are most familiar, differs as we move among various cultures in which English predominates. In Great Britain, the language is interspersed with euphemisms that enable the speaker to avoid expressing strong feelings. For instance, when English persons wish to disagree with someone, they are liable to preface their comments with phrases such as "I may be wrong, but . . ." or "There is just one thing in all that you have been saying that worries me a little. . . ." Another example of this subtle form of speech is the frequent use of an expression of gratitude to preface a request, as in "I'd be awfully grateful if . . ." or "Thank you very much indeed. . . ." This concern also appears in the difference between American and British word choice. Compare the following signs seen in the United States and in England. U.S.: No dogs allowed. Britain: We regret that in the interest of hygiene dogs are not allowed on these premises. U.S.: Video Controlled. Britain: Notice: In the interest of our regular customers these premises are now equipped with central security: closed circuit television. Or, U.S.: Please Keep Hands Off Door. Britain: Obstructing the door causes delay and can be dangerous.

Differences between British and American language also appear in word meanings. Although some words are spelled and pronounced the same, they have different meanings. For instance, the words *boot, bonnet, lift,* and *biscuit* in British English translate properly into American English as car trunk, car hood, elevator, and cookie.

The relationship between language and culture by now should have begun to emerge. Both language acquisition and language meaning are directly related to our experience. These experiences are unique to each of us not only because of the differences we encountered as individuals while we were growing up and learning to use our language, but also because of what our culture has exposed us to. In short, each of us learns and uses language as we do because of both our individual and cultural backgrounds.

ARGOT

The Nature and Use of Argot

We indicated earlier, when discussing the Sapir-Whorf hypothesis, that language is a guide to dealing with and understanding social reality.[8] From this notion comes the idea that cultures evolve different languages because their social realities are different, and their unique languages are best suited to describing and dealing with their specific social realities. This process works at all levels of culture but is most prevalent among nondominant co-cultures.

Co-cultures are groups of people that exist within a society but outside of the dominant culture. Their social realities and values are generally quite different from those of the dominant culture. The process of language evolution in co-cultures, therefore, tends to mirror points of view and lifestyles quite different from those of the dominant culture; so we can examine co-cultures in terms of their language, values, and behavior. This method of analysis recognizes that experience and language work in combination.

A co-culture's use of language, the words its members select, and the meanings of those words offer us insight into the experiences of that co-culture. Because culture helps determine and shape our surroundings, it plays a crucial role in our deciding which experiences we learn to name. In many co-cultures, the name given to the experience clearly demonstrates how co-cultures perceive and interact with the dominant culture.

When we examine co-cultures, we find that their language frequently takes on added significance, a significance that lies in the need of co-cultures to have a language that permits them to share membership and to participate in their social and cultural communities. They need a means to identify themselves and their place in the universe, as well as to permit them to communicate with one another about their unique social realities. They do this by sharing modes and styles of verbal behavior. This form of language is known as **argot,** and we shall examine some of the forms of argot that various co-cultures use in the United States.

Argot is a more or less secret vocabulary peculiar to a particular group. In many respects, if a group cannot demonstrate an argot, it cannot be considered a co-culture. One major difference between an argot and a foreign language lies in the relationship between sounds and meanings. In a foreign language, the sounds are different but the referents are the same. In English the sound of the thing we sit at to eat dinner is *table.* In Spanish, it is *mesa.* In other words, the sounds are different, but the thing is the same. In argot, the sounds remain the same but the meanings change. Simple words may have multiple meanings unique to the social reality of the group. The word *pot,* for instance, may refer to the pot you smoke, to the pot that hangs over your belt, or to the pot in which you cook your dinner. The sound remains the same, but the meaning differs significantly. A second major difference between argot and dominant languages is the cultural reference. One can assume specific cultural identifications when referring to dominant languages such as English, Spanish, French, German, Chinese, Japanese, and Arabic. Here, the name of the language suggests the accompanying culture. But when we examine argot, we find that it does not refer to a specific dominant culture but to co-cultures such as black Americans, gays, prostitutes, prisoners, the hard-core poor, gangs, the drug-using community, and women.

Co-cultures in the United States that use argot are those that, by the norms of the **eurocentric,** monogamous, heterosexual, middle-to-upper-class dominant culture, exhibit some form of deviant behavior. This "deviant behavior" takes a variety of forms. Prisoners, for example, who have become deviants by breaking the law, have an argot. Hobos and vagabonds, not criminals by most standards, are also removed from the dominant culture, and hence they too have an argot. The important point is that argot is a language form limited to a particular co-culture whose members are outside the dominant culture. One way to gain insight into any co-culture, therefore, is to examine its use of language. "Argots are more than specialized forms of language, they reflect a way of life. . . . They are keys to attitudes, to evaluations of men and society, to modes of thinking, to social organization and to technology."[9]

Argot, then, is but one way in which language and behavior are linked together. And "because vocabulary is a part of language that is most immediately under the conscious manipulation and control of its users, it provides the most accessible place to begin exploration of shared and disparate experiences."[10]

Functions of Argot

Argot serves several functions for the nondominant co-culture. First, argot assists countercultures in developing a means of self-defense by providing a code system that helps them survive in a hostile environment.[11] Because many co-cultures function in a hostile environment, members of the co-culture use argot for communicating with each other in a manner that is difficult for outsiders to understand. The European Jews' use of Yiddish during harsh periods of discrimination is an obvious example of argot as a means of defense.

There are, however, even more subtle and contemporary instances. Prostitutes, because they are engaged in an illegal profession, also must use language for concealment. They must not only conceal the sexual acts themselves, but they must camouflage discussion of the acts to avoid arrest. Argot serves this purpose. The following might be a typical conversation between a prostitute and a pimp. "I have a steak if you're interested. I tried for some lobster but couldn't get it." Translated: *Steak* means a client who will pay fifty dollars to be with the prostitute. A seventy-five dollar client is often called *roast beef,* someone willing to pay one hundred and fifty dollars is a *lobster,* and a three-hundred-dollar client is labeled *champagne.*[12]

In a similar manner, black Americans have evolved a distinctive language frequently referred to as **Ebonics.** This language contains a variety of terms denoting different ways of talking that depend on the context. Each way of talking is characterized by its own style and function. Through the study of Ebonics, we can gain insight into the black perspective and condition and develop an understanding of the values and attitudes that drive verbal behavior within the black community.

Rapping is an extremely fluent way of speaking. It is always lively and possesses a unique personal style, frequently taking the form of a narrative or story to describe some event in a particularly colorful manner. Rapping also may be used as a device to obtain something one desires or to create a favorable impression.

Rapping is not an interactive style of communication but rather a very functional activity. One does not rap with someone but *to* someone. Rapping may serve either an expressive or directive function. In the expressive form, a speaker attempts to project his or her personality onto the current social setting. In the directive form, the rap becomes persuasive and attempts to manipulate and control others. Rapping may be used to start a relationship by being impressive. It then may become persuasive if the initial impression-creating attempt is successful. A male, for instance, needs to throw an impressive rap when asking a woman for sex. His initial speaking seeks to demonstrate his verbal virtuosity and, if the woman appreciates this, he will transfer from expressive behavior to a directive behavior that becomes an appeal for sex.

Shucking and **jiving** both denote language behavior that blacks exhibit when confronted by the white establishment or authority figures. This language behavior evolved from the blacks' long history of mistreatment by the dominant white culture. Its roots are in fear, a respect for power, and a will to survive. Shucking has become an effective way for many blacks to stay out of trouble, to avoid arrest, or to get out of trouble when apprehended. Shucking and jiving work on the mind and emotions of the authority figure to get him or her to feel a certain way or to give up something that will be to the speaker's advantage. They include talk and gestures that are appropriate for putting someone on by creating a false impression.

Here is an example of shucking. A black gang member was coming downstairs from a club room with seven guns on him, when he encountered policemen who were going upstairs. If they stopped and searched him, they would arrest him. To avoid this, the black said something like, "Man, I gotta get away from up there. There's gonna be some trouble and I don't want no part of it." This shuck worked because it anticipated the policemen's questions about why the gang member was leaving the club and why he was in a hurry. The shuck also gave the police a reason to get to the upstairs room fast.[13]

Much of the colorfulness of the black language comes from the way in which blacks use words to describe their environment. Although the words usually come from the standard English language, their meanings are changed—sometimes even reversed—to reflect the perceptions and needs of the black community. A number of words and their meanings from the Ebonics vocabulary will demonstrate this. *Bad* takes on the opposite meaning and means the very best. *Candy man* refers to a drug pusher. *Charlie* is a term that refers to the white man. *Chickenhead* refers to a female with short-cropped hair; it also may refer to any unkempt or unattractive female. *Don't have papers on me* means that you do not own me or that you are not married to me. *Feel draft* expresses a black's sense of racism in a white person. *Get down* means to engage in a particular activity with enthusiasm. It especially refers to having a fight, having sex, dancing, or taking drugs. The word *haircut* takes on a unique meaning in that it refers to having been robbed or cheated. *High yella* denotes a particularly light-skinned African American, especially a female. *Hors d'oeuvres* does not refer to snacks with drinks but to capsules of the drug Seconal. *Lame* means socially inexperienced or unaware of what is happening. *Nairobi queen* refers to a particularly attractive dark-skinned female. The word *peckerwood* is used to indicate a white person. A *Tom* is any black person who attempts to emulate or to please the white man. *Tom* also refers both to someone who has sold out to whitey and to a black informer. *Woof* means to joke around or to put someone down playfully.

Argot also serves as a cultural storehouse for the hostility the users feel toward the dominant culture. It permits the expression of frustration and hatred without risk of reprisal from the dominant culture, as well as maintaining the identity and group solidarity of a co-culture or counterculture. A co-culture's use of a specialized linguistic code satisfies a number of significant and real needs.

A third major function of argot is to assert a co-culture's solidarity and cohesiveness through a uniform learned language code. Because a degree of secrecy is associated with the use of argot, a sense of identity and pride are associated with the realization that one is part of a group that developed its own private language; a bond forms among those members who understand the code. Homosexuals who know *AC-DC* (bisexual), *Bill* (a masculine homosexual), *Black Widow* (a person who takes love mates away from other gays), and *chicken* (a young male gay) are privy to an argot that is unique to a particular subculture.

The tramp and hobo are also set apart from the main culture, yet they can feel a type of in-group solidarity because they have learned that a *yap* is a newcomer, a *tool* is a pickpocket, a *paper* is a railroad ticket, to be *oiled* is to be intoxicated, and to *lace* is to punch.[14]

Gangs have become prominent as co-cultures in the past several years because of the violence associated with their drug-dealing businesses. Like other co-cultures, gangs have a rich argot, as some examples will demonstrate. *Buster* refers to a gang member who does not stand up for his gang, who sells out his brothers. A *claim* is the area that gang members have staked out as their turf. If persons are asked what they claim, they are being asked which gang they belong to or are associated with. A *claimer* is a person who pretends or wants to be a member of a gang but has not been accepted by the gang. *Crippin'* is a word that members of the Crip gang use and means survive any way you can. *Drive-bys* is a short term for drive-by shootings, which are surprise attacks from passenger cars. Gangs frequently use drive-by shootings to frighten rival gang members or to exact revenge from them. *Flashing signs* refers to using hand signals to communicate with other gang members. A sign may signify membership in a particular gang or it could be a signal that a drug deal is in progress. *Gang bangin'* means participating in any kind of gang activity ranging from hanging out, to dealing drugs, to being involved in drive-by shootings. A *homegirl* is a young woman who hangs out with gang members. *Jump in* is the initiation process whereby a claimer fights members of the gang to which he desires to belong. *Pancake* designates a person who has become a homosexual as a result of his experience in jail. And *strawberry* refers to a female who exchanges sexual favors for drugs.

A fourth function of argot is to help establish groups as real and viable social entities. During the 1960s, for example, when people began taking drugs as a way of life, they gathered at specific locations and immediately developed what became known as the "San Francisco drug language." As these individuals became more than a group of people simply taking drugs, they evolved a rather elaborate glossary of terms—terms that helped transform them from a collection of people into a subgroup. Some of their terms were *Bernice* for cocaine, *hay* for marijuana, *heat* for police, *pipe* for a large vein, *roach* for the butt of a marijuana cigarette, *octagon* for a square person, *lightning* for achieving a high, and *head* for a heavy drug user.

Women are another segment of our culture that uses language differently. Their language usage does not truly constitute an argot, but we include them here because of the need to understand how culture affects women in our society. Like any other group, women are susceptible to the conditioning applied by their culture. Because of their coexistence with the dominant male culture, they have learned linguistic ways of adapting to their cultural roles.

Women frequently use linguistic devices to avoid having to take a strong stand or to keep from being too direct or forceful. They may make an assertion that expresses their position, but then temper it with a tag line. "That was a good movie—*wasn't it?*" "This is a good dinner—*isn't it?*" To avoid directness or forcefulness, women also use more qualifiers than men do when speaking. Such phrases as "*Maybe* we should go . . . ," "*Perhaps* you are driving too fast . . . ," "I *guess* we can visit your mom first . . . ," and "I *sort of* don't want to do this" indicate this use of qualifiers.

In mixed conversation women talk less frequently than men, and they get the floor less often. When they do get the floor, they hold it for shorter amounts of time. Women interrupt less than men, and they have less control over the flow of the conversation. They tend to use language that is more precise than men's by including more adverbs, adjectives, and intensifiers. And finally, women use less profanity than men do.

Women have a tendency to ask more questions to keep a conversation going than men do. Again, this is a part of their learned behavior and expected role. Questions such as "What did you do yesterday?" or "How was your drive over?" typify their use of language to keep a conversation going.

When examining the argot of various co-cultures, it is important to keep two things in mind. First, you will quickly discover that there is a great deal of overlap. This does not negate the notion that argot is a community's unique language. Instead it tells us that an individual may be a member of several co-cultures simultaneously. For instance, a person may be a hard-core poor, black, drug-using, gay prostitute who is in prison. This particular person then shares membership in the black, hard-core poor, gay, prostitute, drug-using, and prison co-cultures. Another person might be a convicted white, drug-using armed robber serving a prison term. This person is a member of the drug-using and prison co-cultures.

Second, we must remember that argots change. As the dominant culture becomes familiar with the specialized code being used, the co-culture will usually eliminate the word or phrase from its private glossary. Hence, many of the examples we cited in the last few pages may no longer be in use in the co-culture we are discussing. This need to alter words does not diminish the importance in studying argot. It is not a single word that is significant, but rather the idea that the words and phrases selected offer us valuable insight into the experiences of these groups, experiences to which many of us might not have access.

FOREIGN LANGUAGES AND TRANSLATION

The translation of one language into another is far more complex than most people realize. Most people assume that text in one language can be accurately translated into another language, so long as the translator uses a good bilingual dictionary. Unfortunately, languages are not this simple, and direct translations in many cases are difficult if not impossible because (1) words have more than one meaning, (2) many words are **culture-bound** and have no direct translations, (3) cultural orientations can render a direct translation into nonsense, and (4) a culture may not have the experiential background to permit translation of experiences from other cultures. For instance, how does one translate Atlantic Ocean into the Hopi language?

A major problem in translation is that although messages may provide adequate interpretations of original text, there usually is no full equivalence through translation. Even what may appear to be synonymous messages may not be equivalent.[15] There are several problems in the search for equivalence, including vocabulary, idiomatic, grammatical-syntactical, experiential-cultural, and conceptual equivalence. A brief glimpse of each should demonstrate some of the major difficulties in securing an adequate translation.

Vocabulary or lexical equivalence. Dictionary translations rarely reflect the language of the people. One of the goals of translation, of course, is to convey the meaning and style of the original. Problems can arise with the use of highly trained translators because their language style may not be representative of the original style. Translators also need to deal with the nuances of words and with words that have no equivalence in another language. For instance, there are really no good equivalent Tagalog language terms for *feminine* and *domestic*. On the other hand, the Tagalog words *hiya,* which relates to shyness, embarrassment, shame, and deference, and *pakikisama,* which relates to getting along with others and conformity, are difficult to translate into English.[16]

Idiomatic equivalence.   Idiomatic expressions are culture-bound; they do not translate well. Consider this example of an Italian idiom translated literally into English: "Giovanni sta menando il cane per l'aia." Translated, this becomes "John is leading his dog around the threshing floor." A better translation, with greater correspondence of meaning, would have been "John is beating around the bush."[17]

Grammatical-syntactical equivalence.   Sometimes difficulties arise because there are no equivalent parts of speech in the language into which a message is being translated. For example, the Urdu language has no gerunds, and it is difficult to find an equivalent form for an English gerund.

Experiential-cultural equivalence.   Translators must grapple not only with structural differences between languages but with cultural differences as well. The problem of transferring between cultures requires that the translator walk a fine line between the need for precision and the need for keeping the original author's approach or attitude. More importantly, the translator needs to consider shared experiences. *Peace* has various meanings for peoples of the world according to their conditions, time, and place; so does *war.* The meanings that we have for words are based on shared experiences. The ability of a word to convey or elicit meaning depends on culturally-informed perceptions by both source and receiver as message processors. When we lack cultural equivalents, we lack the words in our vocabulary to represent those experiences. For instance, when the vocabulary of a tribe in a mountainous jungle region has words for rivers and streams but not for oceans, how do you translate the notion of an ocean? Or what does a translator do when he or she is faced with the task of translating the Bible verse "Though your sins be as scarlet, they shall be as white as snow" into the language of a tribe that has never seen snow?

Conceptual equivalence.   Another difficulty in translation lies in obtaining a concept match. Some concepts are culture-specific (**emic**) or culture-general

(etic). By definition, it is impossible to translate perfectly an emic concept.[18] So different, for instance, are the cultural experiences that many words cannot be translated directly from Spanish into English. Strong affection is expressed in English with the verb *to love*. In Spanish, there are two verbs, *te amo* and *te quiero*. *Te amo* refers to nurturant love, as between a parent and a child or between two adults. *Te quiero* translates literally into English as "I want you," which connotes an ownership aspect not present in the English expression *I love you*. Commonly used to express love between two adults, *te quiero* falls somewhere between the English statements *I love you* and *I like you*. Neither *te amo* nor *te quiero* has an exact English equivalent.

The Mexican Spanish language also has at least five terms indicating agreement in varying degree: *me compromento* (I promise or commit myself), *yo le asequro* (I assure you), *si, como no, lo hago* (yes, sure, I will do it), *tal vez lo hago* (maybe I will do it), and *tal vez lo haga* (maybe I might do it). This agreement concept ranges from a durable agreement that everyone recognizes to agreement being unlikely. The problem, of course, is to understand the differences between *me compromento* and *tal vez lo haga* in their cultural sense so that one can render a correct version in another language. If, for instance, we were rendering English translations of these Mexican Spanish terms, we could expect all sorts of misunderstandings and confusions to arise if we simply translated each of these phrases of agreement as "OK." About the only way in which an emic concept can be translated is to attempt to relate it to etic concepts by trying to tie it into the context in which the concept might be used.[19]

Language translation is difficult, and it is easy to make mistakes. One of the better illustrations of a mistake is that of a missionary preaching in the West African Bantu language who, instead of saying "The children of Israel crossed the Red Sea and followed Moses," mistakenly said "The children of Israel crossed the red mosquitoes and swallowed Moses." When translation is inept it can also have extreme consequences. Near the end of World War II, after Italy and Germany had surrendered, the Allies sent Japan an ultimatum to surrender. Japan's premier announced that his government would *mokusatsu* the surrender ultimatum. *Mokusatsu* was an unfortunate word choice because it could mean both "to consider" and "to take notice." The premier, speaking in Japanese, apparently meant that the government would consider the surrender ultimatum. But the English-language translators in Japan's overseas broadcasting agency used the "to take notice" meaning of *mokusatsu.* Consequently, the world heard that Japan had rejected the surrender ultimatum rather than that Japan was considering the ultimatum. The possible mistranslation led the United States to assume Japan was unwilling to surrender, and the atomic bombing of Hiroshima and Nagasaki followed. We realize that there has been much speculation on the reasons for the United States' use of the atomic bomb in the years since World War II, but it is quite possible that if the translators had selected the other meaning, the atomic bomb might not have been used in World War II.[20] This example vividly illustrates the difficulties that can be found in foreign language translation and demonstrates the serious consequences that can follow inept translation of words with multiple meanings.

Language translations frequently produce misunderstanding or incomprehension because of cultural orientations reflected in the language. For instance, the Quechua language of Peru uses orientations to past and future that are the opposite of those in the English language. Quechua visualizes the past as being in front of or ahead of one because it can be seen. It visualizes the future as being behind one because it cannot be seen. This is just the opposite of Americans, who speak of the past being behind them and the future being ahead of them. If this aspect of cultural orientation were not known or if it were ignored, it could lead to incomprehensible translations about time, the past, and the future. It might even imply that people must look behind them if they are to be able to see what normally lies ahead of them.

A final problem of language translation arises when it is necessary to work with a professional interpreter. Proper use of an interpreter can enhance our ability to communicate with people of other cultures, but misuses of an interpreter can lead to serious consequences.

A good interpreter needs special, highly developed skills. He or she must be able to translate a message so that others understand it as though it had not been translated. This means that the interpreter must be skilled in understanding not only the words of the language being translated but the emotional aspects, thought processes, and communicative techniques of that culture as well.

The effective use of an interpreter requires the establishment of a three-way rapport. Rapport must exist between the speaker and the interpreter, between the speaker and the audience, and between the interpreter and the audience. This is an extremely difficult state to attain because of the complexity of translation in real time. Consider what an interpreter must be doing simultaneously. When the speaker says a phrase, the interpreter must listen to that phrase. While the speaker says the next phrase, the interpreter must not only be translating the first phrase, but must also be listening to the second phrase. Then while the speaker is saying the third phrase, the interpreter must remember the first phrase, be interpreting the second phrase, and listening to the third. This procedure goes on and on throughout the process of message delivery; and it requires that the interpreter be able to remember not only what the speaker has just said, but what he or she may have said several minutes ago, because the interpretation of the latest words spoken may reflect a reference to what the speaker said several minutes earlier.

In selecting an interpreter, there are several qualities or qualifications you should seek. First is compatibility. You need someone with whom you are comfortable. This means a translator that is neither domineering nor timid. Second is ethnic compatibility. You need a translator who is of the same tribe, religious group, or ethnic background as the people for whom he or she will be translating. Third, your translator should speak the same dialect as the people for whom he or she will be translating. And finally, the translator should have specialized experience in your field and its terminology.

Learning to help an interpreter can make speaking through an interpreter a much easier experience. You can do several things to make your interpreter's task easier. Before the meeting you should brief him or her on the tone, substance, and purpose of the presentation. You should review any technical terms that will be used. Ask the interpreter to brief you on any cultural differences in eye contact or other nonverbal behaviors that may be important in your presentation. Ask about local customs pertinent to your presentation, such as appropriate time of day for the presentation and how the audience regards time. Ask about unwritten rules of conversation. In Muslim countries, for instance, it is considered impolite to ask a man about his wife or wives. During the presentation, speak slowly enough for the interpreter to understand and to follow you. Speak in relatively short sentences and pause often, and look at the audience while you speak, not at the interpreter. Prepare yourself to give greetings and farewells in the foreign language. Do not use profanity, obscenities, slang, regional dialect, acronyms, high-tech shoptalk, or colloquialisms. At the end of your presentation, recap the major points and clear up any ambiguities.

SUMMARY

The Nature of Language

- Language allows us to share our internal states of being with others.

The Importance of Language

- Meaning in language varies because all people decide what words mean to them based on their own personal backgrounds.

Language and Culture

- Language serves as a guide to how a culture perceives reality. Cultures evolve different languages because their social realities are different. An important feature of this is high and low context. Each culture's unique language is best suited to describe and deal with its specific social realities.

Argot

- Argot is a co-cultural language code that undergoes constant and rapid change. It is often regional.

Foreign Languages and Translation

- The translation of one language into another is very complex because of differences in cultural orientations, which are reflected in language. Consideration of these differences aids in intercultural communication situations involving translation and interpretation.

ACTIVITIES

1. Ask an informant (yours, or anyone whose native language is not English) for examples of expressions from his or her native language that are difficult to translate into English. Idioms are the most likely category in which to find examples. Try to determine why the difficulty exists. What cultural values might these expressions represent?

2. In small groups, try to come up with as many meanings as you can for each of the following words:

    collar

    bird

    jam

    can

    hit

    tool

    bill

    To what do you attribute the various meanings? Add any other words you can think of that have multiple meanings.

DISCUSSION IDEAS

1. What problems are associated with language diversity *within* a particular country? What are some of the solutions that have been proposed to deal with these problems? Draw examples from the United States and Canada, as well as from any other bi- or trilingual countries you are familiar with.

2. Listen for uses of argot in television programs, movies, and popular music. Write down the examples you hear, as well as the co-culture to which they belong. Indicate what your examples mean, if possible. (In addition to the co-cultures mentioned in this chapter, you may also find examples that you can ascribe to North American *teen* or *youth* culture.)

3. Find examples of problematic translations. Some may be quite amusing. Look for examples in the packaging and user's manuals for products that are manufactured overseas. If you know anything about the structure of the languages from which the examples were translated, try to explain why the mistranslations occurred.

NOTES FOR CHAPTER 6

1. David G. Mandelbaum, ed., *Selected Writings of Edward Sapir* (Berkeley and Los Angeles: University of California Press, 1949), 162.

2. Edward T. Hall, *Beyond Culture* (Garden City, NY: Anchor Books, 1977).

3. C. Arensberg and A. Niehoff, *Introducing Social Change: A Manual for Americans Overseas* (Chicago: Aldine, 1964), 30.

4. M. Dawson, R. Gardiner, et al., *Six Impossible Things* (San Francisco: Field Education, 1969), 73.

5. M. Hildalgo, "Language Contact, Language Loyalty, and Language Prejudice on the Mexican Border," *Language in Society* 15 (1986), 193–220.

6. John C. Condon, *Interact: Guidelines for Mexicans and North Americans* (Chicago: Intercultural Press, 1980), 37.

7. A. Riding, *Distinct Neighbors: A Portrait of Mexico* (New York: Knopf, 1985), 8.

8. Mandelbaum.

9. D. Maurer, "The Argot of the Dice Gambler," *Annals of the American Academy of Political and Social Science,* 269 (1950), 119.

10. Edith Folb, "Vernacular Vocabulary: A View of Interracial Perceptions and Experiences," in *Intercultural Communication: A Reader,* 2d ed., ed. L. Samovar and R. Porter (Belmont, CA: Wadsworth, 1976), 194.

11. Andrea Rich, *Interracial Communication* (New York: Harper and Row, 1974), 142.

12. Larry A. Samovar and Fred Sanders, "Language Patterns of the Prostitute: Some Insights into a Deviant Subculture," *ETC: A Review of General Semantics* 34 (1) (1978), 34.

13. Thomas Kochman, " 'Rapping' in the Black Ghetto," *Transaction,* 6 (February, 1969) 26–34.

14. G. Irwin, *American Tramp and Underworld Slang* (Ann Arbor, MI: Gryphon, 1972), 12–13.

15. S. Bassnett-McGuire, *Translation Studies* (New York: Methuen, 1980).

16. Lee Sechrest, Todd L. Fay, and S. M. Zaidi, "Problems of Translation in Cross-Cultural Research," *Journal of Cross-Cultural Psychology* 3 (1972), 44.

17. Bassnett-McGuire.

18. Harry C. Triandis, "Approaches toward Minimizing Translation," in *Translation Applications and Research,* ed. Richard W. Brislin (New York: Gardner, 1976), 229–43.

19. Triandis.

20. Peter Farb, *Word Play* (New York: Knopf, 1974), 198.

*When I was a child I used to think it was thunder that killed
people; as I grew older I found it was only the lightning that struck,
and the noise of thunder was only noise.*

ANON.

*Do not the most moving moments of our lives find us all without
words?*

MARCEL MARCEAU

CHAPTER SEVEN

NONVERBAL COMMUNICATION: SOUND AND ACTION

In Thailand, to "ask" another person to come near, one moves the fingers back and forth with the palm down. In the United States, we beckon someone to come by moving the fingers toward the body with the palm up. The Tongans sit down in the presence of superiors; in the West we stand up. Crossing one's legs in the United States is often a sign of being relaxed; in Korea it is a social **taboo.** Muslims consider the left hand unclean and do not eat or pass objects with it. Many Asians believe it is good manners to use both hands when offering or receiving objects. Americans believe that all problems can be "talked out." The Buddha maintained that great wisdom arrived during moments of silence.

The point we are trying to make should be rather transparent. We have attempted to demonstrate some of the many ways nonverbal communication differs from culture to culture. Although all human beings can create actions that other people attach meaning to, many of those actions, and indeed the meanings of those actions, are culturally based.

THE IMPORTANCE OF NONVERBAL COMMUNICATION

It might be helpful if we begin our discussion of nonverbal behavior by highlighting some of the reasons this form of communication is so very important to the study of intercultural communication. We open with this assertion: Nonverbal communication clearly plays an important role in our lives. Barnlund highlights this observation.

> Many, and sometimes most, of the critical meanings generated in human encounters are elicited by touch, glance, vocal nuance, gestures, or facial expression with or without the aid of words. From the moment of recognition until the moment of separation, people observe each other with all their senses, hearing pause and intonation, attending to dress and carriage, observing glance and facial tension, as well as noting word choice and syntax. Every harmony or disharmony of signals guides the interpretation of passing mood or enduring attribute. Out of the evaluation of kinetic, vocal and verbal cues, decisions are made to argue or agree, to laugh or blush, to relax or resist, to continue or cut off conversation.[1]

Consciously and unconsciously, intentionally and unintentionally, we send and receive nonverbal messages. In addition, we make important judgments and decisions concerning the experiences of others—experiences they often express without words. For example, we decide about the quality of our relationships through these nonverbal messages. In our Western culture the distance between us and our partners, and the amount of touching we engage in, helps us define the closeness of that relationship. Even what places on the body we are allowed to touch signals how the parties perceive their relationship. Nonverbal communication is so very subtle that a shifting of body zones can also send a message. The first time you move from holding hands with your partner to touching his or her face, you are sending a message.

Nonverbal communication is also important in that we use the actions of others to learn about their **affective** or emotional states. If we see someone with a clenched fist and a grim expression, we do not need words to tell us that this person is not very happy. If we hear someone's voice quaver and see his or her hands tremble, we probably infer that the person is fearful or anxious, despite what he or she might say to the contrary. And think for a moment of what a big smile can "say." Our emotions are reflected in our posture, face, and eyes. Be it fear, joy, anger, or sadness, we often express these emotions and feelings to others without ever uttering a word. Most of us rely heavily on what we observe through our eyes. In fact, research indicates that we will believe nonverbal messages over verbal when the two contradict each other.[2] As Heraclitus remarked over two thousand years ago, "Eyes are more accurate witnesses than ears."

Nonverbal communication is significant in human interaction in that it usually creates first impressions. Think for just a moment of how your first judgments of other people are usually based on the nonverbal messages they send you. And more importantly, those early messages usually color the perceptions of everything else that follows. Even whom we select as friends and sexual partners is grounded in first impressions. You approach certain people because of the way they are dressed or how attractive you find them. Although we also use other data in forming long-term relationships, these first impressions nevertheless help us decide if we should pursue the association or terminate it.

Finally, nonverbal communication is important because of its strong link to culture. Even though we have already intimated this point, it deserves further discussion. Hall has written on the fusing of culture to nonverbal behavior.

> I am convinced that much of our difficulty with people in other countries stems from the fact that so little is known about cross-communication. . . . Formal training in the language, history, government, and customs of another nation is only the first step in a comprehensive program. Of equal importance is an introduction to the nonverbal language which exists in every country of the world and among the

various groups within each country. Most Americans are only dimly aware of this silent language even though they use it every day.[3]

Students of intercultural communication should find Hall's assertion familiar. For you should recall that earlier in the book we noted that culture was invisible, omnipresent, and learned. Nonverbal communication has these same qualities. Let us explain.

Hall alerts us to the *invisible* aspect of culture and nonverbal communication by employing the word *silent*. In later writings he also uses the phrase *hidden dimension* to make the same point. He is telling us that nonverbal behavior, like culture, tends to be elusive and frequently beyond our awareness. People in Japan will work long hours without giving it much thought because of their cultural value towards work. North Americans will automatically look at people when they are speaking to them. In both instances (valuing work and using direct eye contact), the actions are habitual.

We remind you that culture is all-pervasive and boundless—it is everywhere and in everything. The same is true of nonverbal behavior, for it too appears in all our communication encounters. The list of potential messages is infinite. Our clothes, jewelry, facial expressions, the hundreds of movements we can make, where and how we touch people, our gaze and eye contact, vocal behaviors such as laughter, and our use of time, space, and silence are just some of the behaviors we engage in that people use as messages. Hence, like culture, nonverbal messages are limitless.

Our final parallel between culture and nonverbal behavior is one that occupied a large portion of Chapter 3. Simply put, we are not born with culture; we *learn* it. The same is true, with but a few exceptions, of our nonverbal behavior. First, a word about the exceptions before we develop the notion of "learning." Research now supports the view that because we are all from one family, a general and common genetic inheritance produces a universal way of expressing most of our basic emotions (for example, fear, happiness, and sadness).[4] More specifically, we are all born knowing how to smile—we do not have to learn it. Most scholars, however, would agree that where, when, and to whom we display this emotion is learned, and hence is influenced by both context and culture. We learn about staring, gesturing in public, wearing perfume, touching various parts of another person's body, and even when to remain silent. Like all other phases of our enculturation process, this learning takes place on both the conscious and unconscious levels. We are told when it is appropriate to wear a hat, and we are learning about dress as a form of nonverbal communication. By observing our parents greet each other, we are learning about touch and affection through imitation.

DEFINING NONVERBAL COMMUNICATION

Since the central concern of this chapter is to examine how and why we communicate nonverbally, and with what consequences, we begin with a definition of nonverbal communication. As you discovered in earlier chapters, there is no shortage of definitions for culture and communication. We fear that the same proliferation of approaches is also characteristic of the study of nonverbal behavior. Therefore, we shall once again select a definition that is consistent with current thinking in the field while at the same time reflecting the cultural orientation of this text. With this as preface, we would suggest that **nonverbal communication** *involves all those stimuli (except verbal stimuli) within a communication setting, generated by both the individual and the individual's use of the environment, that have potential message value for the sender or receiver.* It is not by chance that our definition is somewhat lengthy. We wanted to offer a definition that would not only mark the boundaries of nonverbal communication, but also reflect how the process actually worked. Let us explain how our definition meets this criterion.

Our definition permits us to include unintentional as well as intentional behavior as part of the total communication event. This approach is very realistic in that we send the preponderance of nonverbal messages without ever being aware that they have meaning for other people. In verbal communication we consciously dip into our vocabulary and decide what words to use. Although we often consciously decide to smile or select a specific piece of jewelry, we also send countless messages that we never intended to be part of the transaction (for example, frowning into the sun and someone thinking we are mad, leaving some shampoo in our hair and someone thinking we look silly, accidentally brushing up against someone and that person thinking we are flirting).

Goffman has made evident the authentic fusing together of intentional and unintentional behavior. Although his language is that of the sociologist, his meaning is clear.

> The expressiveness of the individual (and therefore his capacity to give impressions) appears to involve two radically different kinds of sign activity: the expression that he gives and the expression that he gives off. The first involves verbal symbols or their substitutes which he uses admittedly and solely to convey the information that he and the other are known to attach to these symbols. This is communication in the traditional and narrow sense. The second involves a wide range of action that others can treat as symptomatic of the actor (communicator), the expectation being that the action was performed for reasons other than the information conveyed in this way.[5]

Before concluding this section on definitions, we should note that our approach to nonverbal communication limits the study to those stimuli operating in a communication setting where two or more people are interacting. We grant that works of art, ballet, architecture, and the like do possess message value, but those forms are normally not thought of as face-to-face communication.

FUNCTIONS OF NONVERBAL COMMUNICATION

Two points should be clear by now: Nonverbal communication encompasses more than one activity, and it is not limited to one set of messages. This multidimensional aspect of our nonverbal behavior also carries over to the many uses and functions of this form of communication. Let us briefly examine the five primary ways in which we employ nonverbal communication.

Repeating

We often use nonverbal messages to repeat what we have said verbally. This enables us to clarify and emphasize the point we are trying to make. We might hold up our hand in the gesture that signifies "stop" at the same time we actually use the word *stop.* Or we can point in a certain direction after we have just said, "The new library is south of the building." Both the gestures and our words have a similar meaning.

Complementing

Closely related to repeating is the function called complementing. Although messages that repeat can stand alone, complementing behaviors generally add to the words you have selected. They tend to add more information to the point you are trying to make. For example, you can tell someone that you are pleased with his or her performance, but this same message takes on extra meaning if you pat the person on the shoulder at the same time you are offering the verbal compliment. The physical contact places another layer on what is being discussed. Many writers in the area of nonverbal communication will even refer to this as a type of accenting because it accents the idea the speaker is trying to make. You can see how an apology becomes more forceful if your face as well as your words are saying, "I'm sorry."

Contradicting

Sometimes our nonverbal actions contradict our verbal messages. Think of the contradiction when we tell someone we are not nervous at the same time our hands are trembling, our eyes are blinking rapidly, and our face is covered with perspiration beads. In this instance there is a contradiction, and the recipient of the dual messages must decide which message to believe. As we indicated a few pages ago, in most situations it is your nonverbal actions that people accept as manifesting your true intentions.

Substituting

We use substitution in nonverbal communication when we employ some action in place of a verbal message. If you see a very special friend, you are apt to throw open your arms to greet him or her—a substitute for all the words it would take to convey the same feeling. If a group of people are boisterous, you might place your index finger to your lips as an alternative to saying, "Please calm down so that I can speak."

Regulating

We often regulate and manage the communication event by utilizing some form of nonverbal behavior. We nod our head in agreement as a way of "telling" our communication partner that we agree and that he or she should continue talking, or we remain silent for a moment and let the silence send a message that we are now ready to begin our speech. In both of the above examples our nonverbal behavior helps control the situation.

VERBAL AND NONVERBAL SYMBOL SYSTEMS

In the preceding chapter we demonstrated how we use a very elaborate symbol system (words) to represent our experiences, ideas, and feelings. As we have already indicated, we also use nonverbal symbols to do much the same thing. Although both systems parallel each other in certain areas, they are different in many respects. To understand better the workings of nonverbal codes, it will be helpful to review the similarities and differences between the two systems.

Similarities

The most obvious similarity between verbal and nonverbal communication is that both use a culturally agreed-upon set of symbols. The words we use or the marks we put down on paper are intended to stand for something. In this sense, a word only represents a thing or idea in reality. If someone says, "I have an old black dog named Sam," that person is only using symbols to stand for a dark, furry creature that she or he owns.

This same process of symbolization applies to nonverbal communication. If we kiss someone we are fond of (tactile communication), the kiss is only a way of representing our internal state (adoration, affection, love, and so on). It is our attempt at sharing a feeling or idea, just as someone used words to share something about a black dog named Sam.

A second similarity between the two systems is that they are both products of individuals. Whether we speak, laugh, point, touch, or remain silent, we are still generating a message that someone else uses to infer something about us. It is our message, and in that sense it is subjective and personal.

The third similarity might well be a corollary of the first two, but it is significant enough to justify some additional development. In simple terms, both systems have someone attaching meaning to the symbols we have produced. Our final similarity stresses what happens to the other person when he or she receives our messages. We can use words to make people follow certain directions. We say, "Turn right," and the person moves right. Or we can point to the right and the person will also turn in that direction. In each case, by attaching meaning to our symbols, another human being is altering his or her behavior.

Differences

One important difference between verbal and nonverbal communication is found in the biological distinctions at the core of each system. That is to say, biological forces govern many of our nonverbal actions. A young man, wanting to show his mate that he is not alarmed by the rattlesnake on the road, might have a difficult time camouflaging his fear. As his voice goes up an octave and his knees knock, we can see biology winning out over culture. We have much more control, on the other hand, over verbal communication than over nonverbal action. Every language has a rather rigid set of rules and principles governing such language elements as syntax, grammar, and vocabulary. When we use words, we consciously decide when to talk and what to talk about. We don't have this same control over pupil size, blinking, blushing, trembling, and the like.

Another significant difference between verbal and nonverbal systems is the degree to which the units are linked together. *Nonverbal communication is continuous, whereas verbal communication is composed of disconnected units.* Each word and sentence have a distinct beginning and end. We cannot turn off nonverbal actions, be they our movements, dress, or body odor, as long as we are in the presence of another person. This fact should alert all intercultural communicators to the importance of being mindful of the totality of the communication event. An act as innocent as yawning can hurt someone's feelings if that person sees it as a sign of boredom or lack of interest.

A third difference deals with the stage in life when we learn these two systems. We learn nonverbal communication much earlier in life than verbal.

An infant, soon after birth, is able to make some sense out of both the quantity and quality of the physical contact it receives from others. A baby also responds to smiles and waves early in its life. By being exposed to these actions the child is actually learning its culture through the process of imitation. As we noted elsewhere, enculturation takes many forms. To learn verbal communication, a child needs not only advanced muscle development, but also a higher degree of socialization.

Finally, we would suggest that nonverbal messages can be more emotional in their appeal and impact than verbal messages. Your tears, even when perceived by someone from another culture, have a much stronger impact than the words "I am very sad."

NONVERBAL COMMUNICATION: GUIDELINES AND LIMITATIONS

Since the popularization of nonverbal communication as an area of study, there has been an explosion of information and books available to the general public on the subject. Most of this information comes with the best of intentions, but it often distorts rather than clarifies the role of nonverbal messages in human interaction. Although there is much reliable information on the subject, most popular writers feel compelled to offer the type of information that makes clever and witty cocktail chatter. Or they offer advice on "how to dress for success" as a way of further trivializing the subject. Many of these approaches make for a superficial study of this important topic. The intercultural setting, because of its added complexities, magnifies errors. Therefore, as an introduction to our discussion of nonverbal communication, we offer a partial listing of some of the hazards and dangers that can lead to a shallow study of this vital communication component.

Overgeneralizing is perhaps the greatest peril when discussing nonverbal behavior. We act, at times, as if all people, groups, regions, and nations are alike. Admittedly, people are similar in countless ways, but subtle and elusive differences can often set us apart from each other. Variations in occupations, co-culture affiliations, gender, age, education, and the like should alert us to the need to be tentative in drawing conclusions about what a specific action might mean. Our generalizations should be based on a sufficient number of cases to warrant the conclusion we reach. When we read that women smile more than men, we must be aware of the problems associated with this type of conclusion. When the research of others supports our personal experiences, however, we should feel safe in making such claims. In short, one drop of water does not mean it is raining.

A second danger of using superficial information is that although some nonverbal behaviors occur regularly within a culture, other actions *are not part of a culture's everyday repertory.* It might be intriguing to know that in Sung Dynasty China, tongue protrusion indicated mock terror, performed in ridicule, and the tongue stretched far out showed surprise. But in most instances this is not the kind of information we need to remember as students of intercultural communication.

A third potential hazard in studying nonverbal communication stems from the fact that we often are guilty of *making the differences more important than they actually are.* Is it crucial, for example, to know that Menomini Indians show contempt by raising the clenched fist palm downward up to the level of the mouth, then bringing it downward quickly and throwing forward the thumb and the first two fingers? As with our last problem, this type of information might be interesting, but does it help in our day-to-day interactions? The question you should ask of all such descriptions is whether the nonverbal actions make a significant difference when you interact with people from this particular culture.

Finally, there is the problem of forgetting that *nonverbal behaviors seldom occur in isolation.* Although in the remainder of this chapter, and in the next, we shall examine individual messages, in reality these messages are but part of the total communication context. We usually send many nonverbal cues simultaneously, and these cues are normally linked to other verbal and nonverbal messages.

NONVERBAL COMMUNICATION AND CULTURE

Having introduced the topic of nonverbal communication in broad terms, we now are ready to study the relationship between nonverbal messages and culture. This relationship should be obvious if we remember that both culture and most of our nonverbal behavior are *learned, passed on from generation to generation, and involve shared understandings.* Both represent what a collection of people deemed important enough to codify and transmit to the members of that group.

When we view both in this perspective, we can see why culture and nonverbal communication are inseparable. For example, because we have been born and socialized in the United States, our culture has taught us the "rules" of greeting. We know when to shake hands and when it is proper to kiss. The Japanese have learned to greet by bowing and seldom kiss in public. As we have said elsewhere in this book, culture is the teacher, and our behavior is the subject matter of that education.

The alliance formed by culture and nonverbal behavior is meaningful to students of intercultural communication for a number of reasons. First, by grasping important cultural differences, you will be able to gather clues regarding the underlying attitudes and values of a culture. We have already seen that nonverbal communication often reveals basic cultural traits. Even our example of shaking hands versus bowing tells us something of the deep structure of a culture. What produces tears and who gets to see those tears is yet another example of how nonverbal communication can help us understand the message systems a specific culture employs. It is not by chance that Hindus greet each other by placing their palms together in front of them while slightly tilting their heads down. This salutation reveals the Hindu belief that the deity is in all of us, not in a single God. Again, we can witness the bond between communication and culture.

Second, the study of cultural nonverbal patterns also can assist us in isolating our own ethnocentrism. For example, we might feel less offended and less judgmental about the way someone smells if we realize that the meanings attached to smell are culturally based. As way of identifying our own cultural biases, we shall begin our discussion of each nonverbal category by briefly examining North American nonverbal behaviors.

In considering the various types of nonverbal messages, we shall look at two comprehensive classifications. In this chapter we shall examine messages our body generates. In the next chapter our emphasis will shift to messages that grow out of the use we make of our environment—how space, time, and silence communicate.

BODY BEHAVIOR

General Appearance and Dress

From hair sprays to hair pieces, from reducing diets to twenty-four-hour fitness centers, from false eyelashes to blue contact lenses, we show our concern for how we look. Because of our desire to be attractive, we support a multi-billion-dollar industry dedicated to modifying how the world perceives us. And how do we calculate the price we pay in mental anguish over our personal appearance should we not quite measure up to the yardstick culture holds forth? It seems most of us believe the words of philosopher Thomas Fuller: "By the husk you may judge the nut." We all seem to want the husk to be flawless.

Reflect for a moment on some of the ways people in the United States make judgments based on personal appearance, dress, and the curios we carry or place on our body. There is no shortage of research to document just how important appearance is in American culture. When deciding whether or not to strike up a conversation with a total stranger, we are influenced by the way that person looks. We make inferences (often faulty) about another's intelligence, character, social status, and profession from cues related to attractiveness, dress, and personal artifacts. Our culture's obsession with attractiveness is so deep-seated, and begins so early in life, that one study revealed that even very young children select attractive friends over less attractive playmates.[6]

People's clothing also sends us messages about who they are. Every occupation has its official and unofficial uniform. Doctors and nurses generally dress in partial or complete white. Every change of any significance, be it birth, entering school, graduation, interviewing for a job, marriage, or even death, requires a different set of clothes. Ask yourself how you respond to someone in a three-piece suit versus someone in overalls. Some department stores have found that sales increase when the male sales staff wear shirts and ties instead of casual clothes. In one study, customers in a department store failed to notice shoplifting when it was being carried out by people in suits and ties, yet they watched and reported the pilferage when the subjects were dressed in jeans, sandals, and T-shirts.[7]

As you might suspect, we are not alone in our concern with how we look. As far back as the Upper Paleolithic period (about forty thousand years ago) our ancestors were using bone for necklaces and other bodily ornaments. From that period to the present there is historical and archaeological evidence of people's fixation with their bodies. They have painted them, fastened objects to them, dressed them, undressed them, and even deformed and mutilated them in the name of beauty. As the anthropologist Keesing has noted, "The use of the body for decoration appears to be a cultural universal."[8] But while it is a universal, it lends itself to an amazing variety of possibilities and variations. Face painting is still common in Africa, parts of Asia, and among some American Indian tribes. And of course women in the United States use lipstick and other "paints." Filing or knocking out of some teeth is a sign of distinction in scattered parts of Australia and Africa. The closest comparison we have in our culture is plastic surgery, which is also a form of altering one's natural appearance.

In each of these examples, and there are thousands more, the point is the same: Human beings cover, decorate, and even mutilate their bodies for a host of reasons. In intercultural communication, appearance and objects are important because the standards we apply and the judgments we make are subject to cultural variations. Let us develop this point so that you might be better able to detect how appearance functions in the intercultural context.

We have already seen that decisions regarding appearance are culturally based. In America, for example, we tend to value the appearance of the tall, slender woman. But in some European countries such an appearance signals weakness and frailty; heavier women are seen as more desirable. In Japan, diminutive females are deemed the most attractive.

Clothing, from uniforms to veils, is also part of a culture's communication system, and as such helps us understand both the messages and the value system of a culture. In Mexico, for instance, uniforms are a popular mode of dress. The police, the military, school children, and anyone else who gets the opportunity enjoys wearing a uniform as a way of reflecting group affiliation. Other cultures, however, have a different view of uniforms. In Israel, as a reaction to Nazism, uniforms are very unpopular. Americans traveling in Israel are often shocked when they see a group of Israeli soldiers dressed in everything from short pants to T-shirts with the Batman logo.

In much of the world people still dress in what we perceive as traditional garments. Robes and veils are part of the attire for much of the Arab world. Women in those areas dress in clothing that covers most of their bodies. This is an expression of the cultural value of modesty. Recently, Princess Diana of England committed a cultural blunder while visiting Kuwait: During a formal dinner she revealed a portion of her uncovered legs.

The influence of culture on appearance and dress is often so subtle that we tend to overlook its significance. Even within co-cultures, nonverbal communication has nuances that help define these co-cultures. Some writers contend that differences in women's and men's clothing in the United States are due to more than physical differences. The male-dominated culture, goes the argument, has since the Victorian period encouraged women to wear clothing that restricts their movements, limits their activity, and produces an image of submissiveness and frailty.[9]

We all know from personal experience that the color of someone's skin can influence how we perceive and communicate with him or her. This information often dictates eye contact, distance, and topic, and controls the amount of time we spend with the person. We end up allowing skin color to determine the messages we send and receive.

We conclude our discussion of appearance with this warning: Learn to be more tolerant of the external differences that confront you. What you might consider a costume and quite garish is very likely the native dress of a particular culture. Whether it be high leather boots, tennis shoes, or no shoes, we have learned to let these and other messages stand for the person. But remember, they are only part of the person. They are, in the final analysis, only cues that the individual gives off. We all are much more than we present.

Body Movements (Kinesics and Posture)

People have always known that action communicates. More than two hundred years ago Blaise Pascal wrote, "Our nature consists of motion; complete rest is death." We have now begun to make sense out of that motion. More specifically, studies in **kinesics** have begun to formally investigate and codify body movement. Kinesic cues are those visible body shifts and movements that can send messages that influence communication. This influence can be direct (holding up your palm and pointing it at someone to signal you want them to "stop") or indirect (fiddling with coins and keys in your pocket as a sign of nervousness). In most instances, however, our actions are but part of the total communication encounter and work in combination with other nonverbal cues and even with our words.

The study of kinesics is based on two important assumptions that link movement to communication. These assumptions are important for our purposes because, with only slight variations, all human beings consciously and unconsciously utilize movement in a similar manner.

First, every movement conveys information about the psychological and/or physical states of the person, regardless of that person's culture. A bow, wave, pointed finger, or yawn all have purpose. Although the person who perceives these actions may not always be aware of the reasons behind these movements, they are all related to some internal state. Our movements, with the exception of those associated with certain illnesses, are never random; in a very real sense, they represent the inside "talking" to the outside. And just as significant, these actions reflect what is happening now. Be it turning away from someone we feel uncomfortable around or aimlessly shifting from leg to leg, each movement refers to whatever is happening at the moment. Because of this, it becomes crucial for us to interpret accurately the body movements of the people we are around—regardless of their culture.

Second, the ability to read meaning into movement is universal. Think for a moment of the long list of gestures and movements that you use and recognize each day as part of being in contact with others. You wave "good-bye" to a friend and use a different movement of the arm to wave "hello" to a family member as you arrive home, you point to the salt shaker at the table so that someone will hand it to you, you shrug your shoulders to tell someone "I don't know," you shake your head from side to side to say "no" and up and down to say "yes." In each of these instances you are using movement as a message.

With these assumptions of kinesics before us, we shall now examine a few of the more common body movements used in the United States and the reactions they elicit. Since scholars have suggested that we can make as many as 700,000 separate physical signs, any attempt at cataloging them would be frustrating and fruitless. Our purpose is simply to call your attention to some nonverbal messages that are common in North America.

One frequent use of movement is to express our attitudes towards others. A great deal of research indicates that when we signal, either intentionally or unintentionally, feelings of affiliation, friendship, warmth, and rapport, we will have more direct body orientation, lean forward with increased regularity, and be relaxed rather than stiff.[10]

Body movements may also indicate the intensity of an emotional state, particularly distress. The argument for the link between movement and emotional state is that each primary motive is linked to a distinctive pattern of behavior. These behaviors are basic to all of us. As we grow older and become enculturated, we usually learn to exercise some control over the outward signs of our emotions; however, the body always needs to "show" how it feels. A depressed mood, for example, seems to be revealed by fewer movements of head and hands but many leg movements. We often exhibit nervous states by fussing with objects such as rings, coins, and keys. Tapping and drumming with the fingers on the body or a table is another way we display tension.

Other movements occur while we talk or listen. These are the actions we engage in as a means of highlighting or underscoring our verbal messages. Visualize, for example, the kinds of hand gestures you have seen people use when uttering such statements as "Come closer," "Back up," and "Please get that snake out of here!" Notice how people's bodies move when they listen to an exciting story. We use all parts of our body to clarify spoken language or to provide feedback to the words of others.

Finally, we have all learned a long slate of physical acts that can fully take the place of spoken words. These are called **emblems.** Not only do emblems stand for a word or series of words; they also represent the type of movement that we most often employ with conscious intent. That is to say, when we fold our arms across our chest and tuck our head down we want the other person to know we are cold. Or if we hold up a tight fist we are trying to tell someone that the moment calls for a fight or challenge. Perhaps the most important characteristic of emblems, at least for our purposes, is that they are grounded in cultural experiences. In nearly all instances you need to be a member of the culture, or at least be familiar with the nonverbal language of that culture, in order to understand the gesture or movement being displayed.

Because cultural differences can cause many communication problems, we shall return to the use of emblems later in this chapter. For now we simply want to remind you that each culture displays certain unique aspects of movement and posture as part of its cultural experiences. To understand better both the movements and the experiences, let us now look at a few cultural differences in (1) posture and sitting behavior and in (2) movements of the body that convey specific meanings (gestures). Before we begin, we must point out once again that in most instances the messages the body generates operate in combination with other messages and are seldom as precise as our explanations make them seem. We usually smile and say "hello" to a friend at the same time. And in Mexico the multiple-messages concept is illustrated when asking someone to wait for "just a minute"(*Un momento, por favor*): The speaker also makes a fist and then extends the thumb and index finger so that they form a sideways letter *U*.

Posture and sitting habits offer insight into a culture's deep structure. In many Oriental cultures, the bow is much more than a greeting. It signifies that culture's concern with status and rank. Although it appears simple to the outsider, it is actually rather complicated. The person who occupies the lower station must begin the bow, and his or her bow is deeper than the other person's. The superior even determines when the bowing is to end. When the participants are of equal rank, they begin the bow in the same manner and end at the same time.

Even in the United States we can see how posture is tied to cultural attitudes. For instance, in the United States, where being casual and friendly is valued, people often fall into chairs and slouch when they stand. In many European countries, such as Germany, where lifestyles tend to be more formal, a slouching posture is considered a sign of rudeness and poor manners. For the native Hawaiian, it is bad manners to assume a stance with your arms behind your back or on the hips.

Cultures also differ in the body orientations they assume during communication. Anyone who has interacted with Arabs realizes that they use a very direct body orientation when communicating. The Chinese, on the other hand, tend to feel uncomfortable with this style and will normally carry out their business in a stance that is less direct.

The manner in which we sit can also be a type of communication. For example, North Americans seldom squat. Most settings, both public and private, have facilities for sitting. At home, at work, at Little League baseball fields, at parks, and at bus stops we can count on a place to sit. People in many countries, however, do not sit down to interact. In some rural parts of Mexico, for example, people squat more than they sit. As strange as it seems, the U.S. Border Patrol, being well aware of this cultural variation, uses the "squat" as a way of detecting illegal Mexican aliens. The patrol has spotter planes fly over the mountains of Southern California at low attitudes. From these elevations people in the planes can tell which group of campers are sitting and which are squatting, the assumption being that the squatters have entered the country illegally.

We can even observe variations in sitting behaviors in the simple act of what people do with their legs when in the company of others. In Japan people sit with both feet resting on the floor. People in Thailand believe that since the bottoms of the feet are the lowest part of the body, they should never be pointed in the direction of another person. In fact, for the Thai the feet take on so much significance that people avoid stomping them. So subtle are these cultural variations that the wife of a former president of the United States shocked her Arab hosts by crossing her legs during a public meeting. And in the Philippine Islands, by contrast, a young girl sitting with her legs apart is perceived as a prostitute.

Even within the United States there are slight yet significant differences in how people move, stand, and sit during interaction. Women in many settings will often hold their arms closer to their bodies than will men. They will also keep their legs closer together and seldom cross them in mixed company.

Our posture is not the only aspect of our bodies that sends messages. People throughout the world engage in countless actions that have communication significance. Noting just a few of these differences should help you appreciate the pull of culture on nonverbal communication.

As a preface to our discussion, keep in mind that thousands of cross-cultural examples prove that the meanings of many movements shift from culture to culture. An Arabic specialist once cataloged at least 247 separate gestures that the Arabs use to accompany speech.[11] And in a large study involving forty different cultures, Desmond Morris and his associates isolated twenty common hand gestures that had a different meaning in each culture.[12] Our gestures have so much potential for communication that the co-culture of the deaf in the United States has developed a rich and extensive series of gestures that they use to communicate. For example, to communicate "please," the gesture consists of rubbing the palm of an open hand in a circular motion over the heart. To ask the question "Where?" one shakes the extended index finger back and forth at the wrist, with the palm facing forward.

Many of the movements people engage in relate directly to attitudes that culture has passed on from generation to generation. In the United States, for example, we show status relationships in a variety of ways. We all know the rules for who goes through an open door first, or who sits or stands first. People in the Middle East indicate status nonverbally by which individual views one's back when one turns around. In Oriental cultures, backing out of a room is a sign of high rank among the participants. In the United States we might show humility by a slight downward bending of the head, but in many European countries one manifests humility by dropping one's arms and sighing. Samoans communicate humility by bending the body downward. And we are all aware of the different gestures for derision that Americans use. Some European cultures communicate this same attitude by closing the fist with the thumb protruding between the index and middle fingers. The Russians express this attitude by moving one index finger horizontally across the other.

As you can clearly see, even specific and often small movements of the hand and arm can send different messages, depending on the culture. In Jordan one might symbolize friendship by placing index fingers side by side. In Argentina one twists an imaginary mustache to signify that everything is okay. In the United States, "making a circle with one's thumb and index finger while extending the others is emblematic of the word 'OK'; in Japan (and Korea) it signifies 'money' (okane); and among Arabs this gesture is usually accompanied by a baring of teeth, and together they signify extreme hostility."[13] This same gesture has a vulgar connotation in Mexico, and to the Tunisian it means "I'll kill you."

Even the taken-for-granted signs we make for beckoning are culturally based. In the United States, when a person wants to signal a friend to come, he or she makes the gesture with one hand, fingers more or less together and turned upwards, with the hand making a clockwise motion. In Japan, when beckoning someone to approach, one extends the arm slightly upwards and cups the hand with fingers pointed down, while making a counterclockwise motion. When seeing this gesture, many Americans think that the Japanese person is waving good-bye. In parts of Burma the summoning gesture is made palm down, with the fingers moving as if one is playing the piano. And Filipinos often use a quick downward nod of the head to ask someone to "come here."

Farewell salutations and beckoning gestures are not the only movements that often change meanings across cultures. For example, head movements for acceptance and rejection take opposite forms in Thailand and the United States. Greeks express "yes" with a nod similar to the one used in the United States, yet when communicating "no," the person jerks his or her head back and raises the face. Lifting one or both hands up to the shoulders strongly emphasizes the "no."

Even the size, intensity, and frequency of our actions can be important in communication. Jews, Italians, Middle Easterners, and South Americans are quite animated when they interact. Many Americans, northern Europeans, and

Orientals perceive such energy quite differently, often equating vigorous action with a lack of manners and restraint.

Although we have focused on cultural differences, people throughout the world share thousands of gestures and movements. For example, gestures as obvious as pointing to an object seldom call for an interpreter. One study even suggested that many of the nonverbal messages used in flirting and courting are performed almost universally. Showing sexual interest in Dublin or Mexico City seems to produce the same mannerisms. We point this out so that you will keep in mind that intercultural communication involves understanding the similarities as well as the differences found in nonverbal communication.

Facial Expressions

At one time or another most of us have been intrigued by how the looks on other people's faces have influenced our reactions to these people. The early Greek playwrights and the traditional Kabuki dancers of Japan were keenly aware of the shifts in mood and meaning that facial expressions conveyed. Both approaches to drama used masks and extensive makeup to demonstrate changes in each actor's character and attitude. In a very real sense, when it comes to using our faces, we are all actors—we all put on a variety of masks. To quote the poet T. S. Eliot, we "put on a face to meet the faces that we meet."

The mask analogy is a good one to keep in mind as we explore facial cues. Earlier in this chapter we considered unintentional messages when we noted that at times people find meaning in our behavior when we are not consciously communicating. This is especially true for facial cues. As part of our genetic package each of us acquires a face—a mask, if you will. This face is part of us; it goes where we go and greatly influences how people respond to us. We can manipulate it to let others know how we feel and what we are thinking. It also may send messages that we did not want to send. It is capable of looking happy when we are not happy, and sad when we are not sad.

As we have mentioned, we can alter our facial expressions in countless ways, and of course gravity, illness, and age make other changes. Some of these changes are micro-momentary expressions that are so fleeting that they register only on the subconscious level. Others are momentary—wrinkling the nose, biting the lips, sniffing, yawning, or grimacing. And some last longer, such as a smile or rolling the tongue inside the mouth. Even our wrinkles or our paleness has the potential to be a message.

You can better understand the place of facial expressions in communication if you remember that our interpretation of any action is based on two factors. First, people are more apt to interpret facial expressions correctly if they take the communication context into account. As we have said throughout this book, communication does not take place in a vacuum. The same facial expression may have different meanings at home, at an informal party, at work, or on a date. If someone showed us a photograph of a person's face, with no hint of the context in which the photograph was taken, would we feel confident about guessing what the expression meant? To be accurate in our interpretation we should know what words, if any, were being spoken just prior to the expression. It would also be helpful if we had access to the other nonverbal messages being sent. Were the parties touching, moving, exchanging gifts?

A second consideration focuses on what is referred to as the perceived relationship between the communication participants. What this means is that each of us uses a host of idiosyncratic expressions that make sense only to people who know us. A person may wrinkle his or her nose out of habit instead of as an expression of aversion or disgust, but only those people who know this idiosyncrasy will correctly read the facial expression.

The importance of facial expressions in communication is well established; however, the intercultural implications of these expressions are more difficult to assess. The reason for this difficulty centers around a lingering academic debate. At the core of the argument lies this question: Is there a nearly universal language of facial expressions? One position holds that anatomically similar expressions may occur in everyone, but the meanings people attach to them differ from culture to culture.[14] The majority thesis, which we introduced earlier in the chapter, is that there are universal facial expressions and that people have similar meanings for these expressions. Ekman has clearly stated this point of view: "The subtle creases of a grimace tell the same story around the world, to preliterate New Guinea tribesmen, to Japanese and American college students alike. Darwin knew it all along, but now here's hard evidence that culture does not control the face."[15]

Both positions agree that specific cultural norms often dictate how and when facial expressions are displayed. Even what calls forth a specific expression is related to our cultural experiences. For example, not all cultures have the same definition of what is humorous. What produces a smile in one culture may yield a frown in another culture. Cultures that value the elderly would not find jokes about old people the least bit amusing. The reason for these variations is simple: We learn the rules that govern the use of facial expressions during childhood, and they become habits, learned to the point of being a reflex action and outside of awareness.

Cultural differences in the unmasking of the face are important enough for us to pause for a moment and develop this point in a little more detail. In many Mediterranean cultures, people exaggerate signs of grief or sadness. It is not uncommon in this region of the world to see men crying in public. Yet in the United States white males, at least, suppress the display of these emotions. Japanese men even go so far as to hide expressions of anger, sorrow, or disgust by laughing or smiling. In one study, Japanese and American subjects revealed the same facial expressions when viewing a stress-inducing film while they were alone. Yet in the presence of others the Japanese manifested only neutral facial expressions. The Chinese are yet another cultural group that does not readily show emotion. Chinese children, for example, are conditioned to use the face to conceal rather than reveal emotion. The Oriental concept of "saving face" is an extension of this attitude.

Even within a culture, there are groups that use facial expressions in a manner that differs from that of the dominant culture. Hopi Indians, for example, tend to be less dramatic in the way they express themselves, and as such are not as animated as the non-Indian population.

There are also gender differences in the use of the face. Summarizing the research on these differences, Pearson notes that compared to men, women use more expressions and are more expressive, smile more, and are apt to return a smile more when someone smiles at them.[16]

Eye Contact and Gaze

In drama, fiction, poetry, or real life, eyes have always been a fascinating topic. From Shakespeare's "Thou tell'st me there is murder in mine eye," to Bob Dylan's "Your eyes said more to me that night than your lips would ever say," to the musical ballad "Your lips tell me no, no, but there's yes, yes in your eyes," the eyes have always communicated. Even "the evil eye" is more than just an expression. In one study, Roberts examined 186 cultures throughout the world and found that 67 of them had some belief in the evil eye.[17]

The number of messages we can send with our eyes is almost limitless. We have all heard some of the following words used to describe a person's eyes: direct, sensual, sardonic, expressive, intelligent, penetrating, sad, cheerful, worldly, hard, trusting, or suspicious. The meaning of a glance can range from inauspiciousness to downright rudeness. The quantity and quality of our interpersonal relationships are affected by our establishing eye contact, avoiding eye contact, looking downcast, shifting our eyes, squinting, staring straight ahead, or even closing our eyes. According to Leathers, there is ample evidence to conclude that in North America the eyes serve six important communication functions. They "(a) indicate degrees of attentiveness, interest, and arousal; (b) influence attitude change and persuasion; (c) regulate interaction; (d) communicate emotions; (e) define power and status relationships; and (f) assume a central role in impression management."[18]

Most people, regardless of the culture, use eye contact and gaze basically for the same reason: to see whom we are with so that we can adapt our behavior as needed. Once we grant this common characteristic of eye contact, we are prepared to examine a number of instances in which one's cultural experiences *alter* the use of eye contact and gaze.

Most studies, as well as our personal observations, tell us that culture modifies how much eye contact we engage in and who is the recipient of the eye contact. People in Western societies expect the person they are interacting with to "look them in the eye." There is even a tendency to be suspicious of someone who does not follow the culturally prescribed rules for eye contact. Direct eye-to-eye contact is not a custom throughout the world. In Japan, for example, children learn to direct their gaze at the region of their superior's Adam's apple or tie knot.[19] As a result, when Japanese people communicate, they will not use eye behavior in the same way as the English or Americans. You can appreciate some of the potential problems when Westerners attempt to do business with a group of people who believe it is a sign of disrespect to hold prolonged eye contact with their communication partners.

The Japanese are not the only people who learn to avoid sustained and direct eye contact. The Chinese, Indonesians, and rural Mexicans will also lower their eyes as a sign of deference, and believe that too much eye contact is a sign of bad manners. Arabs, on the other hand, look directly into the eyes of their communication partner, and do so for long periods of time. They believe that such contact shows interest in the other person and also helps assess the truthfulness of the words the other is speaking. The desire to use the eyes to evaluate honesty has led to a series of stories of how Turkish rug merchants and Las Vegas gamblers use pupil size to read the minds of their clients.

Eye behavior is so important in Korean culture that Koreans even have a special word (*nuichee*) to underscore its importance. Koreans believe that the eyes have the "real" answers to what a person is feeling and thinking.

A culture's male-female relationships also help determine customs of eye contact and gaze. In many Asian and Arab cultures it is considered taboo for women to look straight into men's eyes. Most men, out of respect for this custom, do not stare directly at women. This is a stark contrast to men in France and Italy, who stare at women in public. In North America the prolonged stare is often a part of the nonverbal code that the co-culture of the male homosexual employs. An extended stare at a member of the same sex, at least in the United States, is often perceived as sexually suggestive and as a signal of interest.

A few other differences in the use of eye contact in the United States are worthy of our consideration. For example, many American Indians have an impression of eye contact that is often at odds with the dominant culture. The Hopi interprets direct eye contact as offensive and will usually avoid any type of staring. The Navajo dislike unbroken eye contact so strongly that they have incorporated it into their creation myth. The myth, which tells the story of a "terrible monster called He-Who-Kills-With-His Eyes," teaches the Navajo child that "a stare is literally an evil eye and implies a sexual and aggressive assault."[20]

Differences in the use of eye contact also characterize communication between black and white Americans. When speaking, blacks use much more continuous eye contact than do whites. Yet the reverse is true when blacks are listening. That is to say, whites make more continuous eye contact when they are listening than do blacks. This difference is even more pronounced among black children who are "socialized into *not* looking when being spoken to."[21]

There are also gender variations in how people use their eyes to communicate. Studies on gender differences have established that women look more at their communication partner than men do, look at one another more, hold eye contact longer, and appear to value eye contact more than men do.[22]

So delicate is our use of eye contact that we seldom realize the modifications we make. For example, next time you are talking with a disabled person, perhaps someone in a wheelchair, notice how little eye contact you make with him or her as compared to with someone who is not disabled.

Touch

Just as our words and movements are messages about what we are thinking and feeling, so touch, too, conveys our internal experiences. The meanings we assign to being touched, and our reasons for touching others, help us gain insight into the communication encounter. As the character Holden Caulfield so aptly notes in the American classic *The Catcher in the Rye:*

> I held hands with her all the time. This doesn't sound like much, but she was terrific to hold hands with. Most girls if you hold hands with them their goddamn hand dies, or else they think they have to keep moving their hand all the time, as if they were afraid they'd bore you or something.[23]

Touch is the earliest sense to mature; it manifests itself in the final embryo stage and comes into its own long before eyes, ears, and the higher brain centers begin to work. Soon after birth, infants also employ all of their other senses as a way of interpreting reality. During the same period, they are highly involved with touching other people. They are being nuzzled, cuddled, cleaned, patted, kissed, and in many cases breast-fed. Tennessee Williams eloquently expressed the power and importance of touch when he wrote, "Devils can be driven out of the heart by the touch of a hand on a hand, or a mouth on a mouth."

As we move from infancy into childhood in North America, significant changes take place that influence our use of touch. First, touch becomes less important than sound and sight as a way of sending and receiving messages. People point to objects and talk to children instead of touching the children. Second, a type of socialization sets in: We learn the rules of touch. We are taught whom to touch and where we can touch. Phrases such as *Don't do that* and *That's not nice* mark the territory of touch. A new set of cultural rules and a new emphasis on other modes of communication replace childhood desires to touch and be touched.

By the time we reach adolescence, our culture has taught us how to communicate with touch. We learn we can shake hands with nearly everyone (making sure it is a firm shake), hug certain people (but not everyone with the same intensity), be intimate with still other people (knowing well in advance the zones of the body that we can touch), and make love to one person (being aware of the sexual regions defined by culture and sexual manuals).

The few existing studies on touch behavior in North American culture have uncovered some interesting findings. For example, a number of factors influence the meaning inferred from a touch. First is the mood or state we are in at the time of the touch. If we are crying when someone touches us, it has different meaning than when we are touched during a festive occasion. Second, our past helps define the contact. If we have grown up in a family that did not touch very much, we are apt to feel uncomfortable when another person touches us. Third, our perceived relationship with the toucher will affect the meaning we attach to the touch. We infer different meanings when we are stroked by a parent, friend, professor, employer, or lover. Fourth, even the duration of the touch alters the meaning. If someone shakes our hand but clutches it too long, the meaning of the touch can change. Fifth, how active or passive the touch is also influences meaning. A hand moving on one's back is very different from a patting motion or a hand that is stationary. Finally, the location of the touch (arm, leg, breast, face, and so on) will influence the meaning of the touch. Here again, each culture tells us precisely what it means when we touch which parts of the body.

We need only watch the news on television or stand at an international airport to know that there are major differences in how cultures use touch. Or we can ask ourselves how often we touch someone whose skin color differs from our own. Blacks in America "give skin" and "get skin," but they do not normally use "skinning" (touching) when greeting white people. And as we noted elsewhere, Muslims eat and engage in joyful activity with the right hand, but to touch another person with the left hand can be a social insult because the left hand is reserved for toilet functions.

The few studies that have been conducted on intercultural touching seem to support the preceding observations and generalizations. In a study of Arab and American student interactions, for example, only the Arab students touched.[24] Another study "noted that the French in their mental hospitals deliberately encourage touching, including massage, whereas body contact in American culture is generally limited to such acts as pulse taking."[25]

This last example illustrates a point we made earlier: that one's cultural experiences define even the location of a touch. For instance, in Thailand and in other places in Asia, the head is sacred and it is offensive to touch someone there. For Muslims the shoulder is an approved zone and is used for hugging—a sign of brotherhood. In Korea, on the other hand, young people are socially forbidden from touching the shoulders of their elders.

Even the simple act of kissing also has cultural overtones. While mouth-to-mouth kissing, as a sexual act, is common in most Western cultures, it is not widespread in the Orient. In fact, the Japanese have for centuries rhapsodized about the appeal of the nape of the neck as an erotic zone. The Japanese have no word for "kissing"—though they now have borrowed from the English language to produce the word *kissu*.

Why do the above variations exist? The answer to this question has been one of the major premises of this book. It is because culture teaches us how to use and how to interpret tactile behavior. Hence, cultural differences in the practice of this form of communication run the full spectrum from cultures that employ very little touching (British, North Americans, Japanese) to those that give full expression to tactile experiences (Latin Americans, Italians, eastern Europeans, Arabs, and so on).

Precise classifications, at least for our purposes, are not nearly as significant as the central idea that cultures use touch differently, and more importantly, that not knowing those differences can create problems. Imagine for a moment how easy it would be for someone from Latin America to find a North American somewhat remote, and even rude, because of his or her reluctance to be touched. This is not an improbable example, for in many parts of South America male friends will often walk arm-in-arm or holding hands.

Co-cultures also have established areas and various definitions for touching behavior. Homosexuals, at least those who have made their sexual preference public, tend to be much freer about touching their partners in the presence of others than are most white, middle-class Americans.

There are also gender differences in how individuals use touch to send messages. As Bates notes, "Much research has indicated that men touch women more than women touch men, both in work settings and in general social interaction."[26] From her research she has also concluded "that women initiate hugs and embraces far more often than men do, to other women, to men, and to children."[27]

Race is yet another determinant of touching behavior. Earlier in this section we referred to the black custom of "giving skin." In addition, a limited number of studies also reveal that black males touch each other more often than do white males. And one study has shown that "black females touch each other almost twice as often as white females."[28]

As we conclude this section on touch, keep in mind that tactile communication, like most other aspects of culture, does not happen by chance. There is a reason that collective cultures touch more than cultures that accent the importance of the individual. Living conditions, climate, economics, historical background, and the like also contribute to how a culture interacts with its own members and with outsiders. As we have stressed throughout this book, it is important to know the antecedents of a particular behavior as a first step to understanding the actual behavior.

Smell

Although we can all grant that vision and hearing receive most of our messages from the outside world, the sense of smell can also be a channel for eliciting meaning. As far back as we have recorded history, some cultures have been covering up one odor with another. Even today, Americans spend billions of dollars making certain that they as well as their surroundings exude the right smell. The reason is obvious—we all know that odor communicates. It communicates not only when we are face-to-face with another person, but it has the unique characteristic of being able to send, or sustain, a message even when the other person is not with us. That is to say, an odor can remain even after a person is gone. As Victor Hugo once noted, "Nothing awakens a reminiscence like an odor."

Smell, like touch, is one of our most basic modes of communication. Most animals use odor as a means of ascertaining the presence of their enemies, attracting the opposite sex, marking their territory, and identifying emotional states. Human beings, even with all the perfumes they use, still give off an odor when they are sexually aroused, and they produce yet another aroma when they are frightened.

Because odor sends a message, it has the potential to help or hinder communication. A number of elements affect the meaning we give to a smell: (1) the strength of the smell in relation to competing fragrances and odors

(French perfume versus an inexpensive after-shave lotion), (2) its distance from the other person, (3) the perceived relationship between the parties involved, (4) the context of the encounter, and (5) the past association we have had with the smell.

Culture influences each of these five variables. A few examples will help illustrate this point. In Bali, when lovers greet one another, they breathe deeply in a kind of friendly sniffing. The Burmese, Samoans, Mongols, Lapps, and some Philippine Islanders smell each others' cheeks to say "hello." It is not uncommon for young Filipino lovers to trade small pieces of clothing on parting, so that the smell of the other person will be a reminder of their affection towards each other. And in Japan, where smell is an important part of the culture, young girls will often play a game involving the placing of five fragrances in tiny boxes. The girl who identifies the most aromas wins the game.

The Chinese, as well as people in some other low-meat-consumption countries, feel that the odor of people from the United States is often offensive. This odor is created by the large amounts of meat we eat. On the other hand, Americans who visit Mainland China are often struck by the strong smell of pork throughout the country. The reason, of course, is that the Chinese eat tremendous amounts of pork.

We can assume from the above instances that there are often vast differences between cultures in their perceptions of odor. Americans are the most blatant example of a culture that is uncomfortable with natural smells. Many other cultures regard natural odors as normal, and most Arabs actually perceive smell as an extension of the person. As Hall notes:

> Olfaction occupies a prominent place in the Arab life. Not only is it one of the distance-setting mechanisms, but it is a vital part of the complex system of behavior. Arabs consistently breathe on people when they talk. However, this habit is more than a matter of different manners. To the Arab good smells are pleasing and a way of being involved with each other. To smell one's friends is not only desirable, for to deny him your breath is to act ashamed. Americans, on the other hand, trained as they are not to breathe in people's faces, automatically communicate shame in trying to be polite.[29]

As with all of our other categories of nonverbal messages, not knowing cultural variations in attitude toward smells can create uncertainty and even ill feeling. For example, recently a young couple from Iran was asked to disembark from an American airplane because other passengers had complained of how they smelled.

Paralanguage

We have all attended, at one time or another, the showing of a foreign film with English subtitles. During those intervals when the subtitles were not on the screen, we heard the actors uttering an unfamiliar language but could still understand what was happening just from the *sound* of the voices. Perhaps we inferred that the performers were expressing anger, sorrow, joy, or any of a number of other emotions. Maybe the sound of the voices could even tell us who the hero was and who was cast in the role of the villain. The rise and fall of voices may have also told us when one person was asking a question and another was making a statement or issuing a command. Whatever the case, certain vocal cues provided us with information with which to make judgments about the character's personality, emotional state, and rhetorical activity. To be sure, we could only guess at the exact meaning of the words being spoken, but sound variations still told us a great deal about what was going on. As an advertisement for phone service declared: "Maybe his voice will give us a clue. Let's talk to him by long distance."

What we have just been considering is often referred to as **paralanguage,** which involves the linguistic elements of speech—how something is said, not the actual meaning of the spoken words. Most classifications indicate that paralanguage consists of three kinds of vocalizations: (1) vocal characterizers (laughing, crying, yelling, moaning, whining, belching, yawning); (2) vocal qualifiers (volume, pitch, rhythm, tempo, resonance, tone); and (3) vocal segregates ("un-huh," "shh," "uh," "oooh," "mmmh," "humm").

As we have already noted, it is extraordinary how many inferences about content and character we can make just from the sounds people produce. For example, paralanguage cues assist us in drawing conclusions about an individual's emotional state, socioeconomic status, height, weight, sex, age, intelligence, race, regional background, and educational level.

As with all other aspects of our nonverbal behavior, culture also influences our use of paralanguage. We only have to look at differences in the use of volume to see the sway of culture on communication. Arabs speak very loudly. Loudness for this culture connotes strength and sincerity, and to speak softly implies that one is frail. The Thai people, as well as people from the Philippines, on the other hand, speak so softly that it almost sounds as if they are whispering. Yet for them a soft voice reflects good manners and education. When interacting with Americans, people from cultures that speak softly often believe the Americans are angry or upset because of their relatively loud speech.

There are also cultural differences in the rate at which people speak. Jews, Arabs, and Italians tend to speak much faster than do the English. Often these discrepancies in rate make people feel uncomfortable.

As we noted earlier in this section, paralanguage consists of much more than volume and rate. The "noise" we make also carries meaning. The Maasai, for example, utilize a number of sounds that have special significance, the most common one being the "eh" sound. This sound, which the Maasai draw out, can have a host of meanings. It can mean "yes," "I understand," or "continue." In Kenya the "iya" sound tells the other person that everything is okay; in Jamaica the "kissing" or "sucking" sound expresses anger, exasperation, or frustration.

Even laughing and giggling send different messages depending on the culture. Although smiling and laughing are signs of joy in all cultures, the Japanese often laugh to hide displeasure, anger, sorrow, and embarrassment.

As with all other forms of nonverbal actions, there are also co-cultural differences in the use of paralanguage. Not only are there the obvious idiosyncrasies with regard to group and regional dialects, but co-cultures can use sound in more subtle ways. For example, white and black children tend to pause at different intervals in conversation. "White children pause at the beginning of clauses or before conjunctions, while black children pause whenever a significant change in pitch occurs. Sometimes these pauses by black children are within clauses."[30]

Differences in paralanguage also mark the communication patterns of males and females. Men tend to speak more loudly and in a lower pitch than women. They are also less expressive and are more likely to drop the *ing* endings from their words.

SUMMARY

The Importance of Nonverbal Communication

- We make important judgments and decisions about others based on their nonverbal behavior.

- We use the actions of others to learn about their emotional states.

- Like culture, nonverbal communication is invisible, omnipresent, and learned.

Defining Nonverbal Communication

- Nonverbal communication is all stimuli (except verbal) within a communication setting, generated by both the individual and his or her use of the environment, that have potential message value for both sender and receiver.

- There are both intentional and unintentional nonverbal messages.

Functions of Nonverbal Communication

- Nonverbal communication has five basic functions: to *repeat, complement,* and *contradict* what we have said; to *substitute* for a verbal action; to *regulate* a communication event.

Verbal and Nonverbal Symbol Systems

- Verbal and nonverbal communication are similar in that both use symbols, both are products of an individual, and both involve someone attaching meaning to the symbols someone else has produced.

- They are different in terms of biology, the degree to which units are linked together, and the stage in life when these two systems are learned.

Nonverbal Communication: Guidelines and Limitations

• Students of nonverbal communication must avoid overgeneralizing. They should not assume that all actions are part of a culture's everyday repertory, they should avoid overemphasizing differences in nonverbal behavior, and they should not forget that nonverbal behavior seldom occurs in isolation.

Nonverbal Communication and Culture

• Nonverbal communication and culture are similar in that they are both learned, passed on from generation to generation, and involve shared understandings.

• Studying nonverbal behavior can lead to the discovery of a culture's underlying attitudes and values.

• Studying nonverbal behavior can also assist us in isolating our own ethnocentrism.

Body Behavior

• Nonverbal messages are communicated by means of body movements (kinesics and posture), dress, facial expressions, eye contact, touch, smell, and paralanguage.

ACTIVITIES

1. Ask your informant to show you examples of his or her culture's use of communicative body movements (kinesics). What similarities are there between your culture and your informant's? What differences are there? What are the potential areas for misunderstanding?

2. In small groups, make an inventory of North American emblems. An example of an emblem is the "OK" gesture: the thumb and forefinger of one

hand form an O, and the rest of the fingers on that hand arch above the O. This gesture can fully take the place of the word OK. What other gestures can you think of like this one? Compare your findings with the rest of the class and make a master list.

DISCUSSION IDEAS

1. In what situations might you need to interpret the nonverbal behavior of someone from another culture? What problems could arise from not being aware of the differences in nonverbal behavior in these situations?

2. Give your culture's interpretation of the following nonverbal actions:
   - Two people are speaking loudly, waving their arms, and using a lot of gestures.
   - A customer in a restaurant waves his hand over his head and snaps his fingers loudly.
   - An elderly woman dresses entirely in black.
   - A young man dresses entirely in black.
   - An adult pats a child's head.
   - Two men kiss in public.

3. How can studying the intercultural aspects of nonverbal behavior assist you in discovering your own ethnocentrism? Give personal examples.

NOTES FOR CHAPTER 7

1. Dean C. Barnlund, *Interpersonal Communication: Survey and Studies* (Boston: Houghton Mifflin, 1968), 536–37.

2. Judee K. Burgoon, David B. Buller, and W. Gil Woodall, *Nonverbal Communication: The Unspoken Dialogue* (New York: Harper and Row, 1989), 9–10.

3. Edward T. Hall, *The Silent Language* (New York: Fawcett Publications, 1959), 10.

4. Paul Ekman, Wallace V. Friesen, and Phoebe Ellsworth, *Emotion in the Human Face* (New York: Pergamon Books, 1971). See also Paul Ekman, Richard Sorenson, and Wallace V. Friesen, "Pan-Cultural Elements in Facial Displays of Emotion," *Science* 64 (1969), 86–88.

5. Erving Goffman, *The Presentation of Self in Everyday Life* (New York: Doubleday, 1957), 2.

6. Ellen Berscheid and Elaine Walster, "Beauty and the Best," *Psychology Today* 5 (March 1972), 42–46.

7. Flora Davis, *Inside Intuition* (New York: Signet, 1975), 177.

8. Felix Keesing, *Cultural Anthropology: The Science of Custom* (New York: Holt, Rinehart, and Winston, 1965), 203.

9. Helene Roberts, "The Exquisite Slave: The Role of Clothes in the Making of the Victorian Woman," *Signs* 2 (1977), 554–69.

10. Burgoon, Buller, and Woodall, 323.

11. "Arabic: The Medium Clouds the Message," *Los Angeles Times*, Feb. 12, 1977, sec. I.

12. Desmond Morris, Peter Collett, Peter Marsh, and Marie O'Shaughnessy, *Gestures: Their Origins and Distribution* (New York: Stein and Day, 1979).

13. Robert G. Harper, Arthur N. Wiens, and Joseph D. Matarazzo, *Nonverbal Communication: The State of the Art* (New York: Wiley, 1978), 164.

14. Davis, p. 47. See also, Ray L. Birdwhistell, *Kinesics and Context* (Philadelphia: University of Pennsylvania Press, 1970).

15. Paul Ekman, "Face Muscles Talk Every Language," *Psychology Today* 9 (Sept. 1975), 35–39.

16. Judy Cornelia Pearson, *Gender and Communication* (Dubuque, IA: Wm. C. Brown, 1985), 250.

17. "The Evil Eye: A Stare of Envy," *Psychology Today* 11 (Dec. 1977), 154.

18. Dale Leathers, *Successful Nonverbal Communication: Principles and Applications* (New York: Macmillan, 1986), 42.

19. Helmut Morsbach, "Aspects of Nonverbal Communication in Japan," in *Intercultural Communication: A Reader*, 3d ed., ed. Larry A. Samovar and Richard E. Porter (Belmont, CA: Wadsworth, 1982), 308.

20. "Understanding Culture: Don't Stare at a Navajo," *Psychology Today* 8 (June 1974), 107.

21. Marianne LaFrance and Clara Mayo, *Moving Bodies: Nonverbal Communication in Social Relationships* (Monterey, CA: Brooks/Cole, 1978), 188.

22. Barbara Westbrook Eakins and R. Gene Eakins, *Sex Differences in Human Communication* (Boston: Houghton Mifflin, 1978), 150–52.

23. J. D. Salinger, *The Catcher in the Rye* (New York: Grosset and Dunlap, 1945), 103.

24. O. M. Watson and T. D. Graves, "Quantitative Research in Proxemic Behavior," *American Anthropologist* 68 (1966), 971–85.

25. Harper, Wiens, and Matarazzo, 297.

26. Barbara Bates, *Communication and the Sexes* (New York: Harper and Row, 1988), 60.

27. Bates, 62.

28. Leathers, 138–39.

29. Edward T. Hall, *The Hidden Dimension* (New York: Doubleday, 1966), 149.

30. Burgoon, Buller, and Woodall, 202.

Time and space are fragments of the infinite for the use of finite creatures.

AMIEL

There is no such thing as an empty space or an empty time. There is always something to see, something to hear. In fact, try as we may to make silence, we cannot.

JOHN CAGE

CHAPTER EIGHT

NONVERBAL COMMUNICATION: THE MESSAGES OF SPACE, TIME, AND SILENCE

In the last chapter we focused on nonverbal messages that grow out of our actions and the actions of others. More specifically, we looked at how the body "talks." In this chapter we shall be concerned with how people employ space, time, and silence as a way of communicating. Although these variables are *external* to the communicator, they are nevertheless utilized and manipulated in a way that sends a message to other people. For example, imagine your reaction to someone who stands too close to you, arrives late for an important appointment, or remains silent after you reveal some personal information. In each of these instances you

213

would find yourself reading meaning into how your communication partner used space, time, and silence. These three factors convey meaning in much the same way that words convey meaning—they tell you something about how the other person perceives you and the setting you are both sharing. Understanding the impact of space, time, and silence on communication, and how cultures use them differently, should help you understand your own behavior and the behavior of others.

SPACE AND DISTANCE

The flow and shift of distance between the people we interact with is as much a part of the communication experience as the words we exchange. Notice how we might allow one person to stand very close to us but keep yet another at a safe range. What we are doing with these reactions is using space and distance to convey messages. The study of this message system, called **proxemics,** is concerned with such things as our personal space, seating, and furniture arrangement. Let us look at all three of these areas and attempt to point out the impact they have on intercultural communication.

Personal Space

Our **personal space,** that piece of the universe we occupy and call our own, is contained within an invisible boundary surrounding our body. As the "owner" of this area we usually decide who can enter and who can't. When our space is invaded, we react in a variety of ways. We back up and retreat, stand our ground as our hands become moist from nervousness, or sometimes even react violently. Our specific response is a manifestation of both our personality and our cultural background. A study of social distance between "gays" and "straights," for example, explored attitudes regarding homosexuals. The researchers found that "straight" students sat farther away from their communication partners when they perceived them to be "gay."[1] In a more symbolic way, the Great Wall of China also manifests a cultural attitude. The wall, intended to keep out "the barbarians," was a statement to the world that China wanted to be left alone. As we weave our way through this portion of the book, you will find that nearly all cultural responses to space are simply extensions of deep-seated cultural attitudes and values. Cultures that stress the individual (England, the United

States, Australia) demand more space than do communal cultures (Latin America, Israel).

Many cultures associate space and values with each other. In some Asian cultures, for example, students do not sit close to their teachers or stand near their bosses; the extended distance demonstrates deference and esteem. Extra interpersonal distance is also part of the cultural experience of the people of Scotland and Sweden—to them it reflects privacy. In cultures such as Greece and Italy, where privacy is less important, people demand less space.

In most instances, the participants in a communication encounter are not even aware of the cultural rules that govern how they respond to and use space. Without ever having to articulate their feelings, they seem to know that space and territory express attitudes regarding status, dominance, affection, and attraction. As we noted earlier, we learn the guidelines that govern our use of space as part of our cultural package; therefore, these guidelines shift from culture to culture. Many eastern Europeans have an entirely different concept of public space than do North Americans. The European will stand very close to a stranger, while the American sees this as a violation of personal "territorial rights."

Another interesting contrast can be seen in the distance between opposite-sex mates in various cultures. In most Western countries, a husband and wife signal their relationship by walking side-by-side. They share personal space. But Sudanese Arab men have their wives walk a few steps behind them. The wife may not even sit beside her husband at mealtime, for the man's personal space is his alone.

In some Middle Eastern countries, we can find ourselves subject to continual shoving and crowding on buses and in most public places, for these cultures demand very little social distance. They have learned unique orientations towards space and privacy. A mixing of these orientations can cause communication problems. In England, for example, a country where people queue up (form lines) for just about everything, Arabs are perceived as rude when they thrust their way to the front of lines.

Seating

Culture influences even the manner in which we organize our seating. Notice, for example, that North Americans, when in groups, tend to talk with those opposite them rather than those seated or standing beside them. This pattern also influences how we select leaders when in groups. In most instances, the person sitting at the head of the table is chosen to be leader. In American groups, leaders usually are accustomed to being somewhat removed physically from the rest of the group, and consequently choose chairs at the ends of the table.

In Chinese culture seating arrangements take on different meanings. The Chinese experience alienation and uneasiness when they face someone directly or sit on opposite sides of a desk or table from someone. It makes them feel as if they are on trial.

In Korea, seating arrangements reflect status and role distinctions. In a car, office, or home, the seat at the right is considered the seat of honor. The Japanese also use seating order as a way of marking rank and order. The most important person sits at one end of the rectangular table, with those nearest in rank at the right and left of this "senior" position. The lowest in class is nearest to the door and at the opposite end of the table from the person with the most authority.

Furniture Arrangement

Furniture arrangement is yet another form of communication—and another form that shifts from culture to culture. In a courtroom in the United States, the witness's chair faces outward, as a nonverbal reminder to the person in the stand that he or she is facing the community—the witness's peers. In Europe the witness's chair often faces the judge, the person to whom the witness must answer.

Furniture arrangement within the home also communicates something about the culture. For example, people from France, Italy, and Mexico who visit the United States are often surprised to see that the furniture in the living room is pointed towards the television set. People from these three cultures believe that conversation is important, and that facing chairs toward a television screen can stifle conversation. In their countries furniture is positioned to encourage interaction, not discourage it.

Even the arrangement of office furniture gives us a clue to the character of a people. In countries that are authoritarian, such as Germany and the Soviet Union, most offices are planned so that business is conducted with the person in power sitting behind a desk. Bankers, lawyers, and government officials seldom venture from the position of power. In cultures that are informal (Mexico, Greece, Israel), where being comfortable is a cultural value, the desk is perceived as a hindrance to communication and visitors often sit to one side of the desk so that it does not serve as a barrier. American business executives have often returned from certain Middle Eastern countries and complained about the discomfort they felt in having to sit on the floor.

Co-cultures also have their own unique use of space. Prostitutes, for example, are very possessive of their territory. When they mentally mark an area as their own, even though it may be a public street, they behave as if it were their private property, and other prostitutes had better keep away. In prisons, where space is limited, controlled, and at a premium, space and territory are crucial forms of communication. New inmates quickly learn the culture of prison by learning about the use of space. They learn that there are rules for entering another cell, that space reduction is a form of punishment, and that lines form for nearly all activities.

Our use of space often indicates our attitude toward the person with whom we are sharing that space. One study, for example, found that when whites spoke to blacks they maintained greater distance than when they spoke to other whites.[2] Many studies have also revealed how men and women use space as a gauge to evaluate preeminence. Women normally allow both men and other women to stand closer to them than do men. Summarizing other gender differences in the use of space, Leathers has noted:

> Men use space as a means of asserting their dominance over women, as in the following: (a) they claim more personal space than women; (b) they more actively defend violations of their territories—which are usually much larger than the territories of women; (c) under conditions of high density, they become more aggressive in their attempts to regain a desired measure of privacy; and (d) men more frequently walk in front of their female partner than vice versa.[3]

So far we have stressed that there are certain consistent patterns in the use of space among members of a particular culture. Edward T. Hall isolated some of these consistencies, at least among the people of North America. He developed a model of personal space and distance (see Table 8-1) that focuses on basic communication distances used in business and social relations. Because people treat social distance according to their cultural experiences, Hall's analysis is of added interest for intercultural communication. Although he made his initial observations a number of years ago, current research tends to support his

Table 8-1
American Cultural Interpersonal Distances for
Various Categories of Interaction

Distance	Type of Encounter	Voice Volume
Very close (3 in. to 6 in.)	Awareness of physical involvement. Love-making, comforting and protecting.	Soft whisper
Close (8 in. to 12 in.)	Details of face are easily visible. Highly personal, seldom used in public.	Audible whisper, very confidential
Near (12 in. to 20 in.)	Can hold and grasp the other person. Many dyadic social interactions occur.	Indoors, soft voice; outdoors, full voice
Neutral (20 in. to 36 in.)	Others keep at arm's length. Most common distance for social conversation.	Soft voice, low volume
Neutral (4 1/2 ft. to 5 ft.)	Most social gatherings and business transactions.	Full voice
Public distance (5 1/2 ft. to 8 ft.)	Business and social discourse more formal. Desks in offices are placed to hold off visitors.	Full voice with slight overloudness
Across the room (8 ft. to 20 ft.)	Used by teachers or speakers at public gatherings.	Loud voice talking to a group
Far distances (20 ft. and more)	Public speaking by public figures.	Hailing distances, public address systems

SOURCE: Edward T. Hall, The Silent Language (New York: Fawcett, 1959).

findings. His scheme serves as an excellent conclusion to this section in that it provides a basis for comparing North American patterns with those of other cultures.

TIME

When Shakespeare wrote, "The inaudible and noiseless foot of Time," he was reminding us of what we all know but often overlook—that although we can't hold or see time, we all respond to it as if it had control over our lives. Because time is such a personal phenomenon, all of us perceive and treat it in a manner that expresses part of our character. If we arrive thirty minutes late for an important appointment and offer no apology, we send certain messages about ourselves.

Cultures also present clues about their temperament by the way they conceive of time. In North America we hear people saying, "He who hesitates is lost," while Chinese all know the Confucian proverb "Think three times before you act." Reflect for a moment on how each of these cultures would perceive time differently.

Although the rules for the use of time might appear natural and automatic, all members of each culture know their application. Let us become acquainted with some of these rules so that we might have a better idea of how they differ from culture to culture. A culture's conception of time can be examined in a number of ways. One includes the basic categories of *formal* and *informal time*.[4]

Formal Time

Formal time involves basic relationships, like learning the numbers of weeks and days in a year. It also includes our outlook toward seasons of the year. Cultural differences regarding the seasons range from the obvious fact that not all cultures use the same calendar, to more subtle differences regarding a culture's view of nature and its impact on formal time. For example, many American Indians use only "phases of the moon, summer and winter solstices, or the fall and spring equinoxes as formal time systems."[5] For the Navajo Indian the shortest measure of time is one day. Only those who have adapted to the ways of the dominant culture calibrate hours, minutes, or seconds.

Informal Time

Informal time has greater implications for human interaction than formal time does. The importance of this category stems from the fact that most of the rules for informal time are not explicitly taught, and usually function below the level of consciousness. Therefore, we must know something about the culture and the context if we hope to comprehend another individual's use of time. The phrase "I'll be home *in a while*" takes on many different meanings depending on the situation and the culture. Punctuality, waiting time, and pace are three good examples of how cultures vary in their use of informal time. Let us briefly look at each.

Argyle clearly illustrates differences in punctuality.

> How late is "late"? This varies greatly. In Britain and North America one may be 5 minutes late for a business appointment, but not 15 and certainly not 30 minutes late, which is perfectly normal in Arab countries. On the other hand in Britain it is correct to be 5–15 minutes late for an invitation to dinner. An Italian might arrive 2 hours late, an Ethiopian later, and a Javanese not at all—he had accepted only to prevent his host from losing face.[6]

Varying concepts of punctuality can also be seen when we compare the cultures of Latin America with Germany. In Latin America one is expected to arrive late to appointments as a sign of respect. This same tardiness would be perceived as rudeness in Germany.

Even our reaction to having to wait is rooted in our cultural experiences. In the United States we have all learned that the "boss" can arrive late for a meeting without anyone raising an eyebrow; if the secretary is late, he or she may receive a reprimand in the form of a stern glance. A rock star or a doctor can keep people waiting, but the warm-up band and the nurse had better be on time.

Cross-cultural differences in waiting time can create frustration and serious problems for those who don't understand that the use of time is a subjective matter. Many North Americans trying to do business in other countries often find that their view of waiting time is incompatible with that of executives from other parts of the world. They often grow impatient with what they perceive as wasted time. We seem to believe in the French proverb "Patience is the virtue of asses."

The Japanese and Chinese, on the other hand, handle time in ways that often appear at cross-purposes with American goals. A waiting period for the Japanese and Chinese can bring delays that run into years. What Americans perceive as procrastination is not a sign of lost interest but a reflection of that culture's view of time. Japan and China are not the only cultures that have different notions about waiting time than those found in Western cultures. In Saudi Arabia or Mexico, an American might find him- or herself sitting in an outer office waiting for hours for a "scheduled" meeting to begin.

We can also ascertain a culture's attitude towards time by examining the pace at which members of that culture perform certain acts and how individuals spend their time. Americans, for example, always seem to be in a hurry—there is always one more thing to do. From fast-food restaurants to microwave ovens, most of us live in the "fast lane." We all grow up hearing people say, "Time is money," and "Don't waste so much time." Other cultures see time differently, and hence live life at a different pace than do most people in the United States. Manifestations of pace take a host of forms. One study, for example, pointed out that even the speed at which people walked reflected a culture's concept of time. People from England and the United States move much faster than people from Taiwan and Indonesia.[7] In parts of Europe it is not uncommon for dinner to take three or four hours. And some tribal groups in Ecuador and Africa attach no urgency to any of the tasks they need to carry out. Because there are no clocks, the people eat, work, play, and sleep at their own pace.

Studying how a culture perceives and uses the concepts of past, present, and future can also offer insight into how that culture communicates. For example, past-oriented cultures such as the British place much emphasis on tradition and are often perceived as resisting change. A statement one often hears in England is "We have always done it this way." The Chinese, with their tradition of ancestor worship and their strong pride that their culture has endured for thousands of years, are yet another culture that uses the past as a guide to how to live in the present. The same, of course, can be said for American Indians, who also value tradition and refer to the past when confronting new situations. We must remember that many cultures, like the Greeks and Chinese, have histories that date back thousands of years, and therefore members of these cultures find it normal to take a long-range view of events. At times their view is so very long that they do not plan for the future.

Filipinos and Latin Americans perceive time from a present orientation, and they emphasize living for the moment. These cultures tend to be more impulsive and spontaneous than others, a tendency that contributes to a casual and relaxed lifestyle. This somewhat cavalier approach to life is often confusing to Westerners, who frequently misinterpret a concern with the present as a sign of indolence and inefficiency.

Cultures with a strong Islamic tradition, because they believe that future events belong to Allah, also tend to live in the present. They have little desire to chart events that they believe are out of their control. This orientation is summarized by the Turkish proverb "Today's egg is better than tomorrow's hen."

The third orientation, which puts great faith in the future, is the one that most North Americans take. As a people, we were not content with the original thirteen colonies. We continued to move west, and once we ran out of land we took to the skies, and from there to outer space. We are all taught to look forward to a future that is bigger and brighter than the present. We can hardly wait to finish what we are doing so that we can move on to something else, and then something else, and something else, and something else. . . . As we noted when we discussed pace, having an eye to the future often produces a very low tolerance for extensions and postponements. What we want, we want now, so we dispose of this moment and move on to the next.

Hindus, although their reasons might be different from those of North Americans, are yet another group that has a future orientation. To the Hindu, and to some degree the Buddhist, this life is one of many, so there is little need for elaborate plans.

A third classification of time as a form of communication is one the anthropologist Edward T. Hall advanced. Hall proposed that cultures organized time in one of two ways: They were either **monochronic** (M-time) or **polychronic** (P-time).[8] Although Hall did not intend these as either-or categories, they do offer two distinct approaches to time.

The first, M-time, is characteristic of northern Europe and North America. As Hall explains, "People of the Western world, particularly Americans, tend to think of time as something fixed in nature, something around us and from which we cannot escape; an ever-present part of the environment, just like the air we breathe."[9] As the word *monochronic* implies, this approach sees people doing one thing at a time. It also "emphasizes schedules, segmentation, and promptness."[10] We must not waste time; we must be doing something or we feel guilty. We behave as if time were tangible. We talk of "saving time," "losing time," or "killing time" as if it were a distinct entity. The clock and the calendar are important instruments for people who abide by this pattern. The time-clock records the hours we must work, the school bell moves us from class to class, and the calendar marks important days and events in our lives.

People from cultures that follow P-time live their lives quite differently than M-time people. P-time cultures, for example, deal with time holistically and place great stock in the activity occurring at that moment. Polychronic people, such as Arabs, Greeks, American Indians, Mexicans, and black Africans, stress people instead of schedules. They do not perceive appointments as iron-clad commitments and therefore often break them. For P-time cultures, time is less tangible and hence feelings of wasted time are not as prevalent as in M-time cultures. This leads, of course, to a lifestyle that is more spontaneous and random—characteristics that often confuse and frustrate Westerners.

Even within the United States there are co-cultures that perceive and use time differently than the dominant culture. Mexican-Americans frequently speak of Chicano time when their timing varies from the predominant Anglo culture. And blacks often use what is referred to as BPT (black people's time), or hang-loose time.[11] This outlook, which has its roots in the P-time cultures of Africa, maintains that priority belongs to what is happening at that instant. Statements such as "Hey, man, what's happenin'?" reflect the importance of the here and now. Prisoners use expressions like *doing a pound, doing time,* and *serving time,* which underscore the importance the clock and calendar hold in their lives.

All of the examples in this section show that a culture's treatment of time often reflects an important attitude or value of that culture. Therefore, understanding how people use time not only helps us comprehend the meaning of specific acts; it also assists us in gathering information about the deep structure of a culture.

SILENCE

The American writer and philosopher Henry David Thoreau once wrote, "In human intercourse the tragedy begins, not when there is misunderstanding about words, but when silence is not understood." His point is well taken and serves as an excellent introduction to this final section. For our position is simple: Silence sends us nonverbal cues concerning the communication situation we are in. Observe the poignant use of silence when the classical composer strategically places intervals of orchestration so that the ensuing silence marks a contrast in expression. Or someone says, "There was not even a sound, not any applause, only deafening and profound silence."

Silence cues, specifically, are all the nonverbal portions of an ongoing interaction in which silence affects the rate and flow of the concomitant verbal exchange. They include all the various kinds and degrees of silence: cold, oppressive, defiant, disapproving or condemning, calming, approving, humble, excusing, and consenting. Silence cues have a meaning all their own that supplements the other forms of human communication.

The meaning we assign to silence is contingent upon a number of factors. First, the duration of a silence can have a considerable effect on our response. If a professor asks a student a question, and that student takes a long time to answer, the duration of the silence will influence the entire situation. The professor, the student, and the other members of the class will all infer meaning from the silence.

Second, the appropriateness or inappropriateness of the silence can be important. If, for example, the silence comes when it is not expected, we might infer a meaning quite different from silence that seems well-suited for the occasion. Third, what has just preceded the silence also has an impact. If, in mixed company and right after church, someone told a tasteless joke and silence followed the punch line, we probably would understand immediately what the silence meant. Finally, the relationship between the participants also will influence the interpretation given to the silence. For example, silence cues occurring at the onset of an initial encounter might convey that the individual was remaining still until he or she decided what the other person was like.

Silence cues affect interpersonal communication by providing an interval in an ongoing interaction during which the participants have time to think, check or suppress an emotion, encode a lengthy response, or inaugurate another line of thought. Silence also helps provide feedback informing both sender and receiver as to the clarity of an idea or its significance in the overall interpersonal exchange. Silence cues may be regarded as evidence of agreement, lack of interest, injured feelings, or contempt. Like olfactory and tactile cues, silence cues transcend the verbal channel, often revealing what speech conceals.

The intercultural implications of silence are as diverse as those of the other nonverbal cues we have been examining in the last two chapters. Our use of and reaction to silence is another one of those aspects of culture that has evolved because of our membership in a particular group. In the United States, talking, watching television, listening to the radio, and other activities involving "noise" keep us from silence. In Greek and Arab cultures, which stress social interaction among friends and family, there is often very little silence. This is in sharp contrast with cultures in which a hushed and still environment is the rule. Let us look at a few cultural variations in the use of silence so that you might better understand how a lack of words can influence the outcome of any communication event.

Eastern traditions view silence much differently than Western cultures do. Easterners do not feel uncomfortable with the absence of noise or talk, and are not compelled to fill every pause when they are around other people. In fact, many of the people who share this concept of silence believe that words can contaminate an experience, and that inner peace and wisdom come only through silence. Buddhism, for example, teaches that "what is real is, and when it is spoken it becomes unreal." And think for a moment about these words of Confucius: "Believe not others' tales, / Others will lead thee far astray." Many Japanese proverbs, such as the following, also underscore the value of silence over words: "Out of the mouth comes all evil" and "A flower does not speak." Compare this perception of silence with the Western idea that the "squeaky wheel gets the grease." We Westerners believe that we must describe all things, and that there is a word or phrase for all feelings and objects.

As you might suspect, a culture's attitude towards silence gets translated into how that culture interacts. The Buddhist wedding, for instance, is basically conducted in silence. And concerning the behavior of a Japanese-American family, Kitano has observed:

> The most distinctive characteristic of Japanese family interaction was, and still remains, the absence of prolonged verbal exchanges. Although some of the common strategies to gain support through manipulation or cajoling were present, very few problems were resolved through open discussion between parents and children. Instead, arguments were one-sided, and most Nisei (children) can remember the phrase *de-mot-to-le* (keep quiet) that concluded them. Verbalization, talking out, and mutual discussion were actively discouraged.[12]

The Eastern use of silence as a form of communication contrasts even more sharply with Italian customs than with American customs. For the Italian, conversation with friends is an important pastime that brings enormous joy. Italians will tell you that their greatest pleasure is cheap—it is talk with friends. They believe that company, talk, and noise are signs of a good life.

Even members of co-cultures living in the United States differ in the use of silence. Many American Indians, for example, believe that silence, not speaking, is a sign of a great person. Johannesen, while discussing the function of silence, notes that the American Indian believes "one derives from silence the cornerstone of character, the virtues of self control, courage, patience and dignity."[13]

From our brief discussion of cultural differences in the use of silence, it should be easy to see how these variations could present problems. If you were unfamiliar with cultures that used a great deal of silence, you would probably feel uncomfortable or even stressed if you had to deal with such a culture. Knowing that there are differences in how cultures treat talk, noise, and silence can assist you in overcoming both anxiety and ethnocentrism.

SUMMARY

Space and Distance

- Cultures vary greatly in their perception and utilization of personal space, seating, and furniture arrangement.

Time

- We can understand a culture's sense of time by learning about how members of that culture view formal and informal time. Attitudes toward time also appear in the way in which people conceive of the past, present, and future. Cultural orientations towards time can be classified as monochronic or polychronic.

Silence

- The use of silence varies from culture to culture. Generally speaking, Eastern cultures value silence over the use of words; in Western cultures, the opposite is true.

ACTIVITIES

1. See a foreign movie. Watch for examples of proxemic differences between the culture that produced the movie and your culture. How far/close do people stand when talking to each other? Estimate the number of feet, if possible, and indicate the relationship of the speakers. How different is this culture's proxemic behavior from that of North America?

2. In small groups, read the following situation and explain what went wrong.

   Jan was in Brazil on business. Ciro, a Brazilian associate, invited her to a dinner party he and his wife were giving. The invitation was for "around 8:00, this Friday night." Jan showed up at Ciro's house at exactly 8:00. Ciro and his wife were still dressing, and they hadn't even begun to prepare the food. Jan, Ciro, and his wife were uncomfortable and embarrassed. What went wrong?

DISCUSSION IDEAS

1. Edward T. Hall describes two different cultural approaches to the use of outdoor public space: centripetal and centrifugal. Paris, France, is an example of a centripetal city: people tend to congregate on the streets, in public

squares, and in outdoor cafés. By contrast, most North American cities are centrifugal, lacking in many of these outdoor public meeting places. What, if anything, does this say to you about the differences in values between the two cultures? Can you think of any other cultures that use outdoor public space the way the French do?

2. How late can you be for the following: A class? Work? A job interview? A dinner party? A date with a friend?

3. Give examples from business or educational settings in which understanding cultural differences in the use of space, time, and silence can facilitate communication.

NOTES FOR CHAPTER 8

1. "Gay is Beautiful—At a Distance," *Psychology Today*, 9 (January 1976), 101.

2. Frank N. Willis, "Initial Speaking Distance as a Function of Speaker's Relationship," *Psychonomic Science* 5 (1968), 221–22.

3. Dale Leathers, *Successful Nonverbal Communication: Principles and Applications* (New York: Macmillan, 1986), 236.

4. Edward T. Hall, *The Hidden Dimension* (Garden City, NY: Doubleday, 1966), 159–60.

5. Judee K. Burgoon, David B. Buller, and W. Gil Woodall, *Nonverbal Communication: The Unspoken Dialogue* (New York: Harper and Row, 1989), 9–10.

6. Michael Argyle, "Inter-cultural Communication," in *Cultures in Contact: Studies in Cross-Cultural Interaction*, ed. Stephen Bochner (New York: Pergamon Press, 1982), 68.

7. Robert Levine, "Social Time: The Heartbeat of Culture," *Psychology Today* (March 1985), 35.

8. Edward T. Hall, *The Dance of Life: Other Dimensions of Time* (New York: Anchor Press/Doubleday, 1983), 42–51.

9. Edward T. Hall, *The Silent Language* (New York: Fawcett Publications, 1959), 19.

10. Edward T. Hall, *Beyond Culture* (Garden City, NY: Doubleday, 1976), 14.

11. John Horton, "Time and the Cool People," in *Intercultural Communication: A Reader*, ed. Larry A. Samovar and Richard E. Porter (Belmont, CA: Wadsworth, 1976), 274–84.

12. Harry H. L. Kitano, *Japanese American: The Evolution of a Subculture* (Englewood Cliffs, NJ: Prentice-Hall, 1969), 72.

13. Richard L. Johannesen, "The Functions of Silence: A Plea for Communication Research," *Western Speech* 38 (1974), 27.

People only see what they are prepared to see.

EMERSON

Ignorance of cultural differences is one of the chief causes of
misunderstanding in a world that is getting more and more
interdependent, on the one hand, and increasingly torn with strife
on the other.

FALI CHOTHIA

CHAPTER NINE

THE INFLUENCE OF CONTEXT: BUSINESS, EDUCATION, AND HEALTH CARE

All communicative interaction takes place within some social and physical context. When people communicate within their own culture they are usually aware of the context, which does little to hinder the communication. But when people are engaged in intercultural communication, the context in which that communication takes place can have a strong impact. Unless both parties to intercultural communication are aware of how their cultures affect the context of communication, they can encounter some surprising communication difficulties. In this chapter we shall examine the influence of context on intercultural communication.

CONTEXT AND COMMUNICATION

We begin with the assumption that communicative behavior is governed by rules. By a rule, we mean a principle or regulation that governs conduct and procedure. In communication, rules act as a system of expected behavior patterns that organize interaction between individuals. Communication rules are both culturally and contextually bound. Although the social setting may determine the type of rules that are appropriate, the culture determines the rules. In Iraq, for instance, a contextual rule prohibits females from having unfamiliar males visit them at home. In the United States, however, it is not considered socially inappropriate for unfamiliar males to visit females at home. Rules dictate behavior by establishing appropriate responses to stimuli for a particular communication context within the larger culture.

Communication rules, which include both verbal and nonverbal components, determine not only what should be said but how it should be said. Nonverbal rules apply to proper gestures, facial expressions, eye contact, proxemics, vocal tone, and body movements.

Unless one is prepared to function in the contextual settings of another culture, he or she may be in for an unpleasant experience. The intercultural situation can produce high stress—both physical and mental. The effects of this stress are called **culture shock,** which is "precipitated by the anxiety that results from losing all of our familiar signs and symbols of social intercourse."[1] Harris and Moran have expanded this definition to "a generalized trauma one experiences in a new and different culture because of having to learn and cope with a vast array of new cultural cues and expectations, while discovering that your old ones probably do not fit or work."[2] Culture shock has been found to be responsible for a one-in-three failure rate for Americans working abroad, and corporate losses have totaled in the millions.[3] More and more heads of international operations are becoming aware that it is a mistake to send people abroad or assign international responsibilities to people who will not work effectively with people of a foreign culture. The cost of training is inconsequential compared to the risk of utilizing people who do not have the requisite skills.[4] Because of the almost infinite variations of time, place, and individual circumstances, culture shock cannot be avoided; but knowledge about communication context and how it varies culturally can reduce its effect. The shock or strangeness will not necessarily go away, but some early training and exposure may soften its impact. It is important to remember that cultural contexts are neither right nor wrong, neither better nor worse; they are just different.

Context is a form of cultural adaptation to a particular setting or environment. We can see the importance of context by observing three basic assumptions about communication. First, communication is **rule-governed.** This means that there are learned patterns of behavior or rules that organize interaction between individuals, and that people expect these rules to govern that interaction. The rules specify such things as turn-taking, voice volume, appropriate dress, formality of language, manners and forms of respect, and bodily action for communicating in various social contexts. Obviously, the rules vary depending on the context. You would normally dress quite differently for an employment interview than for watching a basketball game. Your use of language would also be different. In the employment interview you might frequently use the respectful word *sir* when responding to your potential employer. At the basketball game your language would become less formal, incorporating slang phrases, and possibly swearing at the opposing team or at the officials. Your dress would also be different. For the interview you might wear your "power suit," while at the basketball game jeans and a T-shirt would be acceptable. Your nonverbal behavior would also be different. At the interview you would probably shake hands with the prospective employer, but at the basketball game you might hug your friends or slap them on the back as a form of greeting. As you can see, definite rules govern interaction.

The second assumption is that the context helps to define the rules. As we have seen, rules or expectations differ depending upon the situation. Think for a moment about how such various social contexts as being in a bar, classroom, bank, church, hospital, or courtroom, or at a wedding or a funeral determine which rules of communication are appropriate.

The third assumption is that these rules are culturally diverse. Although cultures have many of the same settings or contexts, they have different rules and, hence, different concepts of what communication behaviors are appropriate when their members are in those settings. The concepts of dress, time, language, manners, nonverbal behavior, and control of the communication flow differ significantly among cultures. To be successful in intercultural communication, it is essential to know something about the rules that govern the interaction. This means that you must know not only the rules of your culture but the rules of the culture of the person with whom you are interacting as well.

If you know the rules, the other person's behavior will make more sense to you, and you can alter your behavior to conform to the rules of the other culture. Ideally, both participants in an interaction will be aware of the rules of each other's culture and will use this knowledge to adapt to each other as best they can.

Having determined that cultures develop rules governing human interaction in specific contexts, we must now gain some insight into the general concept of context. Anthropologist Edward T. Hall has written extensively about context.[5] Although Hall's notion of context applies to the workings of larger cultures in general and to all specific contexts within those cultures, we can adopt his concept as a useful tool to help us understand intercultural communication as it occurs in specific contexts. Hall categorizes cultures as either high- or low-context. Context, however, is really a cultural dimension that ranges from high to low. Figure 9-1 shows various cultures placed along that dimension.[6]

In high-context cultures, most of the information lies either in the physical context or within the people who are a part of the interaction. Very little information is actually coded in the verbal message. In low-context cultures, however, the verbal message contains most of the information and very little is embedded in the context or within the participants. The Oriental mode of communication is often indirect and implicit, while the Western tends to be direct and explicit. In Oriental communication, participants suppose much. Westerners are more prone to make very explicit arrangements and have little capability with nonverbal forms of expression.[7] High-context cultures such as Japan, Korea, and Taiwan tend to be more aware of their surroundings and their environment and do not rely on verbal communication as their main information source. The Korean language contains a word *nunchi*, which literally means being able to communicate through your eyes. In high-context cultures, so much information is available in the environment that it is unnecessary to state verbally what is obvious. Oral statements of affection, for instance, are very rare because it is not necessary to state what is obvious. When the context says "I love you," it is not necessary to state it orally.

There are four major differences between how high- and low-context cultures affect the communication setting. First, verbal messages are extremely important in low-context cultures, and the information to be shared is coded in the verbal message. This information is not readily available from the environment because people in low-context cultures do not tend to learn how to perceive the environment for information. Second, people in high-context cultures

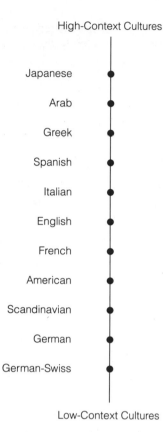

High-Context Cultures

Japanese

Arab

Greek

Spanish

Italian

English

French

American

Scandinavian

German

German-Swiss

Low-Context Cultures

**Figure 9-1   Cultures arranged along the
high-context / low-context dimension.**

perceive low-context people, who rely primarily on verbal messages for information, as less attractive and less credible. Third, people in high-context cultures
are more adept at reading nonverbal behavior and in reading the environment.
And fourth, people in high-context cultures expect others also to be able to
understand the unarticulated communication; hence, they do not speak as much
as people from low-context cultures.

Having looked at the notion of context in general terms, we shall now look
at some rules of context and behavior that shift from culture to culture. In doing
this, we have selected three specific contexts to consider: doing business, the
school, and the health-care setting. We have selected these three contexts

because they are the ones in which most intercultural communication occurs. These are the situations in which you will be interacting with members of other cultures or co-cultures.

THE BUSINESS CONTEXT

The United States finds itself doing more business with other nations throughout the world, so you may soon find yourself working with and doing business with people from many different cultures. The United States is also experiencing a rapidly increasing cultural diversity among its home work force. The American work force is changing dramatically. By the year 2000, women and nonwhites will account for 92 percent of the growth in the American work force, and they will comprise approximately 84 percent of the new workers. Already white males are the minority, comprising only 44 percent of the work force. Foreign-born workers already constitute nearly 20 percent of the work force in California. In the next ten years, nonwhites and foreign-born workers will account for a large part of the growth in the American work force, which will be dominated numerically by Asians, Hispanics, Native Americans, and Pacific Islanders. The work force will also change to accommodate people of diverse religions and lifestyles, as well as people with disabilities.

These changes in the work force have a profound effect upon the ways in which we conduct business and manage our businesses. Cultural diversity is a reality we must face if American businesses are to compete successfully in world markets. To gain some insight into the business context, we shall begin with a look at some of the rules for doing business internationally and the impact of culture upon those rules. Later we shall look at the impact of cultural diversity on the home work force. We shall begin with an international look at normal office routine.

Most Americans with a traditional view of office routine normally think of beginning the day at eight o'clock in the morning, taking a fifteen-minute coffee break about ten o'clock, breaking for lunch at noon, taking another coffee break about three o'clock in the afternoon, and leaving the office at five. We have a normal routine that we believe fits our needs. We also believe that when we are at work we are there to work for our employer and that other concerns and activities must wait until after working hours. This, however, is very much an American cultural view, one that other cultures do not necessarily share. Mexicans, for instance, have a different cultural view about the importance of the family. They hold the family in high esteem, and it is not uncommon for relatives to intrude upon the work scene because they perceive family concerns as more important than business. Business can be done at any time, but family problems must be attended to at once. Muslims in Saudi Arabia may interrupt business for scheduled prayer breaks, and they may conduct several meetings and conversations simultaneously. Germany and the eastern European countries regard privacy highly. Here people work behind closed doors, and one must knock before entering someone's private work space.

Because the **protocol** of doing business varies from culture to culture, it is important to be aware of the protocols operant in the culture in which you are a business visitor. Europeans, for instance, are generally more formal than their American counterparts. An American should never address a European business person by his or her first name unless invited to do so. Introductions should be made using formal titles, and handshakes should be gentle without the vigorous grip, hand pumping, and shoulder slapping typical of Americans. The British give protocol the utmost attention. Appointments are a must, and it is important to be punctual. The British maintain a high respect for formality and the hierarchy of management. First names may be used, but not as freely as in the United States. In social settings it is best not to talk about politics, religion, or the royal family.

Italians follow a different protocol. In Italy, executives are used to traveling and working long hours. Allow plenty of time for business appointments, however, because even the busiest Italian executive may engage you in hearty conversation for several hours. The successful conduct of business in Italy calls for the early establishment of rapport. Lunch and dinner are events that provide the social opportunity to build rapport. Lunch is the most important meal of the day in Italy, and businesses shut down for two to three hours each afternoon. Never refuse an invitation to lunch or dinner, because it will be considered ungracious.

In interpersonal communication situations, Asians usually assess the feelings and state of mind of those present. The harmony of the group is paramount, and they do not want to do anything that would disturb that harmony. Thus, they tend to give their opinions indirectly.[8]

Asiatic modes of communication can seem defensive and situational. Asians' conversations often stop abruptly, or the speaker changes the subject without obvious reason, as soon as he or she feels that the listener does not agree totally with the expressed point of view or that feelings may have been hurt.[9]

The Japanese take business rituals with the utmost seriousness. Knowing what to do in business and social settings is essential in creating a positive relationship with your Japanese host. The Japanese are sticklers on exchanging business cards, and they appreciate bilingual cards. Because Japanese executives tend to wear blue suits with white shirts, it would behoove you to do the same. Business women should stick to conservative suits. One should never approach negotiations casually. The Japanese take these sessions very seriously, and if your approach is casual, the Japanese will perceive that you or your company is not sufficiently interested in the ritual of negotiation. If business is to be discussed over a meal, your Japanese counterpart will usually invite you and serve as the host. If you reciprocate, do not skimp on the restaurant, because the Japanese have a high regard for quality and status.

Japanese management differs from American on several strategies and techniques based on the premise that "human assets are considered to be the firm's most important and profitable assets in the long run."[10] "Management analysts often call the Japanese style of management 'organic.' The employees are like the organs in the human body, while the company itself is the entire body. All parts of the body must perform their intended functions, or the body will suffer."[11] This organic concept inspired Japanese management's policy of lifetime employment, or *shohgaikoyoh*,[12] and its emphasis on group membership/teamwork; outsiders sometimes perceive it as paternalism, groupism, and familyism.[13] "Work is organized around groups of people instead of around individual skills,"[14] and management encourages group autonomy to avoid reliance on experts to solve operational problems.[15] Experts are consulted only to gain specialized knowledge and not to aid in solving problems. This management approach also builds a sense of employee commitment and loyalty to the organization "fostered by Confucianism; the feudal clan, which demanded the warrior's total commitment and loyalty."[16]

Chinese protocol is similar to that of the Japanese. Introductions are made with a slight bow and a handshake. The Chinese are quite formal and use full names and business titles for all first-time introductions. They are hard bargainers, but once parties have reached an agreement, they will not waiver. The Chinese frequently wish to communicate in their own language, so the employment of an interpreter may be necessary.

Cultures vary also in the notion of time and of "getting down to business." American, Australian, German, English, Israeli, Swiss, and Scandinavian cultures, for example, treat time as a valuable, tangible, and limited resource. Like money, time is saved, wasted, given, taken, made, spent, run out of, and budgeted. Because time is so valuable, one must use it productively and compartmentalize it into efficient intervals of activity.[17] But the process of getting down to business is rule-governed, and it differs among cultures. In Oriental countries such as Japan, China, and Korea—as well as Middle Eastern countries such as Saudi Arabia, and Latin American countries such as Mexico, Brazil, and Chile—the cultural rules specify that people take their time before becoming engaged in doing business. In many of these countries, business meetings begin with extensive social interaction over many cups of coffee or tea to establish social rapport. The development of this rapport does not mean a mere five or ten minutes of conversation; there is a lot of small talk, hospitality, and becoming comfortable with each other before engaging in business activities. It may take hours, or perhaps even several meetings during which the business objective may not even be mentioned, to establish an appropriate rapport.

The evaluation of how to spend time differs culturally. Americans work by schedules. Given a deadline, they race to meet or beat it. Giving a task a deadline heightens its importance and creates a sense of urgency. But deadlines elsewhere may produce opposite results. An Arab may take a deadline as an insult; for Arabs consider the drinking of coffee and chatting as doing something, whereas the American sees it as doing nothing. Ethiopians attach prestige to activities that take a long time.[18] Copeland and Griggs provide an example of the extreme to which the concept of time may vary culturally.

A Chinese official matter-of-factly informed an ARCO manager that China would one day be the number one nation in the world. The American said he did not doubt, considering the size of the country and its population, and the tremendous technological progress that will be made, but he asked, "When do you think that China will become number one?" The Chinese responded, "Oh, in four or five hundred years."[19]

We cannot overstress the importance of establishing good social relationships before conducting business. The quality of relationships strongly affects the conduct of business. Foreigners need to assess any business associate and most likely will not make a deal purely on the basis of the best price or product, but rather on personal estimation. From Italy to China, extra personal involvement is important. Many foreigners feel that if both parties can be friends, then business between them will flow naturally and smoothly.[20]

Many Oriental languages distinguish between levels of speech according to age, social status, and patterns of social interaction. Only after one knows someone's status, age, and gender, for instance, will he or she be capable of communicating in the appropriate cultural manner.[21]

Cultural rules also govern the ways in which business negotiations take place. Perceptions of both the concept and the process of negotiation differ culturally. For instance, in the Persian language, the word for "compromise" does not mean a midway solution that both sides can accept, as it does in English. Instead, it means surrendering one's principles. Also, Arabs see a mediator as a meddler, someone who is bargaining uninvited. In 1980, United Nations Secretary-General Kurt Waldheim flew to Iran to deal with the hostage situation. National Iranian radio and television broadcast in Persian a comment he was said to have made upon his arrival in Tehran indicating that he had come as a *mediator* to work out a *compromise*. Less than an hour later, angry Iranians were stoning his car.

Indians and Middle Easterners enjoy the process of negotiation, which they see as an act of bargaining in which there is give and take. People set out to obtain the best deal they can, and they enjoy the process of striking a bargain. The influence of Islam gives the Saudi businessman a strong sense of honor and of personal dignity. Although Saudis are very tough and skilled negotiators, they will honor an agreement to the letter—and, of course, they expect the same in return.

Chinese or Japanese raised in a traditional family setting, on the other hand, may not like negotiation. This may be due in part to their propensity to make group decisions, but it is also antithetical to their communication style, which avoids face-to-face confrontation. The Chinese and Japanese will often conduct their negotiations by letters and written proposals, and reach a decision before face-to-face negotiations. Letters are important to the Chinese because they help establish a relationship. Face-to-face negotiations then become a ceremony at which the parties can sign the agreement, and there is no face-to-face confrontation. In the past, Japanese and Chinese have even resorted to the use of go-betweens so they could personally avoid the conflict associated with negotiation.

A part of business negotiation that also differs culturally is the pace of conversation and the form and content of presentations. A Saudi Arabian executive will not permit business to consume his life, and the American business person would be greatly mistaken to expect any business matters automatically to command a Saudi's immediate attention. Asians prefer a reflective or slow pace. They often let the other party begin, so that they can respond to arguments and also set the pace once the other side has had its say. The Chinese are prone to seeming passive and asking a lot of questions. They probe for information and conceal any eagerness they may feel. They listen carefully and give subtle hints about their requirements for reaching an agreement. French and Korean business persons prefer to give their arguments first and then their conclusions. Americans begin with their position and then develop the evidence to support it. They like to develop the big picture, whereas Chinese and Japanese tend to be very detail-oriented. Japanese business people often do not trust Americans because the Americans omit perceived essential details.

There are also cultural rules that govern the degree of formality appropriate to business transactions. Americans tend toward informality and relaxed atmospheres. Mexicans place a great deal of value on form, rank, status, and ceremony. Arab executives are well groomed and immaculately dressed. In their mind, appearance and charisma carry great weight, and they expect foreign executives to dress according to the highest standards of their own countries. The Japanese have a high regard for status; they prefer to address people formally by their last names. Status also determines who speaks first.

Compromise is another aspect of business that is governed by culturally determined rules. Among Germans and eastern European cultures, there is little room for compromise. Scandinavians tend to make offers or bids that reflect what they believe to be a fair price. They place an offer on the bargaining table with the expectation that the other party will recognize and accept its fairness. Arabs, on the other hand, tend to ask prices that are higher than they expect to get so that they may engage in the give-and-take of negotiation before settling on an acceptable price.

A problem that has caused no little difficulty for Americans engaged in foreign business is the matter of gift-giving. From the American Puritan perspective, gift-giving is akin to bribery and thus is wrong. In fact, there are even laws that prohibit gift-giving in certain situations. Other cultures, however, see gift-giving as the lubricant that eases the effort of negotiation. In Asian and Middle Eastern cultures, gift-giving is a part of the tradition of doing business and is expected. The American view of gift-giving has often made it difficult for Americans to do business overseas.

Culture also influences matters of trust. Americans have a tendency to trust everyone until there is reason to withhold their trust. Japanese and other Asian cultures are more prone to trust people only after they have demonstrated their trust. The French are particularly lacking in trust and require everything to be written down. They may not trust oral commitment.

Finally, culture determines who engages in business transactions. Americans often select negotiators based upon their knowledge and expertise in both negotiating and the subject of the negotiation. We want good negotiators who know what they are talking about. Other cultures use criteria such as power, authority, gender, status, and age to determine who negotiates. In some Oriental cultures, where age is revered, negotiators are often selected because of their age and the status that goes with age.

In Mexico and many Middle Eastern countries, people are selected to be negotiators because of their rhetorical skills. Among Arabs, "strong manhood is co-extensive with strong rhetoric."[22] Educated and illiterate alike have extraordinary mastery of their language, expressed through a rich vocabulary and well-rounded, complex phrases. In Western countries, gender is no longer much of a factor in choosing negotiators; but in Middle Eastern and Asian countries, where women have little status, the negotiators are nearly always men.

Authority is an important variable that can influence negotiation. The Chinese concepts of authority can create difficulty for American business people during negotiations. The Chinese negotiator has very little authority to vary from the position his or her supervisor has chosen, except through additional conferences.[23] This, in the mind of the American, slows down the process and wastes time.

So far, we have looked at the problems of international business and the hurdles we encounter when doing business with other nations, but there are problems within the United States as well. Each day, the United States is becoming more of a multicultural nation, and the American work force is becoming increasingly culturally diverse. Post–World War II migrations have resulted in a large influx of peoples from all parts of the world. The **eurocentric** viewpoint predominant for so long is no longer viable. This means that the old ways of conducting business within the country also must change.

Within the culturally diverse American work force, there are going to be problems between groups of employees and between employees and their supervisors because they do not understand each other's cultural behaviors. These differences can lead to misperceptions, misunderstandings, suspicions, and bruised feelings. Managers and supervisors must learn to recognize the variety of cultural dimensions that operate within their work force. It is incumbent upon business to develop cultural awareness and for managers and co-workers to develop the knowledge of cultural diversity that will permit the multicultural work force to function successfully in America.

Inherent in a culturally diverse work force are racial, ethnic, and gender prejudice. Many members of the American work force have grown up with negative beliefs about other races and ethnic groups as well as the role and place of women. This perception is not peculiar to Anglos; it is common across races and ethnic groups. Managers must adapt to the diversity among their workers and develop programs that will reduce racial, ethnic, and gender tensions. Cultural awareness and sensitivity programs for all employees can help accomplish this.

There are also problems with oral and written communication. Because many workers are new to the United States, they may have difficulty with the English language. Their command of the language may be inadequate, which can result in misunderstood instructions. American management must begin to develop multiple language abilities either through language study or the recruitment and hiring of bi- or multilingual managers.

Another aspect of multiple languages in the work place is the suspicion and feelings of uneasiness that can develop when some members of the work force speak a language that other workers cannot understand. Whether it be on the assemble line, in an office, or in the cafeteria, people speaking languages other than English can create feelings of resentment. Again, management has the task of defusing these situations by sensitizing the work force and bringing its members to accept the necessity and validity of multiple languages in the work place.

Workers may also differ greatly in nonverbal behavior, such as dress and appearance. A black wearing a cornrow hairstyle or a Hindu wearing a turban can cause others to feel uncomfortable because they do not understand the self-significance of a person's appearance. Diverse nonverbal behavior may also appear in the form of greetings that employ special handshakes or embraces. Again, whatever is different may arouse suspicion. The manager's task is to alleviate the suspicions through cultural awareness and the encouragement of cultural expression.

With the rapid increase of women in the work force and the emergence of the feminist movement, which is striving for gender equality, a new concern about the proper treatment of women has resulted in legislative actions. Most of this concern has to do with sexual harassment. Although sexual harassment is usually directed at women by men, it also includes the harassment of men by women and the harassment of homosexuals. Sexual harassment includes behavior such as unwanted sexual advances and requests for sexual favors in exchange for employment, promotions, and recommendations. Conduct such as leering, making sexual gestures, and displaying sexually suggestive objects or pictures, cartoons, or posters also constitutes harassment, as does verbal abuse in the form of derogatory or discriminatory remarks regarding one's sex or a sexual minority, or about an individual's body. It is also illegal to use sexually degrading words to describe an individual, to write suggestive or obscene letters, notes, or invitations, and to make real or implied threats of reprisal following a negative response to verbal or physical contact of a sexual nature.

THE EDUCATION CONTEXT

The classroom is an important context in which cultural influences are much in evidence. Systems of formal education are cultural products designed to meet the perceived needs of their parent societies. In the United States, a system has evolved that generally prepares middle-class children to participate in their own culture. When students from other cultures and lower socioeconomic classes enter this educational system, the system frequently considers them to be unprepared or deficient if their cultural experiences do not match those of the mainstream culture. This frequently leads to inadequate provision for dealing with a culturally diverse student population.

In all cultures, schools serve a multidimensional function. First, they shape individuals. As children grow, what they learn and the ways in which they learn influence their thinking and behavior. From the child's view, education is finding a way to certainty. Children want to learn what they need to know to lead successful and satisfying lives.[24]

Schools also are a primary purveyor of a culture's history and traditions from generation to generation. Schools are asked to teach the formal knowledge a culture deems necessary: history, government, science, art, music, and how to survive. This is true whether we are talking about a country as large, developed, and complex as the United States or about a people who live in small tribal societies in the midst of a South American jungle. What schools teach as history, government, science, art, music, and how to survive differs considerably, of course, from culture to culture. The teaching of history and government reflect a culture's unique history and form of government. The basis of survival in the United States, as we present it in our educational system, is to obtain the education and skills necessary to secure a job that provides sufficient income to live comfortably. In the jungle tribe, the survival skills may be more along the lines of how to set an animal snare, how to fashion a functional bow and arrow, or how to recognize which plants are nutritious and which are toxic.

The educational system of a culture also teaches the informal knowledge of the culture. This teaching involves not only the schools but the home as well. By the time children are ready to attend school, they have already been exposed to and have internalized many of the basic values and beliefs of their cultures, learned the rules of behavior that are considered appropriate for their role in the community, and are continuing to become socialized.[25] In school, children continue this process and learn the rules of correct conduct, how to treat one another, sex-role expectations, respect, and all of the other informal matters of culture. This process continues the education that began at home and furthers the development of cultural values and cultural world view.

We shall now examine some of the ways in which other cultures educate their children, then turn our attention to the problems inherent in the American educational system as it tries to cope with the multicultural diversity emerging rapidly in our classrooms. We begin by examining what cultures teach and how they teach it.

What Cultures Teach

Most cultures that have formal education systems tend to teach about the same things. The differences tend to be in terms of emphasis rather than content. Education in China emphasizes the Chinese language, mathematics, science, engineering, and technology, as well as music, drawing, and physical education. The Chinese also include stiff doses of politics and foreign languages, especially English. Mexico places a strong emphasis on acquiring skills in arts and crafts and in technical and vocational fields, and encourages cultural awareness through the study of folklore, music, and dance. Mathematics and natural sciences receive less emphasis. French schools strongly emphasize language and literature. The Japanese schools emphasize the Japanese language, mathematics, science, social studies, music, arts and crafts, physical education, morals education, and the English language.[26] Russia focuses on politics, Soviet patriotism, science, mathematics, art and the love of beauty, and physical fitness. Russian schools feature a weekly lesson in labor, which may include how to use scissors, sewing, clay modeling, the construction of simple machines, working in the school garden, or doing "socially useful" work in the community.[27] Russian children even study the discipline of soldiering by the age of seven. In Libya, war has been so important that young children go to camp to learn weaponry and slogans of hate.

But children learn more at school than curriculum content. They also learn values. Children learn about cooperation and competition. American children learn a great deal individually and try to outdo other children. They learn the values of striving, competition, and success. Mexican children, on the other hand, grow up within cooperative environments that emphasize strong family ties. These children are not always as competitive as Anglos; they often do not compete in the classroom and may not always work as well when left unsupervised. It has been found that Mexican children sometimes bring with them a set of educational experiences that can undermine their academic adjustment and success in the United States, unless instructors understand these experiences. Because of the Hispanic value toward education, as many as 45 percent of all Mexican-American and Puerto Rican students who enter school never finish, and as many as 40 percent of all Hispanic students who leave school do so before reaching the tenth grade.[28]

Japanese children are also raised in a cooperative environment. They learn through cooperative efforts and develop an insight into the interconnectedness of their society. They also learn to see others as being responsible for the good life of society as a whole. Before they open their lunch, Japanese children often sing: "As I sit here with my lunch, I think of Mom. It will be good. I wonder what she made me." The children may then bow their heads, place their hands together, and say: "Buddha, thank you. Honorable father, honorable mother, we humbly thank you." This is a Buddhist exercise that trains children to visualize the web of interconnectedness in their society by thinking about all the people who helped bring the food to them: the farmer, the truck driver, the person who made the truck tires, the road workers, the grocers, and the like.

Cultural values are also reflected in the types of jobs and skills that a culture emphasizes. In the United States, where talking, arguing, and fixing blame on others is important, there is one lawyer for approximately every 350 Americans. In Japan, where harmony and working things out are important values, there is one lawyer for approximately every 11,000 people.

The esteem in which teachers are held varies culturally. The Vietnamese have extremely high respect for their instructors and consider them to be honored members of society. They see the instructor as a symbol of learning and culture. Mexican students also hold their teachers in high esteem, especially in rural areas of Mexico, where the instructor is seen as a community resource and as a possible leader. In Germany, students value the personal opinion and evaluation of the instructor as highly as do students in underdeveloped nations. It is not customary to disagree with or to contradict a teacher. Canadian students, on the other hand, question their teacher if they do not like the answer he or she gives to a question. And students in an Israeli kibbutz readily criticize an instructor if they feel that he or she is wrong.

A culture's value of education is also reflected in the educational system. In Japan, students attend school 240 days or forty-eight weeks a year. In the United States, students attend school for about 180 days or thirty-six weeks per year. In Japan 65 percent of the children average five or more hours of homework each night. In the United States only about 25 percent of school students average five hours of homework. Teacher salaries in the United States are at the average of all wage earners. In Japan, by national law, teachers are in the top 10 percent of wage earners.

Conformity is another value the schools of some cultures reinforce. In Russia, for example, children all wear the same uniforms, observe the same rules, study the same subjects, and even use the same textbooks throughout that vast country. This reflects a strong value for conformity and standardization. Identified as one of the main tasks of the Soviet educational system is the unification of an ethnically diverse population. This is in opposition to the United States, where there are strong forces at work attempting to ensure that the public schools recognize and help maintain cultural diversity. In addition, individual school districts rather than a national agency control local schools and have a great deal of influence over their curriculum.

The value of conformity is also practiced in Japanese schools where children sit at tables and work together rather than sitting at individual desks, as in the United States. The Japanese are dedicated to the proposition that students learn best in groups and by repetition and drill. As early as preschool, Japanese children have group experiences and learn how to work together cooperatively.

Thus far, we have seen how what schools teach differs culturally. But as yet we have not looked at how teaching and learning differ culturally. We shall turn to this issue next. Inasmuch as we have shown that cultures differ in what they teach, you should not be surprised to learn that there are also major differences in how cultures teach.

How Cultures Teach

In the United States, teachers talk or lecture to students about 75 percent of the time. Teachers talk much more in China, Japan, and Korea. In those cultures, learning is passive, and students are expected to do a great deal of rote memorization. In cultures such as Russia, China, and Japan, teachers will read to the students and then ask questions. In Mexico, students do a great deal of talking and learn through group interaction.

Schools also differ culturally as to how students participate in learning. Participation involves taking part, joining in, and sharing. How one participates, however, is another matter. Japanese students participate by the "silent receipt of information."[29] Discussions are short, with rapid turn-taking. Speaking too much is a sign of conceit and superficiality, and being considered an individual is not desirable in the collectivist Japanese culture. This emphasis upon silence and minimal participation springs from the Buddhist tradition, which values meditation and silence and has led to the incorporation of quiet time into the school curriculum. Silence in the classroom is important to the Vietnamese, Cambodians, and Chinese as well. "Cultures reflecting a Buddhist tradition hold that knowledge, truth, and wisdom come to those whose quiet silence allows the spirit to enter."[30]

In the United States, the opposite is true. Classrooms tend to be noisy, and we tend to see talking by each child as a way of promoting individuality. Arab students, with their "emphasis on spoken language, with poetry and oral eloquence being particularly prized,"[31] participate enthusiastically in discussions among themselves; but because they are taught to listen to their teacher, they will speak in class only if given a specific opportunity.

Many cultures do not have textbooks. This is particularly true in countries where the economy does not permit such a luxury. Learning in Vietnam involves lecturing, listening, taking notes, memorizing, and reciting. Student presentations and discussions are extremely rare, and students refrain from volunteering answers in class. In Mexico and India, for instance, teachers read from a book and students recite after them or write down what the teachers say in a notebook. In the United States, much teaching is now being done through the use of television, films, and interactive computers.

The nonverbal aspects of the classroom also affect how teaching takes place. In Japan, China, and Russia, for instance, students dress in uniforms. In the United States, most students dress as they please, not wanting to look too much like someone else. But this is starting to change. Some school districts are adopting voluntary uniform codes to free children from the stress of looking unique and original and from the cost of high-fashion clothes. The adoption of uniforms also serves another purpose. In areas where there are gang activities, children dressed in school uniforms are easily distinguished from gang members who may be displaying their gang colors. In the case of gang drive-by shootings, the children are less likely to be shot because they will not be inadvertently wearing the colors of a rival gang.

Space, distance, and time are also cultural variables in the classroom. In the United States, teachers tend to stand at the front of the classroom while they are teaching. In Mexico, teachers move about the room. Russian teachers seem to be rooted to one spot in the classroom. In some cultures, schools follow rigid time schedules, with bells or buzzers announcing the change of activity or classes. In other cultures time is less rigid, and in some there is no time schedule at all.

Some cultures impose rigid structure and formality in the school setting. In Mexican classrooms, as well as in Germany, southern Italy, and the West Indies, students rise when an instructor enters the room and address him or her with an appropriate greeting. These cultures constantly observe and enforce etiquette with little variation. The other extreme appears in Israeli kibbutz learning environments, where students move from their desks or leave the classroom at will to sharpen their pencils or to get a drink. They talk among themselves even during oral lessons and hum to themselves while writing.

Interaction patterns also differ culturally. Vietnamese and Arabic students are taught not to interact with members of the opposite sex. In many instances classes are segregated by gender. This, of course, has produced some problems for international students from these cultures when they come to the United States to study and find themselves in groups of mixed gender. Formality differs also. In Germany, Mexico, and Italy, for instance, students rise when the teacher enters the room. In Russia students sit with their arms folded, holding that school is not the place for fun. American and Israeli schools tend toward informality.

All schools in all cultures teach ethnocentrism. This seems inescapable, but what is more interesting are the manifest, invisible, and subtle ways in which it is taught. For instance, the next time you look at a world map, notice that the United States is prominently located in the center of the map, unless, of course, you are looking at a Chinese or Russian map of the world. The teaching of history is common to all cultures, but which history do they teach? By teaching a culture's history to schoolchildren, a society is reinforcing all of its beliefs, values, and prejudices. Each culture attempts to glorify its historical and scientific accomplishments and to downplay the accomplishments of others. Schools in the United States emphasize the English language and devote very little attention to learning a second or third language. What subtle message does that give students about the position of English in the world and the importance of other languages?

Perhaps one of the most subtle influences is the teaching of great thought. In the United States, this has traditionally involved a male-dominated, eurocentric point of view. A listing of the great books of the world will almost certainly turn out to name only authors who are Western, white-skinned, and male. This leaves the impression that the rest of the world has or is doing nothing, and that therefore "we are the greatest."

A similar reflection of this appears in Russia. On a child's first day of school, he or she will receive a small postcard with a greeting: "Dear little friend, today you sit for the first time at your school desk. From the bottom of our hearts we wish you to learn well in order to be a great benefit to our wonderful Motherland. Your senior comrades."

Another cultural variable that affects classroom interaction and teaching methodologies is **cognitive style.** Cognitive styles are individual differences in cognitive organization and functioning. Three particular cognitive styles that can be present in the classroom are **field-dependence/field independence, reflectivity/impulsivity,** and **tolerance/intolerance** for ambiguity. In field-dependent cognition the field dominates the perception of its parts; people seek relationships. Field-independent cognition employs strategies to isolate elements of the field; it is analytical.[32] "Cross-culturally, the extent of the development of a field-independent style . . . is a factor of the type of society and home in which the child is reared."[33] Field-dependent cognition is prevalent mostly in traditional, high-context, collectivist societies, while field-independent cognitive styles predominate in low-context, highly industrialized, individualistic societies.[34]

Reflectivity and impulsivity have to do with whether individuals seek answers slowly or whether they make quick guesses. In cultures that emphasize reflectivity, if one guesses or errs, it is an admission of not having taken enough time to find the correct answer. This can result in a painful loss of face. "Such styles are often accompanied by a relativistic approach to 'truth' in which several choices or answers on True/False tests may represent 'correct' answers."[35] Low-context cultures such as the United States more often encourage impulsivity. Here students frequently learn by trial and error, and risk-taking and creativity are rewarded.

Tolerance or intolerance of ambiguity relates to open-mindedness about differences and contradictions. Cultures such as India are high in toleration for ambiguity, as exemplified in the statement "One must know that one's judgements are true only partially and can by no means be regarded as true in absolute terms."[36] In American culture, there is little tolerance for ambiguity. Here the emphasis is on correct/incorrect, yes/no choices in which there is always an answer. In most instances, it seems culturally that field-dependence, reflectivity, and tolerance of ambiguity group together, as do field-independence, impulsiveness, and intolerance of ambiguity.

Having gotten a good idea of what cultures teach and how they teach it, we shall now turn our attention to the problems of educating the culturally diverse student population emerging in the United States.

Problems in Educating a Culturally Diverse Population

California, like many states, is no longer home to a predominant majority of average white Americans. In California, whites currently account for only 58% of the total population, and white school-age children are already a minority. Latinos represent 31% of the public school enrollment, African-Americans account for 9%, and Asians and others total 11%—51% of California's school-age children are non-white.[37]

As the United States follows the trend in California, it will face an immense set of educational challenges. First, preschools and elementary schools are having to respond to changing patterns of men's and women's work, a high divorce rate, and a growing concern for the needs of single-parent families. More importantly, however, we face a student population whose cultural diversity and language differences are having an impact on traditional educational systems and creating challenges for teachers, counselors, and administrators hardly ever before imagined. Vietnamese children, for instance, whose culture has taught them not to interact with the opposite sex, may be labeled as uncooperative when they are reluctant to join in a coeducational physical education game.

One of the first problems we shall have to face with a culturally diverse student population is that cultural attitudes and world view will produce diverse ideas about the purpose and value of school. One of the first cultural differences to have an impact on the school is the concept of time. Native Americans and Latino students tend toward a polychronic concept of time. They are oriented to doing things when they think the time is appropriate. Classes begin and end when it is appropriate, not when a clock or calendar designates that they should begin or end. This cultural characteristic, as well as a strong family orientation, may well explain why some Mexican students enrolled in United States schools who travel to Mexico at the beginning of the winter holiday season to visit their relatives for Christmas do not return until sometime in March. The values that drive this behavior obviously have precedence over any values that see education as being of prime importance.

Language diversity is another problem that seems overwhelming. Students arriving on an almost daily basis from such diverse countries as Mexico, Peru, Thailand, Korea, Vietnam, Cambodia, Laos, and China—students who may speak no English—place a tremendous burden on the schools. On top of this, some of these students may be beyond the normal age for starting school. Students frequently arrive from abroad at age twelve, never having been to school and not speaking any English, and are placed in junior high schools at a grade level that matches their age. This practice is a disservice to both the newly arrived student and to the other students as well. The question, of course, is what do you do with such a student. One obviously cannot put a twelve-year-old child in kindergarten. This child would not function well in such a placement. The obvious answer is for some sort of instruction in the child's own language— an ideal that is currently quite impractical. Instruction in the child's language presupposes teachers fluent in that particular language; and although educational laws might mandate such placement, the reality is that there are not enough qualified teachers to carry out the mandate. The problem is that the schools have numerous non-English speaking students who are not able to learn because they do not know what is happening.

Another difficulty that affects some children is that they have few role models who value education. For many students, the importance of an education is inherent in the culture, and students approach school highly motivated to participate and learn. In other cultures, however, education is not very important, and it is hard to motivate students from these cultures. Here is where adequate male and female role models from their culture are crucial. We need to do much, therefore, to ensure that role models are available to stimulate and motivate children toward obtaining the education they need in order to function in society.

The public-education sector needs to do much to keep children in school. This requires, however, that the educational system meet the felt and perceived needs of the children. Communication must be a bridge between people. Unfortunately, too frequently the bridges between teachers and students are acutely shaky.[38] We do not pretend to have a solution to this problem, but it does seem obvious that we must revise curricula so that we can free ourselves of the eurocentric approach to education and make our schools responsive to the needs of a culturally diverse student population. We must recognize that not everyone is interested in or capable of mathematics and science beyond the level necessary for getting along in the world. Curricula must be available recognizing that some students have educational needs that are different from those that prepare one for going to college to study science or engineering. We must foster reforms that provide educational objectives for these children so that they do not drop out and so that they may develop the capacity and skills to enter the work force and earn a decent living.

We must recognize that cultural diversity brings about situations for which teachers, counselors, and administrators are not prepared. A recent occurrence in a California junior high school illustrates this. A nearly hysterical Hispanic student told the school principal that he was possessed by a demon. The student spoke little English and could not express himself adequately to the principal. Other Spanish-speaking students with fluency in English talked to the student and confirmed that he believed he was possessed. The other Hispanic students suggested calling in a witch doctor who could deal with the demon. Situations such as this are new, unexpected, and cannot be dealt with by school personnel without special training. The difficulty here is to anticipate the problems and train the school personnel first. Unfortunately, however, it is usually only after the problems occur that new training comes about.

Another cultural problem in educating a culturally diverse population, as we already know from Chapters 7 and 8, is that nonverbal behaviors differ culturally. But unless teachers are familiar with the behaviors associated with the cultures of the children in their classrooms, they may not know what a child is doing, what a child means, or how to interpret a child's nonverbal communication. This can lead to difficulties in evaluating a child. When teachers receive no volunteered answers or head nods from Vietnamese students, for example, they may perceive these students as possessing low intellectual ability. The absence of feedback from these children restricts classroom interaction.

In the United States, students typically raise their hand if they wish attention. But in Jamaica, for instance, students snap their fingers to indicate they know an answer to a question. Teacher-student eye-contact rules also vary culturally. In the United States, children normally look their teachers in the eye while talking with them. How often have we heard someone say, "Johnny, look at me when you speak." But in other cultures, to look someone in the eye may be a sign of disrespect, the sign of respect being to avert one's gaze or to look at the ground or floor. This is quite typical of Asian cultures as well as some Caribbean cultures. If teachers are not aware of this, they can make the mistake of chastising a student for disrespect when the child was displaying his or her culture's sign of respect.

Instead of assuming all students fit the same cultural mold, educators must realize the danger of such thinking and develop an appreciation and awareness of the cultural differences among their students. Students from diverse cultures may experience conflict and frustration when trying to assimilate the practices, rules, and norms of a different culture's classroom environment. Students from a culture where the instructor is the only source of information may not have learned the self-motivation required when asked to read from four or five textbooks, and may be perceived as lazy. Children who are not progressing as fast as others in certain subjects may not be slow but rather may be lacking preparation in those subjects from their past curricula. "Children who are socialized by most of these institutions [American schools] and whose home values are not given institutional recognition may tend to experience conflicts regarding their self-identity and may come to regard their own culture as inferior and undesirable."[39]

In the classroom, students of different cultural backgrounds may react to the same stimulus, but their responses may be different because of the effect of their culture upon their perceptions. These effects may be negative for both the student and the teacher. Students with a Buddhist tradition of silence may have difficulty in adjusting to classroom discussion. If called upon to speak, they may feel embarrassed or ashamed, and the teacher may feel that the student does not understand or comprehend the material. The student may actually understand the material completely but be experiencing a conflict in cultural rules.

In dealing with children from culturally diverse backgrounds, we must remember the effect of that background on the child. Children socialized in cultures that prioritize group achievement, cooperation, obedience and deference to authority, and persons over objects tend to be externally motivated and dependent on praise and reinforcement from significant others. They are more readily responsive to a humanistic, socially oriented curriculum.[40] On the other hand, cultures that emphasize individualism, assertiveness, personal initiative, and material well-being are likely to produce more analytical, competitive, impersonal, individualistic, and task-oriented students. Teachers must match their teaching styles and strategies with their students' learning styles.

One final thought is that not only must the public schools work toward meeting the diverse needs of a multicultural America, but the culturally different students of the 1990s must continue the struggle of informing America that their differences are to be respected. Their quest for education is not a quest for total cultural denial but a quest to participate in American life.

THE HEALTH-CARE CONTEXT

The health-care setting is another important social context on which culture has an impact. Culture plays an important role in defining illness and its treatment. Because of this, when health-care practitioners must treat patients from different cultures, major communication problems may erupt that can cause difficulty in the treatment of the patient. Problems can also arise when people fail to seek medical treatment because of their cultural orientation toward health care. They may, for example, neglect to obtain prenatal care or fail to seek treatment for a serious illness that is a danger to both self and others. In this section we shall look at some of the cultural differences in the definition and treatment of illness and then look at some of the intercultural communication difficulties that can arise in the health-care setting.

The concept of illness differs considerably from culture to culture, as do concepts and practices of treatment. A culture's world view has a great deal to do with concepts of illness, death, and dying. Such factors as the importance of a single life, the acts of fate, and conceptions of heaven or afterlives have an impact on how people view illness, the use of medication, and dying. The Hindus of India, for example, do not perceive death as a dramatic event. One's death means that one will soon be reborn in his or her next life. Christians in Europe and the Americas look upon death differently. Although there is the Christian message of salvation and heaven, Christians nevertheless perceive death as an unhappy event. For Muslims, death is the passage to heaven, and the Islamic religion paints such a lovely picture of heaven that people are prepared to die to go there.

Highly technological and scientific cultures such as the United States, Canada, England, much of Europe, and parts of Asia, view illness as an infection or disease that can be treated by some form of intervention, which may be in the form of medication, surgery, or physical therapy. In low technological and scientific cultures, however, a lay view of illness is likely to hold forth.

Lay theories of illness usually are part of wider concepts about the origin of misfortune in general. They tend to be based on beliefs about the structure and function of the body and the ways in which it can malfunction. These notions of illness frequently have an internal logic and consistency that help victims of illness make sense of what has happened and why. In most cultures, concepts of illness are part of a complex body of inherited folklore.

In general, lay theories of illness place the cause of ill health within the individual patient, in the natural world, in the social world, or in the supernatural world. Social and supernatural causes tend to be a feature of non-Western cultures, while natural or patient-centered explanations are more common in the West. In some cases illness is ascribed to combinations of causes or to interactions between these various worlds.[41] In India, for instance, common colds, headaches, stomach aches, scabies, gonorrhea, and syphilis are regarded as natural diseases. But persistent headaches, intermittent fevers, continued stomach disorders, rickets and other wasting diseases among children, menstrual troubles, and repeated miscarriages are attributed to supernatural forces.[42]

Social world theories typically blame other people for one's illness. This is typical of small-scale societies where interpersonal conflicts are frequent. The most common causes of illness in these societies are witchcraft, sorcery, and the evil eye. Witchcraft beliefs are particularly common in Africa and the Caribbean. Here, people are believed to possess mystical power that permits them to harm others. Sorcery is the power to manipulate and alter natural and supernatural events with the proper magical knowledge and performance of rituals. Sorcerers exert their power consciously for reasons of envy or malice. They cause illness through certain spells, potions, or rituals. Low-income African Americans often ascribe ill health to sorcery known as voodoo, hoodoo, crossing up, fixing, hexing, or witchcraft. The evil eye as a cause of illness is reported throughout Europe, the Middle East, and North Africa. Italians call it the *mal occhia*, Hispanics the *mal de ojo*, and Arabs the *ayn*. In the Middle East the evil eye is found among all communities whether Islamic, Jewish, Christian, or Zoroastrian.

People ascribe illnesses from the supernatural world to the direct actions of supernatural entities such as gods, spirits, or ancestral shades. Low-income black

Americans often describe illness as a reminder from God of some behavioral lapse such as neglecting to go to church regularly, not saying one's prayers, or not thanking God for daily blessings. They see illness as a "whuppin'," a divine punishment for sinful behavior. On this basis, neither home remedies nor a physician are considered useful in treating the condition. A cure involves acknowledgment of sin, sorrow for having committed it, and a vow to improve one's behavior.[43]

Just as illness is perceived differently from culture to culture so is the treatment of illness. Throughout human history, there have always been individuals who claimed to be able to give assistance for certain kinds of illness. Even in countries where professional medical care is highly developed, individual healers, some of whom have little if any scientific training, continue to practice their real or alleged skills and to attract a clientele who would describe themselves as well-educated.[44]

In highly technological and scientific cultures such as the United States, Canada, and much of Europe, there is a strong tendency to use human intervention against illness. This ranges from many forms of surgery to a variety of medicines that fight disease, and has developed to such an extent that many people are of the opinion that there is a pill to cure almost everything.

But even in high-technology societies, the approach to treatment is frequently quite different from one culture to another. In the United States, with its tradition of a "can do" spirit and value for change, we see medicine as aggressive, and we are willing to try anything that might work to save or prolong a life. We even go to the extent of prolonging the life of people in comas with irreversible brain damage, people who would die without costly and sophisticated life-support systems.

French physicians follow in the intellectual footsteps of Descartes, putting more stock in the theory that underlies a treatment than any experimental evidence that it actually works. The French also are keenly sensitive to bodily aesthetics. This sensitivity is a major reason doctors tend to treat breast and other types of cancer by radiation rather than by surgery. The French also have a high regard for a woman's childbearing ability and, consequently, perform hysterectomies only for cancer and other serious conditions.

Physicians in Great Britain also perform less surgery than do physicians in the United States. Under the English form of socialized medicine, there are also rules that govern who can receive certain forms of treatment. For instance, people over the age of fifty-five may not receive kidney dialysis treatments. Of course, those who can afford private care may receive such treatment at their own expense.

The Japanese do not believe in organ transplants. If one is ill with an organ disease, they will not resort to a transplant to save a patient's life. The Japanese also have a tradition of not telling patients that they have a terminal illness. They argue that the revelation of a bleak diagnosis will result in depression and even provoke suicide. Even Emperor Hirohito was unaware that he was dying from cancer. The extent of this value in Japanese culture is revealed by the fact that a Japanese court ruled recently that patients did not have the right to have a physician fully inform them of their disease.

In less technological societies, treatment frequently involves merely making someone comfortable until the illness runs its course. The patient will either recover or die, and the purpose of medicine is to make the patient as comfortable as possible until fate determines the final outcome.

The Chinese make extensive use of herbs and acupuncture. This use is not restricted to Chinese living in China but extends to the Chinese living throughout the world. Many shops in San Francisco and Los Angeles specialize in Chinese herb medicine, which provides a large export market for China.

In India, when people get sick they go to see either an Akyur-Vedic or homeopathic person. These healers use natural forms of medicine, which can be effective sometimes. There is still a fear and reluctance to go to real physicians, especially among women. The medical settings are primitive except in big cities, where there may be decent hospitals. Physicians have little shops in the streets, and after a very rudimentary examination will give you some pills from their own stock.

The Soviet Union has employed psychic powers to heal the ill. The government has united as many as thirty thousand psychic healers at one time to pool their powers and to provide healing for the ill. The Soviets have spent as much as 350 million dollars on psychic research.

Other cultures place much faith in the healing talents of traditional medicine men. This is particularly true among tribal societies that have not accepted modern medicine. People rely on plants and herbs as ways of treating illness, as well as on "magic" prayers and chants by their tribal healers. When some of these people receive treatment in modern societies, they will often throw away the prescribed medicine and use their traditional herbs and plants instead.

Among Vietnamese and other Asian cultures there is a widely practiced remedy called spooning or coining. In the spooning treatment, a spoon is rubbed vigorously back and forth across the body of a patient, most often on the back and the back of the neck. Coining involves using a coin about the size of a quarter, which one rubs on the back of the neck, the stomach, the chest, the upper arms, and even along the forehead and temples. This activity is called "rubbing out the wind" because of a cultural belief that a bad spiritual wind is responsible for ill health, and that vigorous rubbing with the spoon or coin can excise the wind from the body. This practice has caused difficulty in American schools because spooning and coining can leave bruises and ridges that look suspiciously like strap marks. In a number of cases, teachers have referred Asian children to authorities because they feared that the children were the victims of child abuse.

The Navajo conception of health is very different from ours. For the Navajo, health is a sign of a correct relationship between an individual and his or her environment, which consists of the supernatural environment, the world around him or her, and fellow human beings. The Navajo associate health with good, blessing, and beauty, which are the main values in Navajo life. Illness, on the other hand, bears evidence that one has fallen out of this delicate balance by breaking one of the taboos that guide the behavior of Navajos. Illness may also be due to contact with the ghosts of the dead, or even to the malevolence of another Navajo who has resorted to witchery. The Navajo do not make the distinction between religion and medicine that we do; for them, they are aspects of the same thing. This is an important cultural fact that many workers in the health field have failed to realize; as a result, many doctors and nurses have antagonized their Navajo patients.[45]

Among the Navajo, the individual who is sick does not act on his own. The family takes matters into its own hands once it realizes that one of their number is sick. After the diagnostician has indicated the root of the illness, he or she calls for a *singer*. Singers are the men who carry out the ceremonials designed to bring the dangerous illness under control, to drive out evil, and to attract the good and beautiful. The diagnostician will suggest what *sing* should be performed, and the family goes off to find a singer who knows the required ceremony. The family is all present during the sing, which may last from one to nine nights, depending on the nature of the illness and the economic position of the family. Relatives and friends come to the ceremony and take part in the chants and prayers the medicine man and his assistant have chosen. By association, they too receive positive benefits from the cure, and in turn the presence of the family and friends is reassuring to the patient, who feels they are all working to restore his or her health. [46]

With the influx of people from Southeast Asia and southern China there has been a marked increase in the use of **shamans,** who are traditional folk healers much like the medicine men in American Indian tribes. The shaman tradition can be traced all the way back to Paleolithic times. Shamans believe that the world is alive with spirits, that trees, mountains, lightning, and rivers are animate creatures able to communicate with humankind. An intimate relationship between humans and animals is also part of their view. Because animals are kindred creatures, shamans can share and exchange spirits with them; hence, they sacrifice animals during ceremonies of healing. Many problems arise in the United States when shamans use chickens, dogs, snakes, and buffalo horns as part of the healing tradition.

As you can see from this discussion of cultural diversity in the treatment of illness, there are many differing perceptions of illness and its proper treatment. This can lead to communication failures when health-care personnel and patients come from different cultures. In the remainder of the chapter we shall see how some of these difficulties have manifested themselves in the arena of health care.

When the cultural backgrounds of the health-care provider and the patient are different, the treatment, especially in an emergency situation, can cause the patient great anxiety. An African woman who came to the United States to live with her son provides an excellent example. She spoke no English, and her beliefs about medicine were firmly rooted in African culture. While her son was away from the home, she became ill. A neighbor found her and rushed her to the hospital. Not speaking the language or understanding what was happening, the woman was terrified, and she was mortified when strangers removed her clothes and started probing her body. She could be of no assistance in the diagnosis or even indicate where her pain was located. The emergency-room physician finally prescribed a tranquilizer. When the nurses tried to give the woman the medication in pill form, she became even more agitated and would not take the medicine, so the physician prescribed an injection. When she refused to lie still for this, she was tied down and given the shot. From that point, she huddled in a ball under the covers of her bed and the head nurse observed that the patient was likely to die from fear if not from her illness. The mother's condition worsened and exploratory surgery was scheduled. The physician was hesitant to proceed, however, until he had informed consent from the patient or from the son. He tried to explain nonverbally what he was going to do to the patient. Taking a knife, he gestured over her stomach, and she began moaning and screaming. This continued for hours until the son finally reached the hospital. The son was horrified at the manner in which his mother had been treated. Her African beliefs held that medicine in pill form was the white man's magic and should never cross the lips of a true believer. In addition, in her view the knife-wielding physician had threatened her, as it was taboo in her country to penetrate the skin with a knife. The well-intentioned health professional had threatened two of her important beliefs, and this had caused her much distress.[47]

Cultural differences can cause another difficulty in health care by prescribing who can look at a nude woman. In some cultures only the husband may see his wife nude. This can cause difficulties in seeking treatment because taking a woman to a physician who must examine her violates that prescription. There have been cases in the United States in which women have almost died because they could not bring themselves to seek care from a medical system that required them to be examined by a physician.

Cultural norms about openness and self-disclosure are other dimensions of interaction that one must consider. In some cultures it is not permissible to talk about female diseases or problems. Women from Mexico frequently are unwilling to talk to American physicians about birth control or childbirth. And quite frequently, many elderly patients feel too embarrassed about their illnesses to talk to physicians.

When working with patients it is important for health-care providers to take the time to establish a trusting relationship. A female proctologist and a male client need to establish trust before an examination. Likewise, the traditional Chinese female and the hurried American male gynecologist must do the same. Some blacks believe that members of their race have been used as guinea pigs in medical research, and it frequently is necessary to build trust in the provider-patient relationship to allay those fears.

In general, the health-care professional who is working with clients or with other health-care personnel from other cultures can employ techniques that will facilitate better communication. In the first place, it is useful to remember that most people are ethnocentric in their first contacts with and approaches to an alien way of living. To most people, their way of life is a precious possession. To outsiders who have their own habits and assumptions, this way of life or culture often appears incongruous and misguided. Health-care professionals often transfer from their own cultural background their expectations of how people will behave or ought to behave in certain crises or illnesses. Most importantly, one must take the time to discover what kinds of special verbal or nonverbal information are necessary to establish effective interaction. What are the space needs of the individual from the other culture? Does he or she respond to touch? Are there special rules of protocol that one should follow? [48]

SUMMARY

Context and Communication

- Culturally derived rules specify how communication is to take place by prescribing the appropriate behaviors in given contexts.

- In the business context, rules regarding such things as time, the protocol of doing business, and formality vary from culture to culture.

- In the education context, culture determines what students learn and how they learn it. These differences can lead to problems in educating a culturally diverse population.

- Culture plays an important role in defining illness and its treatment.

ACTIVITIES

1. Discuss the differences, if any, in approaches to health care between your informant's culture and your own. Present him or her with a list of typical North American ailments and discuss the way in which they would be treated in both cultures. Possible conditions to discuss include depression, obesity, anemia, cosmetic surgery, cancer (and particular kinds of cancer, such as breast or uterine), and allergies. Try to find cultural values that explain the differences in treatment, if any. Did you mention any diseases

that your informant could not even find an equivalent for in his or her culture? How do you account for this?

2. In small groups, read the following situation and analyze it in terms of cultural values with regard to health care.

A young American journalist based in Europe had a fibroid tumor in her uterus. She consulted a French doctor, who wanted to perform a myomectomy, an operation wherein the tumor is removed but the uterus is left intact and functional. Home on vacation, she next consulted a U.S. doctor, who immediately wanted to perform a hysterectomy. [*]

DISCUSSION IDEAS

1. Give examples from your current course materials and textbooks that reflect North American ethnocentrism.

2. Discuss ways in which your current educational setting embodies North American cultural values such as competition and individuality.

3. A college instructor has a new foreign student in his class, a young Nigerian. The Nigerian consistently looks down at the floor when the instructor addresses him. The instructor is confused by this behavior, and feels that maybe the Nigerian student is not paying attention to him. Explain the problem in terms of cultural values with regard to the educational setting.

[*]This example is adapted from an incident related in the book *Medicine and Culture,* by Lynn Payer (Henry Holt, 1988).

NOTES FOR CHAPTER 9

1. K. Oberg, "Culture Shock: Adjustment to New Cultural Environments," *Practical Anthropology* (1960), 177.

2. P. Harris and R. Moran, *Managing Cultural Differences* (Houston: Gulf, 1987), 207.

3. Harris and Moran.

4. L. Copeland and L. Griggs, *Going International: How to Make Friends and Deal Effectively in the Global Marketplace* (New York: Random House, 1985), xx.

5. Edward T. Hall, *Beyond Culture* (Garden City, NY: Doubleday, 1976).

6. Copeland and Griggs, 107.

7. Jan Servaes, "Cultural Identity in East and West," *Howard Journal of Communication* 1(1988), 68.

8. Servaes, 68.

9. Servaes, 68.

10. N. Hatvany and V. Pucik, "Japanese Management Practices," *Organizational Dynamics* (1981), 8.

11. K. Tanisuichi, "Japan's Cultural Imperatives," *International Marketing* (1989), 64.

12. M. Misawa, "New Japanese-style Management in a Changing Era," *The Columbia Journal of World Business* (1987), 9–17.

13. S. P. Sethi, H. Namiki, and C. L. O. Swanson, *The False Promise of the Japanese Miracle* (Boston: Pitman, 1984).

14. J. S. Bowman, "The Rising Sun (Part 1)," *The Personnel Administrator* (1986), 67.

15. Hatvany and Pucik, 16.

16. Sethi, Namiki, and Swanson, 10.

17. Copeland and Griggs, 8.

18. Copeland and Griggs, 9.

19. Copeland and Griggs, 10.

20. Copeland and Griggs, 15.

21. Servaes, 65.

22. R. Patai, *The Arab Mind,* rev. ed. (New York: Scribner's, 1983), 49.

23. Stanly B. Lubman, "Negotiating in China: Observations of a Lawyer," in *Communicating with China,* ed. Robert A. Kapp (Chicago: Intercultural Press, 1987).

24. J. Henry, "A Cross-Cultural Outline of Education," in *Educational Patterns and Cultural Configurations,* ed. J. Roberts and S. Akinsanya (New York: David McKay, 1976).

25. M. Saville-Troike, *A Guide to Culture in the Classroom* (Rosslyn, VA: National Clearinghouse for Bilingual Education, 1978).

26. E. Ignas and R. Corsini, *Comparative Educational Systems* (Itasca, IL: F. E. Peacock, 1981).

27. I. Thut and D. Adams, *Educational Patterns in Contemporary Societies* (New York: McGraw-Hill, 1964).

28. H. Fuentes, "Hispanics' Dropout Rate an 'Alarming' 45% in High Schools," *The San Diego Union,* Dec. 16, 1984, 1, 6.

29. L. Damen, *Culture Learning: The Fifth Dimension in the Language Classroom* (Menlo Park, CA: Addison-Wesley, 1987), 315.

30. Janis F. Andersen, "Educational Assumptions Highlighted from a Crosscultural Comparison," in *Intercultural Communication: A Reader,* 4th ed., ed. Larry A. Samovar and Richard E. Porter (Belmont, CA: Wadsworth, 1985), 162.

31. M. Farquharson, *Ideas for Teaching Arab Students in a Multicultural Setting.* Paper presented at the annual meeting of the Teachers of English to Speakers of Other Languages, March 1988, Chicago, IL (ERIC Document Reproduction Service No. ED 296 575), 5.

32. H. D. Brown, *Principles of Language Learning and Teaching,* 2d ed. (Englewood Cliffs, NJ: Prentice-Hall, 1987), 85.

33. Brown, 86.

34. M. Ramirez, "Cognitive Styles and Cultural Democracy in Action," in *Toward Multiculturalism: A Reader in Multicultural Education,* ed. James S. Wurzel (Yarmouth, MN: Intercultural Press, 1988), 198–206. See also Brown and Damen.

35. Damen, 302.

36. Nemi C. Jain, "Some Basic Cultural Patterns of India," in *Intercultural Communication: A Reader,* 5th ed., ed. Larry A. Samovar and Richard E. Porter (Belmont, CA: Wadsworth, 1988), 108.

37. N. S. Mehta, S. Monroe, and D. Winbush, "Beyond the Melting Pot," *Time*, April 9, 1990, 28–31.

38. J. Mills, R. Mills, and N. Simpson, *Cross-cultural Conflict in Higher Education*, NADE Research Report No. 4 (Chicago, IL: National Association for Developmental Education; ERIC Document Reproduction Service No. ED 274 383), 35.

39. N. Asuncion-Lande, "Implications of Intercultural Communication for Bilingual and Bicultural Education," *International and Intercultural Communication Annual 2*, ed. Fred Kasmir (Falls Church, VA: Speech Communication Association, 1975), 63.

40. G. Gay, "Interactions in Culturally Pluralistic Classrooms," in *Education in the Eighties: Multiethnic Education*, ed. J. Banks (Washington, DC: National Education Association, 1981), 42–53.

41. C. Helman, *Culture, Health and Illness: An Introduction for Health Professionals* (Boston: Wright-PSG, 1984).

42. M. Read, *Culture, Health, and Disease*, (London: Tavistock Publications, 1966), 27.

43. Helman.

44. Read, 15.

45. Read, 25–26.

46. Read, 10.

47. G. Kreps and B. Thornton, *Health Communication: Theory and Practice* (New York: Longman, 1984), 190–91.

48. Kreps and Thornton.

III

KNOWLEDGE
INTO ACTION

*It does me no injury for my neighbor to say there are twenty gods,
or no God.*

THOMAS JEFFERSON

Not unless we fill our existence with an aim do we make it a life.

REICHEL

CHAPTER TEN

ACCEPTING DIFFERENCES AND APPRECIATING SIMILARITIES: A POINT OF VIEW

We conclude this book in much the same way we started it—by calling your attention to the obvious, yet often overlooked, fact that changes in transportation, information systems, political dynamics, and economics have created a world where people from diverse backgrounds are confronting each other with a regularity that is unique to this period of history. The manner in which we face and respond to these contacts influences our lives in subtle and profound ways. That is to say, the results of these contacts range from individual touch points that may offer us a new friend whose experiences we find exhilarating, to understanding alternative concepts of life and death so that we can escape the tragic consequences of global annihilation.

We can also visualize our reasons for wanting to improve the quality of our intercultural encounters by placing individual motivations on a continuum. You may choose to amend your communication behavior because this can bring you personal gain, such as a better career because you understand differences in international negotiation styles, or because you see the humanitarian benefits of interacting with other cultures so that together we can overcome the fact that "40,000 babies die each day from malnutrition and disease."[1] You may, of course, have many reasons for wanting to improve the way you interact with "strangers." Regardless of the motivation that moves you to action, knowing how to communicate with different cultures is a worthwhile pursuit. It is also one you have been practicing for the last nine chapters. In this final section of the book we simply ask you to continue those efforts. We believe that such improvement is not only desirable but possible. Let us begin this final chapter by explaining why we believe that the power to become a more effective intercultural communicator is all yours—should you elect to use that power.

A PHILOSOPHY OF CHANGE

Our strong belief that improvement is possible is based on three interrelated assumptions that lie at the heart of human behavior: (1) the brain is an open system, (2) we have free choice, and (3) our behavior influences other people. Although we examined these three axioms in Chapter 2, they deserve further scrutiny so that we can see why they are the force behind this chapter.

The Brain Is an Open System

In Chapter 2 we pointed out that one of the most engrossing aspects of the human brain is that there is no upper limit to what it can receive and store. As we move from moment to moment in our lives we can, and in fact do, learn from each experience. If we tell you, at this moment, that the first word in the dictionary is *aal* and that it stands for an "East Indian shrub which yields a red dye," you now know something you did not know before you read this sentence. Although our example is rather superficial, it nevertheless illustrates the idea that we can always learn. Our ability to learn, and to change, is indeed a rare gift. It means that we are not condemned to one outlook, only one way of acting, or one set of "truths" for all of our lives. Rather, it heralds the notion that change is as much a part of the living process as is breathing. Cultures may differ in the degree to which they welcome change, but change is unavoidable in nature and in human relationships. Accepting the axiom that we are always learning and changing should assist you in developing a philosophy that mirrors an observation Plutarch advanced over two thousand years ago: "All things are daily changing." You can use change to improve the way in which you send and receive messages.

We Have Free Choice

Having just developed the idea that learning and change are inevitable, we now offer another truism about human behavior that extends the concept one step further. This supposition, while complex in how it is acted out, is elementary in its stating. We can articulate it in four words: We have free choice. This notion should prompt us to recall that most of what we do in life, from selecting a single word when we speak, to deciding on a mate, we do of our own feel will. Although countless events in each of our lives seem out of our control, we freely choose most of what we do, and fail to do. Reflect if you will on the two examples we used a few lines ago. We said that each word we choose is under our jurisdiction. We could, for example, have used the word *control* instead of *jurisdiction* in the last line, but chose the word *we* wanted—it was *our* choice. The same idea even applies to the influence we have over our actions. Even though many actions are habitual, when we greet a stranger we can still decide to smile, frown, look the person in the eye, or glance down.

Our second example, that of mate selection, also underscores the degree of freedom we enjoy in conducting our lives. We decide what traits we want in a mate and who measures up to that yardstick. Although selecting a lover might be harder than selecting what words to use, the principle is the same—we have free will. How we use that freedom is also a matter of choice, and we should also add that the degree of choice is also a matter of our cultural background. For example, North Americans have a great deal of choice in nearly everything from the selection of clothing to careers. In many parts of the world, however, people have much less freedom than we. In China and India it is not uncommon for parents to help select marriage partners for their children. Yet even with these cultural differences, we all must make decisions. As George Moore wrote, "The difficulty in life is the choice." This final chapter will urge you to *choose* to improve your intercultural communication skills.

Communication Has a Consequence

Our final introductory edict is yet another one of those ideas that takes us back to Chapter 2. In that chapter we discussed how each of our actions, be it a word or a movement, produces a response from our communication partner(s). That is to say, the way we communicate and what we communicate has an effect on someone else. Here at the end of the book we wish only to remind you of that fact, and to show you later in the chapter how it directly relates to the topic of improvement.

By remembering that the brain is an open system, that you do have choices, and that your actions affect others, you can begin to appreciate the power you have over whether or not you improve your communication behavior. To assist you in your efforts toward becoming a more effective communicator, we have come up with four closely related goals and purposes. First, we shall review some potential problems facing anyone who is engaged in intercultural communication. Second, we shall explore the resolution of these problems and offer some advice for improvement. Third, because communication is such a personal activity, we shall see how a new ethical stance toward other people and cultures can make us more effective intercultural communicators. And finally, we shall explore the future of intercultural communication—a future that will see our intercultural contacts increase and intensify both at home and abroad.

POTENTIAL PROBLEMS IN INTERCULTURAL COMMUNICATION

It is not by chance that we used the word *potential* in the title of this section. We selected the word as a way of underscoring the idea that every intercultural encounter contains the ingredients for both success and failure. We have reviewed the literature relevant to intercultural communication obstacles and isolated six problems that seem to afflict many intercultural encounters. We shall look at that research when we discuss the success dimension in the second segment of this chapter. We should point out before we begin our discussion of potential problems and solutions that our own cultural experiences will undoubtedly color the pictures we draw. As two white male college professors born and raised in North America, we have experienced the "hidden grip" of culture that influences all of our lives. Although we have tried to assume a global orientation, we want to alert you to the Western bias that may occasionally, and we hope only accidentally, creep into our commentary.

Seeking Similarities

We can perhaps best clarify this initial problem by asking you to think about your personal communication behavior—more specifically, what sort of people you choose to be around and how you select your friends. Most likely you gravitate toward people who are a lot like you. Although this observation is not profound, it is nevertheless true. For decades the research on initial attraction and the development of friendships has revealed an overwhelming tendency among all of us to seek out people whom we perceive to be much like ourselves. It is a very natural inclination when meeting someone to think about talking about a topic that both parties might enjoy; and should those topics prove interesting, it is equally natural for friendships to form and evolve. Attraction, both physical and intellectual, is stronger when you and your communication partner parallel each other in a number of ways.

The connection between intercultural communication and our bias to solicit friends and acquaintances who mirror our personality should be obvious. As we have said throughout this book, a culture gives its members specialized patterns of communication—patterns that are often dissimilar to those of people from other cultures. Because of these cultural differences, we often confront individuals whose background and experiences seem so odd that we are not attracted to them. Hence, culture, by its very nature, often separates us from people with a history different from our own. The poet Emily Dickinson vividly described this separation when she wrote, "The Soul selects her own Society— / Then— shuts the Door— / To her divine Majority— / Present no more." Her message is crystalline: We prefer our own kind and avoid the unfamiliar. Imagine what this does to intercultural communication.

Uncertainty Reduction

Our second potential problem grows out of a body of research done under the heading of **uncertainty reduction.**[2] Even though the theory was first presented in 1975, researchers have tested it for the last fifteen years. The communication axioms this theory has generated are clear and are directly related to intercultural communication.

Berger and Calabrese summarize this theory by writing, "Central to the present theory is the assumption that when strangers meet, their primary concern is one of uncertainty reduction or increasing predictability about the behavior of both themselves and others in the interaction."[3] According to the theory, all of us have a high need to understand both the self and the other when facing interpersonal situations. By means of communication we gain that understanding; we reduce uncertainty and gain insight into our partner by "increasing predictability." Gathering information to increase this predictability is difficult when one is confronted with people from other cultures. As you have learned in this book, the information is often unfamiliar or even strange. If you don't understand what a certain action means, how can you use that action to reduce uncertainty? Hence, cultural differences often make the reduction of uncertainty very difficult.

Diversity of Communication Purposes

Communication problems often occur because we all have different reasons and motivations for deciding when and why to communicate. These reasons range from the simple to the complex, and cover purposes as diverse as seeking the time of day from another person to "having our say" as a means of experiencing an emotional catharsis. In the intercultural setting this diversity of purposes can present problems. For example, on a superficial level we might be misunderstood if, while traveling in Turkey, we were to approach an elderly female dressed in traditional apparel and ask her to recommend a hotel or restaurant. Such an advance, by a male stranger, would be highly inappropriate, and our innocent reason for making contact could be misconstrued.

The second example, that of an emotional outburst, is even a better illustration of diverse communication purposes. In our culture we often use communication to "get things off our chest" or to "clear the air." In many other cultures communication is not used for these purposes. Quite the contrary, these types of feelings are left unexpressed for a number of reasons, each one demonstrating how diverse cultures are in their use of communication. First, many cultures believe verbal explosions disrupt the natural peace and harmony that exists between people, and therefore do not employ communication to express personal feelings.

Second, there are cultural differences in how much one actually must express. You will recall that elsewhere in the book, when we discussed Hall's notion of high- and low-context cultures, we noted that high-context cultures (east Asian, American Indian, Latin American, and eastern Mediterranean) rely mainly on the physical context and/or the relationships between people for the important information.[4] They believe that explicit verbal utterances are not necessary, and hence use "talk" in ways that are quite different from the low-context cultures of the Swiss, Germans, and North Americans. For high-context cultures, verbal communication alone does not always serve the purpose. Again we can see potential problems arising when people make different uses of the communication process.

Withdrawal

Perhaps this fourth intercultural problem is actually an extension of the first three, for if we can't find similarities and/or we fail to reduce uncertainty, we often withdraw from the communication event. Although it is a rather somber commentary on our times, it appears that "modern life," with its rapid pace, urbanization, massive institutions, and mediated contacts, has created a sense of bewilderment, alienation, and detachment. A common response to disaffection is to retreat rather than confront the cause of the separation. When this happens the consequences are obvious. Communication is impossible when we are separated from other people. We can no longer learn from, support, or persuade people who have withdrawn.

On both the international and domestic levels, withdrawal has often marked the intercultural exchange. History is full of examples of how one nation or group of people refused to attend (withdrew from) an important peace conference. For decades the governments of the United States and the Soviet Union, like East and West Germany, rebuffed each other, only to discover decades later that talking helped both parties. If we examine our own behavior, we might see occasions when, like governments, we withdrew from communication. In many of these instances the other person might have had a different skin color, gender, or cultural heritage. When this happens there can be little communication. In an age when each cultural group has some sway over another, retreat can harm everyone. As the philosopher Flewelling once wrote, "Neither province, parish, nor nation; neighborhood, family, nor individual, can live profitably in exclusion from the rest of the world."

Before we conclude this section on withdrawal we must remind you once again about the Western bias of some of our advice. The concept of "talking things out" and confronting what is "wrong" are two examples of North American communication strategies. As we have noted, in cultures that highly value interpersonal harmony, withdrawal would be quite appropriate. That is to say, there are even cultural differences in the value placed on the act of communicating.

Ethnocentrism

Although we have discussed ethnocentrism throughout this book, it is important enough to the study of intercultural communication to deserve yet further inquiry. In fact, many scholars believe that because we learn ethnocentrism so early in life, and on the unconscious level, it might well be the single major barrier to intercultural communication. Its impact on intercultural communication is buttressed by the fact that all cultures display some signs of ethnocentrism. To appreciate the significance of ethnocentrism as a potential problem, you need only recall two themes we have stressed in each of the preceding chapters. We have continuously emphasized the notion of individual differences and the uniqueness of each person. While granting that we experience the world from inside our skin, however, we have also mentioned the corollary position that culture, by selecting and evaluating certain experiences, helps determine what that world looks like. Culture helps supply us with our perspective on reality. For example, if males in the dominant culture value women who are thin, young, and blond, then they will perceive women who are stout, older, and dark-haired in a somewhat less favorable light. If we perceive openness as a positive trait while another culture fosters silence, we again have perceptual differences. If we value competition and other cultures stress cooperation, we might interpret the way they work in groups quite differently. These three cases—and there are countless others—are examples of how perception influences communication.

When our perceptions are narrow and our subsequent behaviors rigid, we are guilty of ethnocentrism. The link between ethnocentrism and potential communication problems is illustrated in the definition of ethnocentrism Ruhly has advanced. Ruhly defines ethnocentrism as "the tendency to interpret or to judge all other groups, their environments, and their communication according to the categories and values of our own culture."[5] Reflect for a moment on those times when we have placed one cultural group above another because we judged them through the lens of our culture. How do we regard Chinese, Germans, blacks, or gays? In most instances we evaluate them by standards we have learned from our culture.

As we have noted, even the counsel advanced in this chapter contains traces of the enthnocentrism of both authors. The danger of such counsel is that it can be limited, arbitrary, and often false and misleading. It is truly a naive view of the world to believe and behave as if our culture, regardless of what it might be, had discovered *the* true and ultimate set of norms. Jews cover their heads when they pray, Protestants do not—is one more correct than the other? The Catholic speaks to God, the Buddhist has no God—is one more correct than the other? In parts of Saudi Arabia women cover their faces, in the United States they often cover very little—is one more correct than the other? A list of such questions is never-ending. We urge you to remember, however, that it is not the questions that are important, but rather the dogmatic manner in which people often answer them. If we allow ethnocentrism to interfere with our perceptions, our reactions, and our interactions, we will reduce the effectiveness of communication. To be successful, we must be vigilant to the ease with which we negatively judge the actions of others. The danger of ethnocentrism is that it is strongest in political, moral, and religious settings. In these contexts it is easy to let myopic views overshadow rationality. Taken one step further, ethnocentrism might even lead to outward hostility.

Stereotyping and Prejudice

In many ways our final problem is an extension of ethnocentrism, for stereotyping and prejudice have their roots in an orientation that is based on a rigid in-group–out-group distinction. The distinctions, however, and the unfavorable images they foster, often lie below the level of awareness and therefore can go undetected. Although in most cases stereotypes and prejudice work in tandem, it serves our purposes to examine them separately. We hope that an analysis of these two problems will enable you to see the adverse results of letting our cultural predispositions alter the accuracy of our social perceptions.

Stereotypes are the perceptions or beliefs we hold about groups or individuals based on previously formed opinions and attitudes. We should pause for just a moment and make one important point about stereotypes before we go on. Human beings have a psychological need to categorize and classify. The world outside of us is too big, too complex, and too transitory for us to know in any detail. Hence, we classify and pigeonhole as one way of making sense out of that world. As we discussed earlier in the chapter, human beings don't like ambiguity and uncertainty, and therefore employ existing categories as a way of deciding what they think of the group or person they are confronting.

Stereotypes do not develop suddenly; culture forms and molds them. They are made up of bits and pieces of information, yet we store and use them as large conclusions. Often the bits and traits we select consist of positive characteristics. We might, for example, believe that doctors are concerned about the welfare of their clients. However, these are not the types of stereotypes we are concerned with in a section called "potential problems." Our focus is on stereotypes "as rigid preconceptions which are applied to all members of a group or to an individual over a period of time, regardless of individual variations."[6]

Stereotypes are also dangerous because they are oversimplified, overgeneralized, and/or exaggerated. Because they are beliefs that are composed of half-truths, distortions, and often untrue premises, you should be able to realize why we refer to stereotyping as a "potential problem."

If we are not careful, the intercultural setting can become an environment that cultivates negative stereotypes. The intercultural context frequently brings people together who have very little knowledge about each other. When this happens, people often take the easy path and invoke stereotypes. It is both effortless and comfortable to say quickly, "All Jews are . . ." or "He is Mexican; therefore he must. . . ." Such conclusions take very little energy, and also exonerate the individual from any other serious thinking. People are able, often without ever knowing a Jew or a Mexican, to act as if they knew all about these groups of people. Stereotypes represent a lazy method of perception.

Not only is stereotyping an indolent way of perceiving and communicating with other people, but for many it is a defense mechanism and a way of reducing culture shock. Bock has described culture shock as the disturbing sensation of disorientation, frustration, and helplessness that results from direct exposure to an alien and unfamiliar society.[7] When faced with symbols we are not accustomed to, we often revert to stereotyping as a means of overcoming the feelings associated with culture shock.

Prejudice, like stereotypes, varies in direction and intensity. It can be either positive or negative, but once again we shall concentrate on those aspects of prejudice that are most destructive. Plotnik and Mollenauer clearly illustrate the damaging effect of prejudice, and its link to stereotyping, through both the definition and example they provide: "Prejudice refers to an unfair, biased, or intolerant attitude towards another group of people. An example of prejudice would be the attitude that women should not be in positions of power because they are not as logical or competent as men."[8]

Prejudice, again like stereotypes, can take many forms, ranging from those that are almost impossible to detect to those that are clearly blatant. Let us look at a few of these forms so that we might be able to identify them before they impede our communication with other people.

In an essay entitled "Prejudice in Intercultural Communication," Brislin discusses six ways in which prejudice can express itself: (1) red-neck racism, (2) symbolic racism, (3) tokenism, (4) arm's-length prejudice, (5) real likes and dislikes, and (6) the familiar and unfamiliar.[9] Red-neck racism, which Brislin maintains is found all over the world, occurs when "certain people believe that members of a given cultural group are inferior according to some imagined standard and that the group members are not worthy of decent treatment."[10] Symbolic racism finds its expression when members of one culture, or co-culture, have adverse feelings about another culture because they believe the "outside culture" is endangering their group.

Tokenism is a form of prejudice that is often difficult to detect. For when applying tokenism, the prejudiced party does not want to admit that it harbors negative feelings and is, in fact, prejudiced. It will even engage in "token" activities to "prove" its evenhandedness. The term *arm's-length* is very descriptive of the fourth type of prejudice Brislin mentions. In these instances people engage in what appears to be friendly behaviors with out-group members on certain occasions, but hold these same people at "arm's-length" in other environments.

Real likes and dislikes evolve because people actually employ behaviors that members of the in-group find distasteful. When those behaviors arise, such as arriving late if one values promptness, prejudice occurs. Brislin's final type of prejudice, the familiar and unfamiliar, is not as severe as some of the other forms we have been looking at. It deals with instances when people choose to associate only with individuals and groups just like themselves. As we said earlier in this chapter, human beings don't like the unfamiliar, and hence gravitate to what is familiar and avoid what they are unaccustomed to. Again, although this is a mild form of prejudice, it is nevertheless prejudice.

We would suggest that all of Brislin's six expressions of prejudice are restrained and moderate when compared to some of the manifestations of prejudice that the world has witnessed. Perhaps the most vivid example of extreme prejudice can be found in the area of discrimination. In cases of discrimination we observe ethnocentrism, stereotyping, and prejudice bordering on fanaticism. When discrimination replaces communication we see covert behavior that restricts a group's opportunity or access to resources solely on the basis of group membership, color, race, gender, and the like. When a real-estate agent will not show homes to black people who want to live in a certain neighborhood, we have discrimination. When large corporations promote less qualified male managers instead of competent women, that too is discrimination. In these cases the prejudiced person is excluding members of a particular culture, co-culture, or group from certain locations or positions based on preconceived notions.

One of the greatest dangers of discrimination is that it can, when carried to its limits, not only prevent communication but also lead to physical attacks. In extreme cases, such as in Hitler's Germany, the attempt to exterminate an entire out-group is the final step of discrimination.

We would be remiss if we concluded this section on stereotypes and prejudice by leaving you with the impression that all behavior is instinctive. This, of course, is not the case. In fact, one of the major themes of this chapter is that we can conquer the problems associated with stereotyping and prejudice if we expend the energy necessary to know others in alien situations and are willing to accept the simple premise that different may not be wrong, but rather another way of perceiving and dealing with reality.

IMPROVING INTERCULTURAL COMMUNICATION

It seems somewhat ironic that we have a section in this final chapter called "Improving Intercultural Communication," for in a very real sense this entire book has been about improving the manner in which you interact with people from different cultures. However, our suggestions, admonitions, counsel, and proposals in previous chapters have only tangentially related to improvement. Now our recommendations will be very direct. But before we submit specific techniques for improving your intercultural skills, we need to offer a few qualifications related to this entire issue of how to become a more competent communicator.

First, whenever you tell another individual to think or act in one way or another, you run the risk, particularly if he or she listens to you, of making matters worse. To be very blunt, the person may have been better off without your advice. For example, we believe that many of you already know a great deal about intercultural communication, and, in fact, are actually very good practitioners of the art. In these cases we run the risk of spoiling what it took you years to develop. But you need to keep in mind that our intentions are admirable even if the results are catastrophic. What we are saying is somewhat analogous to the Oriental story of the monkey and the fish. It seems that a monkey and fish were very good friends. One day, however, they were separated by a dreadful flood. Because the monkey could climb trees, he was able to scramble up a limb and escape the rising waters. As he glanced into the river he saw his friend the fish swimming past. With the best of intentions, he scooped his paw into the water, snatched his friend from the river, and lifted him into the tree. The result is obvious. From this modest story you can see the dilemma we face; so please remember as we offer advice that, like the monkey, we have the best of intentions.

This second caveat also takes the form of an apology. In this case, however, we share our insecurities with a host of other "experts." We are alluding to the idea that it is difficult to agree on the characteristics of a successful intercultural communicator. Put yet another way, people who study and write about intercultural competence cannot seem to agree on its specific components. Spitzberg has clearly articulated this lack of accord: "Indeed, the literature reveals an unwieldy collection of terminologies, a general lack of specific or practical predictive statements, and a deficit of conceptual explanatory integration."[11]

Much of Spitzberg's concern focuses on the way in which components of intercultural competence are categorized and placed into rather rigid boxes. For example, many discussions of competence divide a person's ability to be competent into three areas: cognitive (knowing), affective (wanting), and behavioral (performing). Other approaches refer to the same areas as knowledge, motivation, and skills.[12] Regardless of the terms they employ, the approaches are all saying about the same thing. Couched in practical language, they mean that someone communicating with a person from another culture would know (cognitive) that a particular culture, for example, conducts business slowly and that this deliberate rate would not upset (affective) the visitor. Finally, the communicator would moderate (behavioral) his or her pace when conducting business with this culture.

Although we believe that the categories associated with intercultural competence have value, we find them too dichotomous and restrictive. We shall still use some of the findings that employ these categories; but our alternative perspective, which we shall soon offer, allows us the freedom to take a more holistic approach to human behavior.

Our final disclaimer deals with questions related to an issue often characterized by the terms **culture-specific** and **culture-general**. Culture-specific and culture-general are not only two contrasting methods of assessing improvement in intercultural communication; they also represent two very different ways to address the entire subject of intercultural communication—both of which have their merits.

The case made for improving through the culture-specific method is a simple one. If you want to study another culture, learn all the distinct and specific communication features of that culture. For example, if you were going to interact with an Arab, you should know his or her specific values in regard to hospitality, pride, honor, and rivalry. You should also know that Islam is a regulator of behavior as well as a religion. You should even learn about the person's language, the argument being that your communication with Arabs will improve if you know that "Arab language abounds with forms of assertion. Metaphors, similes, long arrays of adjectives, and repetition of words are frequently used by the Arabs in communicating their ideas. Repetition of words is especially common in extending or rejecting invitations for coffee, dinner, and the like."[13]

If you were going to Japan, you might benefit from advice about gift-giving, the use of first names, bowing, the removal of shoes, politeness, business cards, and the like. Although we have oversimplified the culture-specific approach to make our point, it should nevertheless be evident that people interested in the culture-specific view of communication want you to gather noteworthy facts about a particular culture.

On many occasions the culture-specific approach to improvement is sound. If you knew in advance that you were going to do business in Germany, then it would behoove you to learn all you could about the specific communication patterns of that culture as they related to the business context. As you have discovered by now, however, the orientation of this book is culture-general. That is to say, we have looked at those aspects of communication that seem to apply to all cultures. To remain consistent with this approach, we shall treat the subject of improvement in the same manner. We believe that some "universal" skills apply across all cultures, and that understanding these basic guidelines for successful interaction you can move into and out of any culture with some degree of confidence. As when we discussed potential problems, the list that follows reflects the coming together of our personal advice and the research in the area of intercultural communication. In short, we are both a conduit carrying you the advice of others and a source of advice ourselves.

Know Yourself

The novelist James Baldwin once wrote, "The questions which one asks oneself begin, at last, to illuminate the world, and become one's key to the experience of others." His remarks serve as an ideal introduction for the portion of this book that urges you to begin your path to improvement with some self-analysis. As with many of the suggestions we offer in this section, the stating of the advice is usually easier than practicing it. We can write the words *know yourself* with very little effort, but putting this assignment into practice takes a great deal of effort. We believe that the application should take two directions: first, know what is in your head; and second, know how you behave around others. Although these two concepts work in tandem, it might be useful to examine them separately.

By exhorting you to know what is in your head, we are not referring to any mystical notions involving another reality, or suggesting you engage in any deep psychological soul-searching. Rather, we are asking you to identify those attitudes, opinions, and biases that we all carry around and that influence the way the world looks to us. If we hold a certain attitude toward homosexuals, and a man who is a homosexual talks to us, our precommunication attitude will color our response to what he says. Knowing our likes, dislikes, and degrees of personal ethnocentrism enables us to place them out in the open so that we can detect the ways in which these attitudes influence communication. This is essential for successful intercultural communication. Hidden personal premises, be they directed at ideas, people, or entire cultures, are often the cause of many of our difficulties.

The second step in knowing ourselves is somewhat more difficult than simply identifying our prejudices and predispositions. It involves discovering the kind of image we portray to the rest of the world. That is to say, how do we communicate, and how are we perceived? We cannot stress the importance of this type of introspection enough. If you view yourself one way, and the people you confront view you another way, serious problems can arise. We have all heard stories of how foreigners view Americans traveling abroad. The "Ugly American" example might be dated and trite, but our experiences continue to reveal its truth. Therefore, if we are to improve our communication and to understand the reactions it produces, we must have some concept of how we present ourselves. If, for instance, you see yourself as cheerful and friendly, but in reality you exhibit an image that is quite different, you will have a hard time understanding why people respond to you as they do.

We suggest that you learn to recognize your communication style. By **communication style** we mean those communication characteristics that are part of your personality. Many communication scholars have attempted to isolate those characteristics so that we could differentiate and evaluate our specific communication patterns. One listing, which Norton has proposed, indicates that we can judge our communication styles according to such criteria as dominance, dramatic behavior, contentiousness, animation, impression-leaving, attentiveness, openness, and friendliness.[14] Barnlund offers yet another interpretation of what our individual and cultural styles include.

> By communication style is meant the topics people prefer to discuss, their favorite forms of interaction—ritual, repartee, argument, self-disclosure—and the depth of involvement they demand of each other. It includes the extent to which communicants rely upon the same channels—vocal, verbal physical—for conveying information, and the extent to which they are tuned to the same level of meaning, that is, to the factual or emotional content of messages.[15]

Our styles even include the way we employ time and space. In short, what we are calling style is simply the manner in which you present yourself and your ideas to other people.

What should emerge from the last few paragraphs is that all of us have unique ways of interacting. Discovering how we communicate is not always an easy task. It is awkward and highly irregular for us to walk around asking people what they think of us. We must, therefore, be sensitive to the feedback we receive, and perceptive in the reading of that feedback. We must learn to ask ourselves questions such as the following: Do I give people my full attention? Do I seem at ease or tense? Do I often change the subject without taking the other person into consideration? Do I deprecate the statements of others? Do I smile often? Do I interrupt repeatedly? Do I show sympathy when someone has a problem? Do my actions tend to lower the other person's self-esteem?

In addition to the above questions, we can gain insight into ourselves by observing the topics we select to talk about when the choice is ours. Our tone of voice, our expressions, our reaction to being touched, and literally hundreds of other factors have an impact on other people. Frequently overlooked, the subtleties of how we act are often the most important variable in human interaction. As Chaucer wrote over five-hundred years ago, "Full wise is he that can himselven knowe."

We conclude this section on introspection by reminding you of one of the major themes of this book—that a great deal of culture and communication takes place below the level of awareness. Therefore, gaining insight into your cultural patterns of communication is difficult, but it is an assignment you nevertheless work at if you hope to improve your intercultural skills.

Consider the Physical and Human Setting

Another continuing theme of this book has been that it takes more than words to convey meaning and intent. Our total personality and all our actions come into play each time we are part of a communication experience. And as we stressed in Chapter 9, even the setting carries meaning. Let us consider for a moment the role of timing, physical setting, and customs on human communication.

Being aware of timing often can make the difference between a successful engagement and one that is characterized by ill feelings, antagonism, and misunderstandings. The effective communicator knows the importance of timing and has developed the skill to determine the appropriate time to talk about this subject or that. You know from your own experiences that there is a right and wrong time to ask your parents for a loan, or to ask someone for a date. Few professors will sympathize with the student who waits until the last week of the semester to announce, "I would like to come to your office and talk about the midterm examination I missed a few months ago." This is poor timing! In short, learn to ask yourself this simple question: Is this the best time to discuss this particular topic with my communication associate?

As we just mentioned, we deemed physical setting important enough to justify an entire chapter. So at this point we need only remind you of the main message of Chapter 9. Develop the skill that allows you to appreciate the fact that communication is rule-governed, and that different cultures have different rules as they move from setting to setting. In many Arab countries, people often conduct business while sitting on the floor. One would not, of course, find this in North America. However, being aware of the physical setting, whether it be a courtroom, classroom, factory, temple, or hospital, can greatly improve the chances that your efforts at communication will be successful.

Considering customs is a skill that we have asked you to develop throughout this book. Remember, your intercultural encounters will, to a large extent, be influenced by the degree to which you can adapt your communication behavior to the situation in which you find yourself. Your experience will not be fruitful if custom calls for you to remain standing when you enter a room, but instead you take a seat. When, if at all, do you bow? When, if at all, do you touch members of the opposite sex? You must take these, and countless other questions of custom, into consideration when interacting with people from different cultures. Because we all have free choice, we can make the necessary concessions to custom, but first we must know the custom.

Seek a Shared Code

In the chapter we set aside for language (Chapter 6), we noted that meanings resided in people, not in words. This basic precept of language serves as a tool for improvement. Stated as a positive axiom for successful communication, both parties should seek a common code. Admittedly, it is difficult to arrive at a common code if you and your communication partner speak different languages. To overcome this problem, our first piece of advice is simply that if you plan to be around people from a foreign culture, try to learn their language. Think about how much more effective you would be if you found yourself doing business in Mexico and could speak Spanish. Should you not speak the foreign language of your communication partner, there are still other considerations when striving for a common code. We have already discussed the issue of translation elsewhere in the book, so our purpose here is to remind you that vocabulary, syntax, and dialects represent only a few of the variables of the spoken code. We must always work toward unfolding that code. We need to understand the picture in the head that the sound or scratch on paper represents. That picture will tell us more about what is being discussed than will the sound of the word.

In Chapter 6 we also made it very clear that the English language contained countless subcodes, and that to improve our communication we must know the specific code the other person is using. If he or she uses an argot that is indigenous to a certain group, we must know that argot as part of the code. If a street person says, "The headknockers never leave us alone," it is important that you know the argot word *headknocker* denotes a police officer.

With the phrase *seek a common code* we also are referring to the nonverbal codes that people use. As you learned in Chapters 7 and 8, nonverbal behaviors also shift from culture to culture. For example, in Japan a female may cover her mouth out of shyness, but in North America we often associate this same action with fear. These differences should not keep us from looking for a common code, particularly in the area of nonverbal communication. Although there are cultural variations in what makes people smile, and even in who receives the smile, one does not have to speak a foreign language to know that a smile carries nearly the same meaning throughout the world. And those of you who have visited other countries know the power of pointing and laughing as ways of "talking."

Learning how to use a common code also means that you develop a **code sensitivity** towards codes other cultures use. For example, if you interact with disabled people, you should learn the long list of what are called the "no-no words." Think for a moment about the impact on a disabled person when you use words such as *crippled, deaf and dumb, deaf mute, normal, unfortunate,* or *victim.*[16] Code sensitivity also applies to foreign cultures. You need to know that practicing your Spanish in Mexico is appropriate, but to bungle the French language in Paris marks you as someone who doesn't understand how much the French value their language.

The skillful communicator is not only perceptive in the use of language, but knows about the nonverbal symbols of a culture. To the Hindu, the burning of incense calls forth meanings that go well beyond the aroma produced by the incense stick. Knowing those meanings can promote successful communication.

Develop Empathy

Many researchers in the area of interpersonal and intercultural competence believe that our success as communicators depends, to a large extent, on our "skill at establishing and maintaining desired identities for both self and others."[17] "Identities" are actually the pictures of ourselves and the other person that we hold in our heads. We have already discussed knowing ourselves; our focus now is on our need to develop **empathy** or role-taking ability. Trenholm explains the importance of this skill, and how it functions: "Competent communicators must be *empathic*—they must be able to assess accurately others' definitions of a situation. The empathic communicator must be able to infer the feelings and needs of others."[18] As with so much of the counsel in this chapter, we are once again faced with a concept that is easier to state than put into practice. For the fact remains, regardless of the advice, that however similar we may appear to be, there is something distinctive and unique about each of us. Our internal states are elusive and fleeting, and we know them only as distorted shadows. Knowing the other person, and predicting his or her reactions and needs, is a difficult and troublesome activity. Adding the dimension of culture compounds the problem.

Our inability to understand completely, to appreciate, accept, and even take pleasure in these individual and cultural differences is but one problem we face in trying to develop empathy. A number of behaviors we often employ appear to keep us from understanding the feelings, thoughts, and motives of another person—regardless of his or her culture. It might be helpful if we paused and examined a few of these so that we might improve our empathetic skills.

Perhaps the most common of all barriers to empathy is a *constant self-focus.* It is difficult to gather information about the other person if we are consumed with thoughts of ourselves. Attending to our own thoughts, as if they were the only ones that mattered, uses much of the energy that we should direct towards our communication partner. However, most of us are guilty of behaving according to the German proverb "Everyone thinks that all the bells echo his own thoughts."

The tendency to note only some features to the exclusion of others often causes us to misuse the data we gather about another person. If, for example, we notice only a person's skin color or that his or her surname is Lopez, and from this limited information assume we know all there is to know about that person, we are apt to do a poor job of empathizing. Admittedly, color and names offer us some information about the other person, but we must consider this type of data along with other information. Although it is an overused analogy, we should remember that most outward features represent only the tip of the iceberg.

Even though we mentioned it earlier in the chapter, we repeat that the *stereotyped notions* concerning race and culture that we carry around in our heads also serve as potential stumbling blocks to empathy. If we believe that "all English people dislike the Irish," we might allow this stereotype to influence our view of an English person. Stereotyped notions are so much a part of our personalities that we must be careful not to allow these unsupported generalizations to serve as our models of other people. We must be careful and not take a laissez-faire attitude; it is too easy to drift to simplistic stereotypes.

We often engage in *behavior that keeps other people from wanting to reveal information about themselves*. This is called defensive communication. If people are "put off" by our actions, they are not likely to disclose very much to us. It is nearly impossible to predict how others will act if, by our behavior, we have created a situation that makes it difficult for them to be natural and open. Because defensive behaviors are so common, it would be useful for us to examine how some of these actions inhibit our ability to empathize.

When we appear to be evaluating other people, whether by what we say or what we do, we are likely to make them feel defensive towards us. If we feel others are judging and evaluating us, we will hesitate to offer information that will foster empathy. Think about how awkward you feel when, after sharing some personal information, the other person quickly lectures you on the foolhardiness of your act. After a few minutes of criticism and ridicule, you will probably decide not to disclose any other private information to that person. In the intercultural situation, you would give someone else the same experience if that person said people in his or her culture did not like standing in lines and you responded by saying, "There must be disorder and disorganization everywhere."

When we appear to want power over another individual, we are employing communication behavior that will make him or her defensive and guarded. In most instances power so permeates the encounter that most of us just assume its presence—unless of course the exercise of power is directed at us. From parent-child relationships to world power politics, we learn about power all of our lives. The methods of exercising power are as diverse as they are widespread. People and cultures have employed guns, bombs, language, space, money, and even history for controlling others. But as we have noted, when power hampers face-to-face interactions, it prevents the development of empathy. In North America it was common for whites to assume power over blacks. It is easy to see how this misuse of power, when employed to control and to determine another's behavior, could restrict openness and communication. "To allow customary subservience or power a place in human interaction is to introduce an inevitable obstruction."[19]

Most of us have an aversion to revealing very much to a person who seems uninterested in us and our ideas. Empathy, which is most effective when it is reciprocal, cannot take place when one of the individuals becomes defensive over the lack of interest the other person shows. Again, we must answer this question: How much do I disclose to a person who shows no interest in me and what I am saying? Remember, there is a direct correlation between the amount disclosed, the data available for knowing the other person, and being able to use that data to accomplish your purpose.

An attitude of superiority, which produces defensive behavior, seldom elicits the kind of information we need for empathizing. Having already spent a great deal of time on the problems associated with ethnocentrism, our task now is simply to remind you of the pitfalls of manifesting superiority. Imagine how defensive you would become if someone from Iran told you that Americans used language in a very dull manner.

Dogmatism is yet another attitude that keeps us from developing empathy. If someone behaved as if he or she had all the answers, even to questions we hadn't even asked, we would probably become defensive. In the case of the dogmatic person, our defensiveness may take the form of silence, or even of responding with some dogmatism of our own. In either case, this defensive behavior will not be conducive to empathy.

Up to this point we have painted a rather dark picture of empathy and the problems related to it. Although it is difficult to know the other person, we can, with practice, develop the necessary skills to overcome these problems. We have mentioned nearly all of these skills in one context or another during the course of this chapter, so at this point we need only tie them together.

The first step in developing empathy is to *accept that there are differences* among individuals and cultures. This assumption leads us to a multiple-reality theory, which holds that not all people have the same view of the world. The second is to *know ourselves*. We have already discussed this in some detail, but we need to mention it here because it works in conjunction with the steps that follow. In the third step, one sets aside the self-identity that is part of knowing ourselves for what is called *suspended self*.

> One way of thinking about this procedure is to imagine that the self, or identity, is an arbitrary boundary that we draw between ourselves and the rest of the world, including other people. The suspension of self is the temporary expansion of this boundary—the elimination of separation between self and environment.[20]

In the fourth step, we *imaginatively put ourselves in the other person's place*. Once we let our imagination inside the other person we are ready for the fifth step—*the empathic experience*. Although this experience is still imaginative, it nevertheless comes close to our own experience and feelings. Finally, we must *reestablish self*.[21] Granting the excitement and exhilaration of sharing another's experience, we must be able to return to ourselves.

By learning how to use the above steps we all might be able to overcome ethnocentric tendencies while becoming more sensitive to the needs, values, and goals of other people.

Encourage Feedback

Being able to invite feedback is another skill that marks the successful communicator. Because we have discussed the importance of feedback to human communication elsewhere in the book, in this final chapter we shall not reexamine its significance but instead focus on how to use feedback to improve communication behavior.

You will recall that feedback enables us to adapt future behaviors because we perceive the responses our earlier messages have produced. Feedback, in the most simplistic sense, is our returning the smile that greeted our original smile. In this sense feedback is useful in that it enables us to correct and adjust our next message. A competent communicator uses feedback both to monitor the communication process and to exercise some control over it. Feedback clearly manifests the three axioms with which we began this chapter—we can learn, adapt, and influence. Put another way, with feedback we see or hear what is happening (learn), we alter our actions (exercise free choice), and improve the encounter (determine a consequence).

Granting that feedback is critical, we must learn to create an atmosphere that encourages other people to offer us feedback—feedback we need in order to adjust our own behavior. Therefore, let us review a number of communication skills that encourage other people to send us messages about the current situation.

We can use nonverbal actions as a way of inspiring others to respond to us honestly. To improve our nonverbal feedback, we must begin by recognizing that it takes many forms. Think for a moment of all the positive attitudes and images you associate with smiling, eye contact, head nodding, leaning forward, and laughing. Although these actions seem very Western, they often produce positive reactions in other cultures. Each of these actions, separately or in combination with verbal messages, creates an atmosphere that tells other people we are interested in them and want to hear what they have to say.

Positive verbal behavior can also encourage feedback. Like our nonverbal messages, our use of words also takes a variety of forms. Asking questions is an excellent method of encouraging feedback about the quality of our previous messages. We can ask specific questions such as, "I recommend that we start the meeting by introducing ourselves. Is that agreeable?" Or we can ask more general questions: "How do you think we should start the meeting?" Further, questions can be used to seek additional clarification. Even the question "Do you understand?" assists in monitoring the level of comprehension. We should warn you before we leave this point that in some Asian cultures the word "no" is seldom used. In Japan, for example, when someone says, "It is difficult," they are actually saying "no." Hence, be very careful when you use language as a probe.

Our use of words also encourages feedback if we relate what we say directly to what the other person has just said. You know from your own experiences that it is a little disconcerting if you tell a friend that you don't feel well, and she or he responds with a remark about needing to study for an examination. When using verbal feedback with someone from a foreign culture, remember to speak slowly, explain things carefully, avoid the use of slang, and choose words carefully. "It is raining cats and dogs, so perhaps we should not go outside," might well confuse someone for whom English is the second language.

We also can encourage feedback by using ourselves as a model of an efficient feedback system. If we offer feedback to others honestly and clearly, it is likely that this example will become contagious, and people around us will do the same.

Using feedback, like developing empathy, takes time. The skill of taking time with a communication partner relates to our common tendency to jump to conclusions. Although this notion of suspending judgments is not new, it does underscore the need to avoid rushing to premature evaluations. In face-to-face interactions, regardless of the other person's culture, we often complete the thought or idea before he or she has even finished talking. If we don't cut a person off with our words or actions, we often do it in our mind, and this prevents us from making effective use of feedback. There is no positive compensation for a quick decision, particularly if we made that decision without sufficient evidence (feedback).

When the parties are from different cultures, the relationship between deferring conclusions and the caliber of feedback available is more manifest. If we do not know the world view, value orientation, symbol systems, and the like of the other culture, we might bolt to a conclusion that limits the worth of feedback. For example, if in our head we do not allow a Jewish person to finish a story, we may well miss the point of the entire transaction; for storytelling, and the embellishing of a simple tale, is an important aspect of Jewish culture. By taking time, we can discover the person's main idea, gather feedback about the current situation, and also perhaps find that we enjoyed the story.

Sometimes silence instead of words will inspire feedback. We have repeatedly seen that every culture has a communication style that is unique. Some cultural styles call for periods of silence and/or long pauses, and you must learn to respect these phases in the encounter. You should try to cultivate the necessary patience to allow the other person to think through his or her ideas. Giving the person this quiet period creates an atmosphere that promotes feedback once the silence is broken. There are even occasions when the silence itself is a form of feedback. The Japanese do not enjoy being hurried when they negotiate. If you can learn to remain silent, you will be sending them some positive feedback about the meeting.

One final reminder on the role of feedback in intercultural communication: Remember that the quality and quantity of feedback cues shift from culture to culture. For example, we can find an abundance of data to use as feedback when we are with cultures that are very amicable and have high levels of self-disclosure. In most Oriental cultures, however, outward displays of emotions and verbal expressions of one's feelings are rare. Hence, in these instances the communicator must be cautious when reading the responses his or her message produces.

Develop Communication Flexibility

Besides the other skills we have discussed, "competent communicators must also develop a repertoire of interpersonal tactics."[22] This means that you need to be flexible and able to adapt your communication behavior to each situation that confronts you. All of us have learned a host of communication tactics as part of the socialization process. We know about tactics ranging from complex forms of bargaining to when and how to "turn on the charm."

Regardless of the techniques we employ, we must learn to be flexible in selecting our words and actions. This same strategy applies to the intercultural context. You need to learn how to respond to conditions, people, and situations as they arise. Having the skills to play these multiple roles means being able to be reflective instead of impulsive when interacting with a culture that moves at a slower pace. It means behaving in a formal manner when encountering a culture that employs a formal style. It means speaking softly instead of in a loud voice when sharing space with people who use a gentle communication pattern. As you can see, there is no end to cultural comparisons that ask you to be flexible. We have woven many of these differences in and out of the entire book. Your goal now is simply to identify these communication differences and make the necessary adjustments to your personalized communication style.

Your efforts at being adaptable will be greatly facilitated if you learn how to tolerate a degree of ambiguity while trying to analyze what role to play. Much of the research in intercultural communication points to the following conclusion: "The ability to react to new and ambiguous situations with minimal discomfort has long been thought to be an important asset when adjusting to a new culture."[23] If you are self-conscious, tense, and anxious when confronted with the unknown, you will use your energy to alleviate your frustration when you should direct it towards being flexible. Again, we remind you that all of us have free choice—use those choices wisely and learn to endure some ambiguity.

Seek Commonalities

Although we have worked against it, this type of book tends to overemphasize the differences between people and cultures. Admittedly, many of these differences are important, or we would not have included them in the book. In many instances, however, if we want to improve intercultural communication we must also learn about likenesses, for indeed we are very much alike. As the great photographer Edward Steichen once noted, "I believe that in all the things that are important, in all of these we are alike." This creed is important, for what we share draws us together and allows us to find common ground and establish rapport. It might be intriguing to know that "an American child sticks out his tongue to show defiance, a Tibetan to show courtesy to a stranger, and a Chinese to express wonderment,"[24] but it is more important to know that they share a series of more crucial characteristics that link them together. The similarities that unite us, and in a very real sense make us one family, range from the obvious to the subtle. For example, it is apparent that all 5.5 billion us share the same planet for a rather short period of time. And there are thousands of other less glaring similarities that still bond us together. Reflect for a moment on just a few universal characteristics that unite us. The skillful use of intercultural communication keeps them foremost in our minds.

As we saw at the end of the 1980s, in both China and eastern Europe, all people desire to be free from external restraint. The craving for freedom is indeed basic. There also seems to be a universal link regarding children and family. We all share the same thrill and excitement at a new birth. Mating and wanting good friends also tie us together. All of us must face old age and the potential suffering that often goes with it; and, of course, we are joined in knowing that death, like birth, is part of life's process. These basic similarities are not the only ones that people share. All cultures love music and art, tell jokes, believe in being civil to one another, and search for ways to be happy.

By now it should be obvious that the list of commonalities is as long as our list of differences. The effective intercultural communicator is aware of general and also specific similarities. To be cognizant of our commonalities, and be able to deal with them on a practical level, is crucial if you seek to improve your communication behavior. There is nothing religious or metaphysical in appreciating and using the fact that all people seek to avoid physiological and psychological pain while searching for some degree of tranquility in life. When you can combine these philosophical truisms with distinct cultural characteristics, you will be able to travel in and out of other cultures with much greater ease.

SOME ETHICAL CONSIDERATIONS

Every chapter of this book has stressed the theme that culture and communication are inseparable, that they are interrelated, like the object and the shadow. Other themes, perhaps not as obvious but just as important, have appeared on almost every page. We highlighted some of these in the beginning of this chapter. Two themes are important enough to warrant yet another examination as we conclude this book. One is the simple yet profound premise that communication is an activity that has a consequence. As we have seen repeatedly, we cannot send messages without those messages influencing other people. Like the sea rolling over the sand, there is change with each wave that makes it to the shore. The same applies to communication—your actions are the wave, the responses of other people are the shifting grains of sand. Quite simply, communication is an instrumental act; and whether it is used to sell cars, get elected to public office, ingratiate yourself to an employer, punish children, or deceive teachers, it will have an impact that is either good or bad, desirable or undesirable, significant or insignificant, but an impact nevertheless. Most cultures recognize the ethical dimensions of communication, as we do in our libel, slander, truth-in-advertising, and campaign practice laws. But just because most of our communication does not involve mass media does not relieve us of considering the effects of our actions in the interpersonal setting.

When we transpose the consequences of our communicative behavior to the intercultural context, the problems and issues are even more complex. Two of these issues are worthy of our consideration. First, in the intercultural environment, because of the diversity of backgrounds, it is much more difficult to assess and predict the type of response our messages and actions will produce. For example, in the United States we have learned, as part of our cultural endowment, how to thank someone for a compliment or a gift. That is to say, we can predict, with some degree of accuracy, what others expect from us and how they will respond to our signs of veneration and appreciation. As we indicated earlier in the chapter, forecasting the responses of other cultures is a far more difficult task. Let us stay with our simple example of saying "thank you." In Arab cultures one is expected to be profuse in offering thanks, while in England one is expected to offer milder thanks when receiving a gift, since too much exuberance is considered offensive. Yet in all three instances (North America, Iraq, and England) what we do will affect the other person.

There even are more striking examples of how appropriateness shifts from culture to culture. As you learned from this book, in many Eastern cultures the desire for harmony overrides nearly all other values. Members of these cultures will do almost anything to keep from disrupting that peace. They will smile and say "yes" even when this message camouflages their true feelings. As you can see, this cultural trait often makes knowing another person quite perplexing. But the troublesome nature of the assignment must not discourage you from trying. For we again remind you, whatever message you send will have a consequence.

Because of the potential power of our messages we must continue to ask ourselves if we are behaving in a way that harms the other person. We must learn to send messages that reaffirm a belief in the intrinsic worth of each individual. This philosophical orientation maintains that all people have the same desire to be happy and to be free from emotional and physical hardships. The question then is simple: Is our communication behavior creating effects that contribute to or detract from that basic goal? It seems to us that anything else would diminish us and our communication partner. Tead's eloquent statement on ethics provides a good summary of our first point:

> Without indulging in too great refinements, let us remind ourselves that communication also has at bottom a moral aspect. It does, when all is said, anticipate a change in the conduct of the recipient. If the change has any large significance it means an interposing or interference with the autonomy of the other person or persons. And the tampering with

personal drives and desires is a moral act even if its upshot is not a far-reaching one, or is a beneficial result. To seek to persuade behavior into a new direction may be wholly justifiable and the result in terms of behavior consequences may be salutary. But the judgment of benefit or detriment is not for the communicator safely to reach by himself. He is assuming a moral responsibility. And he had better be aware of the area with which he concerns himself and the responsibility he assumes. He should be willing to assert as to any given policy, "I stand behind this as having good personal consequences for the individuals whom it will affect." That judgment speaks a moral concern and desired moral outcome.[25]

Our second ethical consideration also has cultural overtones. Simply stated, when changing the other person, we might also be changing the culture he or she belongs to. As Barnlund has noted,

> Technical innovations and scientific discoveries have been found to produce severe dislocations when transplanted into other cultures; less visible, but no less profound, may be the shock waves flowing from introducing alien patterns of friendship, of male-female relations, of attitudes toward work, of unfamiliar modes of decision making.[26]

As we just indicated, this idea is, of course, an extension of our first point, but now we are expanding our analysis. Here again the premise is the same one we started with—intervention produces change. We are referring to possible changes or even "the loss of a life style, an art form, a language, or a religious experience" because of the way we communicated with another culture.[27]

The ethical ramifications of these cultural alterations are significant, and we should not ignore them. There are no objective yardsticks to apply when considering the cultural consequences of your actions on another group of people, but there are some philosophical guidelines that you can use. Although they are much like the ones we suggested for individual interactions, they merit repeating and amplifying.

You need to be ever vigilant about ethnocentrism. Applying the Western world view to all cultures is not only unfair but also limiting. Does it really matter if females shave their legs in one culture and not in another? Or that some people pray five times a day while others don't pray at all? Or that some people pray indoors while others worship outside? Of course not! Yet many of us want everyone we meet to act just like us. If we pray in a church on Sunday, we can't understand why other people need to pray most of the day. When we communicate to them that they should shave their legs, or pray only on Sunday, or pray inside, we might be tampering with the deep structure of that culture; for these changes, and countless others, have a ripple effect. Therefore, you must reflect on your requests and your messages when you "invade" the life-space of another culture. You need to ask these two difficult questions: Are the changes that are built into my message for their benefit or mine? And will these changes contribute to the overall well-being of the person and his or her culture?

Try to view ethical questions from a micro rather than a macro perspective. Each individual is important, for he or she represents his or her culture. Influence that person in a profound way and you are apt to influence a larger segment of the culture. For you are not the only agent of change; your communication partner will create change. Hence, we urge you to be conscious of your actions and meticulous in your selection of words. The people you confront will confront, and be confronted by, members of their culture. A slight alteration of the lines of Tennyson says it so well: "I am part of all that I have met," and they are part of me. In short, your influence does not end when you walk away from your communication partner.

THE FUTURE OF INTERCULTURAL COMMUNICATION

We end this book in the same way we started it—with two declarations regarding intercultural communication. First, a changing world has made intercultural communication an important field of study. And second, those changes will accelerate in the future; they will not diminish. The inescapable nature of these changes is creating a different world than the one we were born into. None of us or our institutions, our professions, our governments, our values, or our belief systems will remain untouched by these changes. What will be the course of these changes, and what will be our individual and collective roles in them? These two questions about the future will take us to the final lines of this book.

Trying to chart the course of future events is a very perplexing assignment. For who among us can say, with any degree of accuracy, what tomorrow will be like? Who ever thought before the 1960s that we would see a person walking on the moon? Or who could have predicted that the Berlin Wall would come down in 1989? Hence, it is not profound when we say the future is, by its very nature, unknown. Yet we must be ready for the future if we and our culture are to prevail. One way to prepare for the future is to use the past, for it tells us something of what lies ahead. For example, we have learned that we must be willing to accept that the powers of science and technology may be almost boundless. Inventors can amaze us with beer cans we can open with one hand, television sets that we can operate without leaving our chairs, and computers that can spell words that we can't. Scientists can even make babies in laboratories and take them to far-off planets. So who knows what science can do in the next few decades? We might even encounter beings from other planetary systems as well as people from other continents. In short, if the past is any gauge, we must be prepared for some very momentous changes in science and technology.

What about intercultural communication's past? How does it help us anticipate and predict the future? The history of intercultural communication, as we illustrated in Chapter 1, is dotted with examples of how contact and change seem to be two sides of the same coin. We believe that the next few decades will be characterized by an acceleration in both communication and diversity. Think for a moment about the implications of *Time* magazine's selection of Mikhail Gorbachev as "Man of the Decade." Gorbachev was selected not because he had created a war that separated people from each other, but rather because "In novel alliance with the *glasnost* of world communications, Gorbachev became the patron of change."[28] The increasing number of intercultural contacts, and the resulting changes they bring, go far beyond the influence of one person. We now remind you of some of the changes we discussed in the first chapter of the book and try to ascertain how they might be a guide to the future.

One does not have to be a professional futurist to know that travel will become more commonplace, communication satellites more abundant, and international mobility much easier in the future. In fact, one of the outgrowths of the 1992 European Economic Community is that members of this trading bloc will be able to pass freely from country to country. Even now tourism is being heralded as the fastest growing industry in the world. Tourism from the Pacific Rim countries alone accounts for 5 percent of the entire world's gross national product.[29] Increasing mobility is also reflected in the fact that in 1989, nearly one-half million foreign students studied in the United States.

Other changes in the world besides travel and advanced communication systems will also increase the amount of contact between people. Perhaps the greatest force contributing to the future of international contact is overpopulation. The world's population, now at around 5.5 billion, is increasing by at least eighty million a year, and might well reach ten billion by 2040. Because this growth is not uniform, it is expected to create a series of problems that will touch us all. About 90 percent of the growth is occurring in developing countries, where under the best of conditions people struggle to even survive. This swelling of humanity is a powerful force driving the people of the world together—or it had better.

More and more we are seeing how the use, or misuse, of the planet affects all of us. The cutting down of trees in India causes several thousand people to die in Bangladesh and forces millions to leave their homes. Overgrazing in one country produces starvation in yet another. And "water-supply arguments between Egypt, the Sudan and Ethiopia, have already prompted Egypt's Foreign Minister to warn, 'The next war in our region will be over the waters of the Nile, not politics.' "[30] Even the United States will not be spared being drawn into these environmental debates. Think of the intercultural implications of the following facts: The United States has 5 percent of the earth's population but uses 26 percent of the world's oil supply, releases 26 percent of the world's nitrogen oxides, produces 22 percent of the world's carbon dioxide emissions, and disposes of 290 million tons of toxic waste.[31] How long do you anticipate it will be before the rest of the world wants to talk to us about our role in global pollution?

The thawing of relations between the United States and the Soviet Union will increase, not decrease, the amount of intercultural contacts that will take place. In the past only the superpowers had to talk. The United States and the Soviet Union represented many other cultures. What happened at the end of the 1980s and the start of the 1990s will only make the world become larger. Instead of two superpowers, elevated to exceptional preeminence by their nuclear arsenals, a proliferation of other countries will emerge. More and more people are going to want to speak for themselves. This means, in short, that the decade of the 1990s will see us all interacting with an expanded list of cultures.

The future of intercultural communication will also be different on the economic level. American business will, more than ever, be international in both scope and outlook. Even now one-third of all U.S. corporate profits are generated by international trade; four of every five new jobs in the United States result directly from foreign involvement; and foreign investments in the United States now total $1.5 trillion.[32] The pace of economic involvement will quicken as the list of international business countries continues to grow. Hence, the business setting will continue to put us into contact with people from different cultures.

Within the United States intercultural contacts through immigration will also increase. Almost 600,000 people a year immigrate to the United States; and with fifteen to eighteen million refugees now wandering the world, the number of immigrants entering the United States will only increase. Projections suggest that ethnic and racial minorities will make up about one-third of the population of the United States by the year 2000. Some demographics are also pointing to the year 2050, when 45 percent of the population could be composed of these ethnic and racial groups.

In the coming years we can also expect demands for equal rights to increase from the growing population of co-cultures. It is estimated that by the year 2000, 84 percent of all women of childbearing age will be members of the work force and will be interacting with the dominant white male culture.

We cannot afford to overlook the consequences of a future that will see an increase in both the number and the importance of our intercultural contacts. This brings us to our second question: What is *your* role in this new and changing world? We propose that it be an active role. Let us explain.

When billions of people are hungry and desperate, and they see millions of other people who appear to be free from such despair, they will care very little about the consequences of their actions. In the 1960s in the United States, and the 1980s in South Africa, the world witnessed a microcosm of this problem. In both instances large groups of people, living in ghettos and feeling out of touch with the dominant culture, sensed their desperation and attempted to destroy many of the cities and institutions in each country. Very little communication was taking place between the affected cultures. We suggest that these same problems now exist on a global scale. Hence, we need to engage in intercultural communication *before* violence becomes the product of misunderstandings and hopelessness.

If we are going to make this world better for all of us, we must accept that the web of life and nature's interdependence involve all creatures—including us. All people and cultures are inextricably connected to each other, and this connection will grow even stronger in the future. Already we are seeing signs of this increased contact, and the dichotomies created by the contact. Everywhere in the world homogeneity and cultural pluralism are attempting to coexist. A teenage girl may dress in blue jeans and a T-shirt with the Batman logo whether she lives in New York, Nairobi, Moscow, or Mexico City. She may listen to the Rolling Stones and drink Pepsi Cola regardless of where she lives. We have seen how international marketing and travel have lowered cultural boundaries. Although there is a real danger in the homogenization that is occurring, we see evidence everywhere that the deep structure of culture is indeed resistant to change, and that people, whether consciously or unconsciously, agree with anthropologist Laura Nader when she says, "Diversity is rich."[33] In the end, people of all cultures long for a place to raise their children, ply their trades, and express themselves aesthetically and socially. When that expression differs from our own, we must respect the rights of people from other cultures. John Comenius expressed this same idea over three hundred years ago:

> To hate a man because he was born in another country, because he speaks a different language, or because he takes a different view of this subject or that, is a great folly. Desist, I implore you, for we are all equally human. . . . Let us have but one end in view, the welfare of humanity.

We ask here at the end of this book that your future include a global philosophy as you move from culture to culture, becoming what Adler calls a multicultural person. "What is universal about the multicultural person is his abiding commitment to essential similarities between people everywhere, while paradoxically maintaining an equally strong commitment to their differences."[34] We are convinced that being able to appreciate both the similarities and differences among cultures, while at the same time enjoying the security of your own culture, is not only desirable but possible. The history of each culture, as well as our private history, provides countless examples of how adaptive we can be. On a personal level, we have seen individuals overcome and adapt to physical disabilities and emotional problems that seemed insurmountable. On a larger scale we have all witnessed Japan adapting to a new world order after the devastating effects of World War II. This tells us that humanity and culture are one and the same, and that both can adapt when the need arises. The need is now! The future of all of us is the same as the future of culture, for culture is the primary way we adapt to our environment. We have fashioned better roads, increased food production, explored outer space, and increased our life expectancy. The world has changed to such an extent that it is now necessary to change ourselves. It is time to accept a world composed of diverse cultures that can learn from each other, take pleasure in each other, and by working together create a planet that will persevere throughout the centuries.

We would ask those who would say that such a view of the future is simplistic and fanciful to provide alternatives. In a world that can now destroy itself with bombs or pollution, we do not consider it romantic or idealistic to issue an appeal for greater understanding. Only by understanding and appreciating the values, desires, and frustrations of other cultures can we shape a future that is fit for our generation and the next, and the next, and the next.

> To me there is something thrilling and exalting in the thought that we are drifting forward into a splendid mystery—into something that no mortal eye hath yet seen, and no intelligence has yet declared.
>
>   E. H. CHAPIN

SUMMARY

A Philosophy of Change

- The belief that improvement in intercultural communication is possible is based on three assumptions: (1) the brain is an open system, (2) we have free choice, and (3) our behavior influences other people.

Potential Problems in Intercultural Communication

- Avoidance of the unfamiliar, the desire to reduce uncertainty, and diversity in communication purposes are some of the potential problems in intercultural communication. The tendency to withdraw because of these problems further complicates intercultural communication. In addition, our own ethnocentrism, which leads to the development of stereotypes and prejudices, is the single major barrier to intercultural communication.

Improving Intercultural Communication

- By following some basic guidelines such as knowing yourself, seeking a shared code, and encouraging feedback, you can move in and out of any culture with some degree of confidence.

Some Ethical Considerations

- Because communication is an activity that has a consequence, we must continually ask ourselves if we are behaving in a way that harms our communication partner or creates change in the culture he or she belongs to.

The Future of Intercultural Communication

- New technology, growth in the world's population, and shifts in the global economic arena will continue to contribute to increased international contacts. Domestic contacts will also continue to increase because of new immigrants and co-cultures demanding recognition.

ACTIVITIES

1. Pick a foreign country that you would like to visit, study in, or do business in. Find out as much as you can about that country's culture with regard to your specific purpose. For example, if you are going as a tourist, you might want to find out about table manners, tipping, and so on.

2. Bring to class news articles you have collected over a week's time that directly or indirectly have to do with problems in intercultural communication. Then, in small groups, discuss what may have caused the problems (for example, withdrawal or ethnocentrism) and how the situations could have been improved.

DISCUSSION IDEAS

1. Find examples in the media (especially television and movies) of subtle stereotyping. Explain how the stereotypes may have developed in terms of ethnocentrism.

2. Define your communication style to the best of your ability by answering these questions:

   - Do I give people my full attention?
   - Do I seem at ease or tense?
   - Do I often change the subject without taking the other person into consideration?
   - Do deprecate the statements of others?
   - Do I smile often?
   - Do I interrupt repeatedly?
   - Do I show sympathy when someone has a problem?
   - Do my actions tend to lower the other person's self-esteem?

   It may help you to record yourself in conversation with another person, or, if you have the means, to videotape yourself.

3. Give a specific example of an intercultural communication experience in which an individual and/or his or her culture might be harmed or changed.

NOTES FOR CHAPTER 10

1. *Time*, Oct. 23, 1989, 63.

2. Charles M. Berger and Richard J. Calabrese, "Some Explorations in Initial Interaction and Beyond," *Human Communication Research* 1 (1975), 99–112.

3. Berger and Calabrese, 100.

4. Edward T. Hall, *Beyond Culture* (New York: Doubleday, 1976). See also Edward T. Hall, *The Dance of Life: Other Dimensions of Time* (New York: Anchor Press/Doubleday, 1983).

5. Sharon Ruhly, *Orientations to Intercultural Communication* (Chicago: Science Research Associates, 1976), 22.

6. Donald R. Atkinson, George Morten, and Derald Wing Sue, "Minority Group Counseling: An Overview," in *Intercultural Communication: A Reader*, 4th ed., ed. Larry A. Samovar and Richard E. Porter (Belmont, CA: Wadsworth, 1982), 172.

7. Philip K. Bock, *Culture Shock* (New York: Knopf, 1970), 1x.

8. Rod Plotnik and Sandra Mollenauer, *Introduction to Psychology* (New York: Random House, 1986), 565.

9. Richard W. Brislin, "Prejudice in Intercultural Communication," in *Intercultural Communication: A Reader*, 5th ed., ed. Larry A. Samovar and Richard E. Porter (Belmont, CA: Wadsworth, 1988), 339–44.

10. Brislin, 341.

11. Brian H. Spitzberg, "Issues in the Development of a Theory of Interpersonal Competence in the Intercultural Context," *International Journal of Intercultural Relations* 13 (1989), 242.

12. T. Todd Imahori and Mary L. Lanigan, "Relational Model of Intercultural Communication Competence," *International Journal of Intercultural Relations* 13 (1989), 278.

13. A. J. Almaney and A. J. Alwan, *Communicating with Arabs* (Prospect Hills, IL: Waveland Press, 1982), 87.

14. Robert Norton, *Communication Style: Theory, Application and Measures* (Beverly Hills, CA: Sage Publications, 1982).

15. Dean C. Barnlund, *Public and Private Self in Japan and the United States: Communication Styles of Two Cultures* (Tokyo: Simul Press, 1975), 14–15.

16. Jim Johnson, "The Press Should Show More Sensitivity to Disabled People," *Editor and Publisher,* Feb. 22, 1986, 64.

17. Sarah Trenholm, *Human Communication Theory* (Englewood Cliffs, NJ: Prentice-Hall, 1986), 112.

18. Trenholm, 113.

19. Arthur L. Smith, *Transracial Communication* (Englewood Cliffs, NJ: Prentice-Hall, 1973), 71.

20. Milton J. Bennett, "Overcoming the Golden Rule: Sympathy and Empathy," Paper delivered at the 29th Annual Conference of the International Communication Association, Philadelphia, May 1979, 31.

21. Bennett, 29–34.

22. Trenholm, 112.

23. Brent D. Ruben and Daniel J. Kealey, "Behavioral Assessment of Communication Competency and the Prediction of Cross-Cultural Adaptation," *International Journal of Intercultural Relations* 3 (1979), 19.

24. Yu-Kuang Chu, "Six Suggestions for Learning about People and Cultures," in *Learning about Peoples and Cultures,* ed. Seymour Fersh (Evanston, IL: McDougal and Littell, 1974), 52.

25. Ordway Tead, *Administration: Its Purpose and Performance* (New York: Harper and Row, 1959), 52.

26. Dean C. Barnlund, "The Cross-Cultural Arena: An Ethical Void," in *Intercultural Communication: A Reader,* 4th ed., ed. Larry A. Samovar and Richard E. Porter (Belmont, CA: Wadsworth, 1985), 395.

27. Barnlund, 395.

28. *Time,* Jan. 1, 1990, 44.

29. *U.S. News and World Report,* Nov. 20, 1989, 68.

30. *U.S. News and World Report,* Dec. 25, 1989/Jan. 1, 1990, 50.

31. "Uncle Sam against the World," *Time,* Dec. 18, 1989, 63.

32. Connie Pryzant, "International Studies Fast Becoming College Necessity," *Dallas Morning News,* Oct. 4, 1989, 27A.

33. Valerie Lynch Lee, ed., *Faces of Culture* (Huntington Beach, CA: KOCE-TV Foundation, 1983), 69.

34. Peter S. Adler, "Beyond Cultural Identity: Reflections on Cultural and Multicultural Man," in *Intercultural Communication: A Reader,* 4th ed., ed. Larry A. Samovar and Richard E. Porter (Belmont, CA: Wadsworth, 1985), 412.

GLOSSARY

activity orientation An aspect of human behavior having to do with the relative importance of activity in a particular culture.

affective Having to do with emotions.

argot A more or less secret and unique vocabulary peculiar to a particular co-cultural group.

attitude A learned tendency to respond in a consistent manner to objects and events; based on beliefs and values.

beliefs A person's convictions concerning the truth of an object or event.

channel   The means by which a message moves from source to receiver; primarily sight and sound.

co-culture   A group of people living within a dominant culture, yet having dual membership in another culture.

code sensitivity   Using language that is appropriate to the culture or co-culture with which one is interacting.

cognitive style   The way in which the brain functions and organizes information.

collectivism   A tight social framework in which people distinguish between in-groups and out-groups.

communication   An act in which meaning is attributed to behavior or the residue of behavior.

communication style   Communication characteristics that are part of an individual's personality, such as attentiveness and openness.

context   The setting and environment in which communication takes place.

cultural calamity   A crisis or catastrophe that forces a culture to change, such as a war.

culture   The deposit of knowledge, experience, beliefs, values, attitudes, meanings, hierarchies, religion, timing, roles, spatial relations, concepts of the universe, and material objects and possessions acquired by a group of people in the course of generations through individual and group striving.

culture-bound   Pertaining to a form, concept, or symbol, the meaning of which is derived solely from the culture in which it is found.

culture-general   Pertaining to all cultures; also, a method of studying intercultural communication in which one deals with the aspects of communication that apply to all cultures.

culture shock   Emotional stress (disorientation, frustration, and a feeling of helplessness) produced by an absence of familiar signs and symbols in social intercourse; usually caused by exposure to a new culture.

culture-specific   Pertaining to a particular culture; also, a method of studying intercultural communication in which one deals with all the aspects of communication of a particular culture that are distinct to that culture.

decoding (also known as **information processing**)   The process by which a receiver attaches meaning to the behaviors a source produces.

deep structure   The underlying values and perceptions of a particular culture.

diffusion   A change within a culture as a result of borrowing from another culture.

dominant culture   The culture of those with the most power in a particular society.

Ebonics   The name given to the language of African Americans.

emblems   Body movements that replace spoken words and are employed consciously.

emic   Pertaining to a concept that is culture-specific and is therefore difficult to translate from one language to another.

empathy   The ability to assess the feelings and needs of others.

empirical   Pertaining to knowledge that is acquired through observation.

encoding   An internal activity in which verbal and nonverbal symbols are selected and arranged according to linguistic rules.

enculturation   The process by which we learn our culture. Also called **socialization.**

Enlightenment   See **Nirvana.**

epistemological assumptions   Assumptions about how we gain knowledge.

ethnocentrism   The belief that one's own group or culture is superior to all other groups or cultures; the tendency to interpret other cultures according to the values of one's own.

etic   Pertaining to a concept that is culture-general and is therefore easy to translate.

eurocentric   Pertaining to a cultural group that derives its beliefs, values, and attitudes from dominant European cultures.

fatalism   The belief that whatever happens is out of the hands of the individual.

field dependence   A cognitive style in which the field dominates the perception of its parts and people seek relationships between things and ideas.

field independence   A cognitive style in which people isolate elements in a field; analytical thinking.

formal time   Calendar and clock time; time concepts that are explicitly taught.

global village   The phenomenon of the world becoming smaller by means of improved communications technology.

high-context   A form of communication in which most of the information to be conveyed is contained in the physical context or is internalized within the people who are communicating.

impulsivity   A cognitive style in which one makes quick guesses.

informal time   The unconscious, individual use of time; it involves concepts such as punctuality, waiting time, and pace.

information processing   See **decoding.**

in-group   The group that one belongs to (relatives, clans, organizations).

intercultural communication   Communication between people whose cultural perceptions and symbol systems are distinct enough to alter the communication event.

interethnic communication   Communication between people who are of the same race but whose geographic origins make them a minority within a country or culture.

international communication   Communication between political structures (nations and governments) rather than between individuals.

interracial communication   Communication between people who are from different races.

intolerance of ambiguity   A cognitive style in which there is a low degree of open-mindedness about differences and contradictions.

intonation   A system of conveying meaning through the rising and falling of the voice. For example, a "yes/no" question in English is expressed by raising the voice at the end of the utterance.

intracultural communication   Communication between members of the same culture, including members of racial, ethnic, and co-cultural groups.

invention   A change within a culture due to acceptance of a new concept or tool, for example.

jiving   See **shucking.**

karma   The cause-and-effect relationship between what a Hindu does in one life and what he or she does in the next life.

kinesics   The study of body movements that have the potential of sending messages.

low-context   A form of communication in which the explicit coded message contains almost all of the information to be shared.

materialism   A belief in the importance of concrete possessions.

message   A set of verbal and/or nonverbal symbols that represent a source's inner state at a particular point in time.

monochronic   Pertaining to a cultural concept of time as segmented and scheduled; monochronic cultures tend to do one thing at a time.

Nirvana   For the Hindus, an internal state of bliss (the highest state) that one achieves through an advanced spiritual life. Also called **Enlightenment.**

nonverbal communication   All stimuli (except verbal) within a communication setting generated by the individual and the individual's environment that have potential meaning for the sender and the receiver.

out-group People who are not members of an individual's group (relatives, clans, organizations).

paralanguage An aspect of speech that has to do with how something is said (by means of such linguistic features as stress, pitch, intonation, volume, and rate), not the actual meaning of the spoken words.

perception The process by which we convert the physical energies in our surroundings into meaningful internal experiences.

personal space The invisible "bubble" of space surrounding an individual and that the individual controls.

phonemic Concerning the level of language involving the sounds that are meaningful to a community of language users.

polychronic Pertaining to a cultural concept of time according to which people deal with time holistically; emphasis is upon the activity of the moment rather than on schedules and timetables.

power distance A cultural value regarding the degree to which a society accepts the fact that power in institutions is distributed unequally.

pragmatic Concerning the level of language that has to do with the rules governing the accomplishment of desired communicative goals.

prejudice Unfair, biased, or intolerant attitudes toward an individual or a group of people.

primary values Values that are the most important in a culture.

protocol Behavioral guidelines within specific settings, such as business.

proxemics The study of how such things as the use of space, seating, and furniture arrangement convey meaning.

rapping A fluent, noninteractive African-American speech style that is used to tell a story, create a favorable impression, or obtain something that one desires.

receiver The person who takes a message into account.

reflectivity A cognitive style in which one seeks answers slowly.

residue What remains as a record of a communicative act.

rule-governed A characteristic of communication according to which learned patterns of behavior or rules organize interaction between individuals.

secondary values Values that are important but occupy second place in a culture's value hierarchy.

self-reflective Having the ability to observe, evaluate, and change one's own communicative performance.

semantic   Concerning the level of language at which meanings are attached to words.

sensory perception   The process of deriving meaning from external stimuli by means of the five senses.

shaman   A traditional folk healer; found in Southeast Asian and southern Chinese cultures.

shucking   An African-American language behavior that involves speech and gestures designed to manipulate an authority figure in such a way that the speaker avoids trouble.

socialization   See **enculturation.**

social perception   The process by which we construct reality by attributing meaning to the social objects and events we find in our surroundings.

source   A person who has a need to communicate.

stereotype   A belief about other groups or individuals based on previously formed opinions and attitudes.

stress   A system a conveying meaning (in verbal language) by emphasizing certain words or syllables within an utterance.

syntactic   Concerning the level of language involving the rules that govern the use of words.

taboo   An action or word that a cultural or social group strongly forbids.

tertiary values   Values that are at the bottom of a culture's value hierarchy.

time-binding   The human ability to use symbols to transmit knowledge from the past to future generations.

tolerance of ambiguity   A cognitive style that emphasizes open-mindedness about differences and contradictions.

uncertainty reduction   The attempt to understand the other person in a communication setting by increasing predictability; brought about by the high need to understand oneself and others in interpersonal situations.

values   Enduring attitudes about the preferability of one belief over another; beliefs that have assumed qualities such as goodness and usefulness.

verbal language   A set of symbols with rules for combining the symbols that a large community uses and understands; it consists of sounds, words, combinations of words, and communicative purposes.

world view   A culture's orientation toward life, death, God, nature, and other philosophical issues related to the concept of "being."

CREDITS

INDEX

Achievement, 126

Activity, 90, 126

Activity orientation, 90

Affective state, 177

Affirmative action legislation, 13

Africans, 134, 261–262

Almaney, A. J., 52

Alwan, A. J., 52

Ambiguity
  in Asian languages, 155
  tolerance/intolerance for,
    251–252

Ancient Greeks, 106

Appearance, 187–189

Arabs. *See also* Saudi Arabians
  direct body orientations of,
    192
  meaning of smell to, 204
  reasoning reflected in
    language use of, 152
  speaking volume of, 205–206
  use of eye contact by,
    198–199
  use of gestures by, 193
  use of language by, 92,
    156–157
  view of space by, 106

Arensberg, C., 152–153

Argot
    functions of, 160–165
    nature and use of, 158–160, 289
Argyle, Michael, 220
Artifacts, 52
Asian Americans, 11
Assumptions, epistemological, 86
Attitudes, 84
Attributions, 28–29
Avoidance, 129

Bali, 204
Barnlund, Dean C., 176, 286, 300
Bates, Barbara, 202
Behavior
    as aspect of culture, 52
    and communication, 274
    and free choice, 273–274
    and human brain, 272–273
    relationship between perception and,
        107, 109
Behavior residue, 28
Beliefs
    definition and description of, 82–83
    influence of culture on, 107–108
Benedict, Ruth, 62–63
Berger, Charles M., 276
Black Americans
    and differences in paralanguage, 206
    Ebonics used by, 160–162
    eye contact used by, 199
    health care and, 257–258, 262
    increased contact with dominant culture,
        12
    and personal space, 217
    population statistics of, 12
    touch used by, 201, 203
    and U.S. history, 134
Bock, Philip K., 281
Body movement, 189–195
Brain, 38–39, 272–273
Brislin, Richard W., 281–282
British
    versus American English, 150
    emphasis on tradition and protocol by,
        221, 237

medical treatment of, 258–259
    view of space, 106
Buddha, 37
Buddhism, 123–125
    ego in, 91
    perception of time in, 152
    role of silence in, 225, 248–249, 255
Business context, 236–237
    aspects of, 53
    diversity in, 237–240
    and negotiation, 238, 240–242
Business negotiations, 238, 240–242, 296

Calabrese, Richard J., 276
Cateora, Philip, 52
Chapin, E. H., 306
Children
    impact of family on, 136–139
    value of education to, 253
Chinese. See also Orientals
    in business context, 238–239, 241
    facial expression used by, 197
    history of, 135
    language of, 155
    meaning of smell to, 204
    perception of time by, 220–221
    stance used by, 192
    and treatment of illness, 259
Choice, free, 273–274
Christianity, 119–120
    concept of death in, 256
Clothing, 187–189
Co-cultures
    emergence of, 11
    function of argot for, 160–165
    impact on dominant culture, 12–15,
        304
    meaning of, 72, 158
    nature and use of argot by, 158–160
Code sensitivity, 289
Cognition
    and classroom interaction, 251
    culture and, 50–51
Coining, 260
Cole, Michael, 50–51
Collectivism, and world view, 128

Color, 106
Comenius, John, 305
Commonalities, 297–298
Communication. *See also* Intercultural
    communication; Nonverbal
    communication; Verbal
    communication
  characteristics of, 31–41
  complex nature of, 26–27
  components of, 29–31
  contextual nature of, 37
  definition of, 28–29
  dynamic nature of, 36–37
  ethnocentrism and, 61–63
  as intentional and unintentional
    behavior, 27–28
  messages of, 34–36
  relationship between culture and, 48
  rules of, 37–38, 233–234
  self-reflective nature of, 38
  symbolic nature of, 33
Communication style, 286–287
Communication technology, 5
Complementing, 181
Compromise, 241
Concepts, 52
Conceptual equivalence, 166–168
Conformity, 248
Conscious learning, 56
Context, 233–236
  attitudes toward, 94
  impact and awareness of, 231
Contradicting, 181
Copeland, L., 239
Credibility, 106
Cross-cultural communication, 70
Culick, S., 93
Cultural calamity, 59–60
Cultural equivalence, 166
Cultural imperialism, 61
Cultural values, 83–84
Culture
  definitions of, 50–51
  differences in, 76–78
  dominant. *See* Dominant culture
  elements of, 52–54
  ethnocentrism and, 61–63

  function of, 49
  and influence on perception, 105–107.
    See also Perception
  language and, 151–158
  learning and, 54–58
  nature of, 59–60, 60–61
  and nonverbal behavior, 176–179,
    185–186
  role in communication, 17, 48,
    76
  study of, 16
  transmission of, 58–59, 105
Culture-bound words, 165
Culture-general method, 284, 285
Culture shock, 232–233, 281
Culture-specific method, 284, 285

Dance, Frank E. X., 26
Deaf individuals, 13, 193
Death, 256
Decoding, 30
Deductive reasoning, 93
Deep structure, 15
Defensive communication, 291–292
Democracy, 127
Diffusion, 59
Diplomacy, 72
Discrimination, 15, 282
Distance. *See* Space
Dodd, Carley H., 54
Dogmatism, 292
Dominant culture, 11
  hostility for, 162
  power of, 71
  in United States, 133, 134
Drug language, 163

Ebonics, 160–162
Economics, 8–10, 304
Education
  of culturally diverse student body, 13,
    252–256
  purpose of, 244–245
  variations in methods of, 248–252
  variations of emphasis on, 245–248

Educators, 247
Efficiency, 126
Ekman, Paul, 196
Elderly people
    perception of, 115
    status of, 138–139
Emblems, 191
Emic concepts, 166–167
Emotional state, 177, 190–191
Empathy, 290–293
Encoding, 29–30
Enculturation, 55–56
Energy consumption, 6
English language, 150, 153, 157–158
Environmental pollution, 7
Epistemological assumptions, 86
Equality, 127
Ethics, 298–301
Ethnicity, 71. See also Interethnic
    communication
Ethnocentrism
    as barrier to communication, 278–279,
        292, 300–301
    culture and, 61–63, 186, 262–263
    definition of, 17, 279
    prejudice and, 15, 71
    teaching of, 250–251
Etic concepts, 166, 167
European Economic Community, 9,
    302
Evil eye, 197–198, 199, 257
Experiential equivalence, 166
Eye contact
    cultural variations in, 95, 178, 197–200,
        234
    in school, 95, 254–255

Face painting, 188
Facial expression, 195–197
Family
    as aspect of social organization,
        136–139
    as influence on perceptions, 87–88
Fatalism, 121, 123
Feedback, 293–296
Femininity, and world view, 127–128

Field-dependent/field-independent
    cognition, 251
Filipinos, 131, 204, 206, 221
Flexibility, 296–297
Folb, Edith A., 71
Folklore, 114
Folktales, 57
Food, 6–7
Foreign languages. See various foreign
    languages
    argot and, 159
    represented in student bodies, 253
    translation of, 165–169
Formality
    American colonist's dislike of, 133
    in business context, 237, 241
    in classroom, 250
    of Germans, 130
    in Spanish language, 155
Formal time, 219
Forms of address, 130
Free choice, 273–274
Freedom, 127
French
    medical treatment by, 258
    use of touch by, 201
Frost, Everett L., 50
Fuller, Thomas, 49, 187
Furniture arrangement, 216–217
Future-oriented cultures, 222

Gangs, 163, 249
Gays. See Homosexuals
Generalizations, 184–185
Germans
    differences between Americans and,
        77–78
    formality of, 130, 192
Gestures, 95, 189–195
Gift-giving, 242
Gissing, George, 31
Global economics, 8–10
Goffman, Erving, 180
Gossip, 115
Government, as influence on perceptions,
    87, 88

Greek language, 157
Greeks, ancient, 106
Griggs, L., 239

Hall, Edward T., 48, 59, 61, 177–178, 204, 217–218, 222, 234
Harris, P., 232
Hawaiians, 192
Head movements, 194
Health care, 256–263
High-context communication, 151, 155
High-context cultures, 234–235, 277
Hinduism, 122–123
    concept of death in, 256
    future orientation of, 222
    world view of, 86
Hispanics. See Latin Americans
History, social organization and, 132–136
Hoebel, E. Adamson, 50
Hofstede, Geert, 51, 127
Homosexuals
    population statistics of, 13
    social distance between heterosexuals and, 214
    use of gaze by, 199
    use of touch by, 202
Hostility, 162
Human brain, 38–39, 272–273
Humanitarianism, 126
Human nature, 89–90

Idiomatic expressions, 166
Illness
    concepts of, 256–258
    treatment of, 258–262
Immigration, U.S., 11–12, 304
Impressions, first, 177
Impulsivity, 251
India, 153, 259
Individualism
    perceptions of, 91
    and world view, 128
Inductive reasoning, 93
Inferences, 32
Informal time, 219–223

Information processing, 30
In-groups, 128
Intercultural communication, 70
    ethical considerations in, 298–301
    forms of, 70–74
    future of, 301–306
    importance of, 4, 272–274
    methods of improving, 283–298
    model of, 74–79
    nonverbal processes and, 94–96. See also
        Nonverbal communication
    perception and, 80–91. See also
        Perception
    potential problems in, 274–282
    study of, 16–18, 69–70
    verbal processes and, 91–94. See also
        Verbal communication
Intercultural generalizations, 16–17
Interethnic communication, 71
International communication, 72
International contact
    economic change and, 8–10
    new technology and, 5
    population growth and, 6–8
Interpreters, 168–169
Interracial communication, 70–71
Intonation, 156
Intracultural communication, explanation of, 72–74
Introspection, 285–287
Invention, 59
Islam, 120–122
    concept of death in, 256
    influence on business dealings, 340
    and perception of United States, 136
    world view of, 117
Italians, 225–226, 237

James, William, 34
Japanese. See also Orientals
    in business context, 238, 240–241
    education of, 246–248
    eye contact used by, 198
    history of, 135–136
    language of, 155
    meaning of smell to, 204

Japanese (*continued*).
and perception of credibility, 106
perception of time by, 220
sex roles of, 138–139
silence used by, 225
and treatment of illness, 259
and use of touch, 202
and World War II, 167–168, 305–306
Jews
history of, 134–135
importance of children to, 139
Jiving, 161
Johannesen, Richard L., 226
Johnson, Frank, 16–17
Jordanians, 194
Judaism, 119

Karma, 123, 125
Keesing, Felix M., 61, 62, 188
Kinesics, 189–195
Kitano, Harry H. L., 225
Kluckhohn, Clyde, 51
Koreans. *See also* Orientals
communication with eyes by, 199,
234
language of, 155
and use of touch, 202
Kroeber, A. L., 51

Labor force
cultural diversity in, 14, 236, 243–244
women in, 244, 304
Language
and culture, 91–93, 151–158
importance of, 149–150
and meaning, 150
nature of, 146–149
shared codes in, 288–290
translation of foreign, 165–169. *See also*
various foreign languages
use of argot, 158–165
Latin Americans. *See also* Mexicans
education of, 246
perception of time by, 221
recent immigration patterns of, 11

Learning
conscious, 56
culture and, 54–58, 248–252
values and, 111–116
Leathers, Dale, 198, 217
Legislation, 12, 13
Lesbians. *See* Homosexuals
Lexical equivalence, 165–166
Low-context communication, 151–152
Low-context cultures, 234–235, 277

Maasai, 206
Management style, Japanese, 238
Marketing trends, 12
Marriage, intercultural and interracial,
14
Masculinity, and world view, 127–128
Material comfort, 127
Materialism, 87
Media, 114–115
Melting pot, 132–133
Messages, 30, 34–36
Mexicans
educational system of, 246
meaning of conversation to, 90,
154
sitting habits, 192
use of Spanish by, 154–155, 167
Miller, Gerald R., 27
Mind-to-mind contact, 32
Mollenauer, Sandra, 281
Monochronic culture, 222–223
Moore, George, 274
Moral orientation, 126
Moran, R., 232
Mormons, 120
Morris, Desmond, 193
M-time, 222–223
Muslims. *See* Islam

Nader, Laura, 305
National languages, 152–153
Native Americans, 85, 106, 152, 260–261.
See also Navajo Indians
Natural resources, 6, 117

Nature
  Asian view of, 114, 117
  relationship of individual to, 85–86
Navajo Indians, 105, 137, 199, 219,
  260–261
Negotiations, 238–239, 240–242, 296
Niehoff, A., 152–153
Nirvana, 123, 124
Nonverbal communication
  appearance and dress as, 187–189
  body movement as, 95, 189–195
  common codes in, 288–290
  culture and, 177–179, 185–186
  defining, 179–180
  eye contact and gaze as, 95, 178,
    197–200, 234
  facial expression as, 195–197
  functions of, 180–182, 294
  guidelines and limitations of, 184–185
  importance of, 176–179
  and paralanguage, 205–206
  in school, 249, 252, 254
  silence as, 223–226
  smell and, 203–205
  time and, 94–96, 218–223
  use of space as, 96, 214–218
  use of touch as, 94–95, 176–177,
    200–203
  verbal communication vs., 182–184
  in work place, 244
Norton, Robert, 286
Norway, 136
Nudity, 262

Olayiwola, Rahman O., 84
Organizations, 128–129
Orientals. See also Chinese; Japanese;
  Koreans
  in business context, 237–239
  facial expression in, 197
  high-context nature of, 151, 155, 234
  meaning of humanity to, 89
  perception of self, 91
  thought patterns of, 93–94
  use of time by, 220–221
Out-groups, 128

Paralanguage, 205–206
Past-oriented cultures, 221
Pearson, Judy Cornelia, 197
Perception
  activity orientation and, 90
  attitudes and, 84
  beliefs and, 82–84
  explanation of, 80–82, 103–105
  human nature and, 89–90
  of physical objects, 105
  of self and others, 90–91
  sensory, 86, 104
  social aspects of, 78–79, 105–107
  social organization and, 87–89
  values and, 83–84
  world view and, 84–87. See also World
    view
Personal space, 96, 106, 214–215,
  217–218. See also Space
Personal titles, 130
Phoneme, 147
Physical objects, 105
Physical setting, 287–288
Plotnik, Rod, 281
Polychronic culture, 222, 223
Population growth, 6–8, 303
Posture, 192, 193
Power, 292
Power distance, 129–130
Practicality, 126
Pragmatic level of language, 147
Prejudice
  as barrier to communication, 279–282
  harmful nature of, 15, 79
  racial, 71
  types of, 281
Present-oriented cultures, 221
Primary values, 110–111
Privacy, 237
Problem solving, 93–94
Profanity, 164
Progress, 126
Prostitutes, 160, 217
Protocol, 237
Proverbs, 112–114
Proxemics, 214. See also Space
P-time, 222, 223

Public schools
    diversity of student bodies in,
        252–256
    minority students in, 13
Punctuality, 219–220

Quechua language, 168
Questioning, 164

Races
    communication between, 70–71
    differences among, 70
    stereotyped notions regarding, 291
Racism, 281. *See also* Prejudice
Rapping, 161
Reasoning
    as component of culture, 93–94
    expressed through language, 152
Receiver, 30
Reflectivity/impulsivity, 251
Regulating, 182
Religions
    and beliefs and values, 108
    overview of major, 119–126
    and world view, 116–119
Repeating, 180–181
Residue, 28
Rhetorical skill, 92, 156, 242
Roberts, Helene, 198
Ruben, Brent D., 35, 56
Ruhly, Sharon, 279
Russia, 135

Samoans, 193–194
Sapir, Edward, 151
Sapir-Whorf hypothesis, 151
Saudi Arabians. *See also* Arabs
    business negotiations with, 240, 241
    communication patterns of, 156–157
    and role of women, 81
Sayings, 112–114
Schools
    diversity of student bodies in, 252–256
    function of, 244–245

minorities in public, 13
nonverbal communication in, 249, 252,
        254–255
Science, 127
    influence of world view on, 85–86
Scribner, Sylvia, 50–51
Seating, 215–216, 288
Secondary values, 110–111
Self
    family teachings regarding, 139
    perceptions of, 90–91
Self-motivation, 91
Semantic level of language, 147
Sensory perception, 86, 104
Setting, physical, 288
Sex roles
    taught by family, 137
    and world view, 127–128
Sexual harassment, 14, 244
Shamans, 261
Shintoism, 117
Shucking, 161–162
Silence
    in educational setting, 248–249, 255
    as encouragement for feedback,
        295–296
    as nonverbal communication, 223–226
Similarities, 275
Singer, Marshall R., 80
Singers, Navajo, 260–261
Sioux Indian language, 152
Sitting behavior, 192–193
Smell, 203–205
Smith, Alfred G., 69
Socialization, 55
Social organization
    family as aspect of, 136–139
    and history, 132–136
    perception and, 87–89
Social perception. *See also* Perception
    aspects of, 105–107
    explanation of, 78–79
Social relationships, establishment for
        business, 239–240
Solidarity, 162–163
Sorcery, 257
Source, 29

Soviet Union
   education in, 246, 248–251
   medical treatment in, 259
   relations between United States and,
      303
Space
   in classrooms, 249
   and furniture arrangement, 216–217
   perception of, 96, 106
   personal, 96, 106, 214–215, 217–218
   and seating organization, 215–216
Spanish language, 154–155, 167
Spitzberg, Brian H., 283–284
Spoken language, 148. *See also* Language
Spooning, 260
Squatting, 192
Standard of living, 127
Status, 82, 240
Steinberg, Mark, 27
Stereotyping, 279–282
Subculture, 72
Substituting, 181
Success, 126
Suspended self, 293
Symbolic racism, 281
Symbols
   as core of communication, 33, 91–92
   portability of, 58
   in verbal and nonverbal communication,
      182–184
Syntactic level of language, 147

Taboos, social, 118, 175
Tactile communication, 94–95, 176–177,
      200–203
Tagalog, 165–166
Tead, Ordway, 299–300
Technology
   and global economic interdependencies,
      8–10
   impact on international contact, 5
   influence of world view on, 85–86
Television programs, foreign-language,
      12
Terpstra, Vern, 53, 54
Tertiary values, 110–111

Thai
   language of, 153–154
   sitting behavior of, 193–194
   speaking volume of, 206
   and use of touch, 202
Thought patterns, 93–94
Time
   concepts of, 94–96, 239
   and education, 249–250, 252
   formal, 219
   informal, 219–223
   use of language to describe, 152
Time-binding, 33–34
Timing, 287–288
Tokenism, 281
Tourism, 5, 302–303
Transcultural communication, 70
Translation, of foreign languages, 165–169
Travel, 302–303
   and increased awareness, 5
Trenholm, Sarah, 290
Triandis, Harry C., 50
Trust, 242
Tunisians, 194

Uncertainty, 129
Uncertainty-avoidance societies, 129
Uncertainty reduction, 276
Uniforms, 187, 188, 249
Unintentionality, 27
United States
   body movements used in, 190–194
   cultural diversity in, 11–15
   dominant cultural values in, 126–127
   educational challenges in, 252
   foreign business in, 10
   impact of immigration on, 11–12, 304
   impact of intercultural contact on,
      303–304
   labor force in, 14, 236, 243–244
   role of history in, 132–134

Values
   definition and description of, 83–84, 109
   dominant U.S., 126–127

Values (*continued*).
   influence of culture on, 108–111
   methods of learning, 111–116, 246
   and world view, 127–131
Value system, 109
Verbal communication. *See also*
     Communication; Language
   encouraging feedback by positive, 294
   high- and low-context, 151–152,
     155
Verbal communication (*continued*).
   nonverbal communication vs., 182–184.
     See also Nonverbal communication
Verbal processes
   and language usage, 91–93
   and patterns of thought, 93–94
Vietnamese language, 152, 154
Violence
   transmitted by mass media, 114–115
   and U.S. history, 133
Vocabulary, 165–166

Waiting time, 219–220
Waldheim, Kurt, 240
Weinberg, Harry L., 33–34
Whorf, Benjamin, 151
Witchcraft, 257
Withdrawal, 277–278

Women
   body movement in, 193
   contact with dominant culture, 13, 304
   and differences in paralanguage, 206
   and education, 250
   eye contact by and with, 199
   in labor force, 14, 242, 244
   language usage by, 164
   perceptions of, 81
   as separate culture, 73
   use of personal space by, 217
Women's movement, 81, 244
Words, 146–148
Work, 126
Work force. *See* Labor force
World view
   and concept of illness, 256
   and cultural values, 126–131
   effects of, 116–126
   explanation of, 84–85, 116
   and perception of environment, 85–87
World Watch Institute, 7
Written language, 148. *See also* Language

Yiddish language, 160

Zaire, 153